Parenting and the Goods of Childhood

Parenting and the Goods of Childhood

LUARA FERRACIOLI

OXFORD
UNIVERSITY PRESS

Oxford University Press is a department of the University of Oxford. It furthers the University's objective of excellence in research, scholarship, and education by publishing worldwide. Oxford is a registered trade mark of Oxford University Press in the UK and certain other countries.

Published in the United States of America by Oxford University Press
198 Madison Avenue, New York, NY 10016, United States of America.

© Oxford University Press 2024

All rights reserved. No part of this publication may be reproduced, stored in a retrieval system, or transmitted, in any form or by any means, without the prior permission in writing of Oxford University Press, or as expressly permitted by law, by license, or under terms agreed with the appropriate reproduction rights organization. Inquiries concerning reproduction outside the scope of the above should be sent to the Rights Department, Oxford University Press, at the address above.

You must not circulate this work in any other form
and you must impose this same condition on any acquirer.

CIP data is on file at the Library of Congress

ISBN 978-0-19-761270-5

DOI: 10.1093/oso/9780197612705.001.0001

Printed by Integrated Books International, United States of America

Contents

Acknowledgments   vii

PART I. PROCREATION, ADOPTION, AND PARENTING

Introduction   3

1. Justifying Procreative Parenting   6
   1.1. Introduction   6
   1.2. Two Challenges   7
   1.3. On the Value of Procreative Parenting   12
   1.4. Procreation and Reasons for Love   16
   1.5. Back to the Challenges   20
   1.6. Alternative Responses   24
   1.7. Conclusion   26

2. The Right to Parent and Moral Commitment   29
   2.1. Introduction   29
   2.2. On Procreation and Parenthood   31
   2.3. Three Desiderata for a Correct Theory of Moral Parenthood   33
   2.4. On Moral Commitment   39
   2.5. Committing to a Child   42
   2.6. Objections   46
   2.7. Conclusion   51

3. The Opportunity to Parent and Adoption   53
   3.1. Introduction   53
   3.2. The State and Procreation   54
   3.3. The State and Adoption   65
   3.4. Implications   69
   3.5. Objections   73
   3.6. Conclusion   78

PART II. CHILDHOOD GOODS

Introduction   83

4. Carefreeness   87
    4.1. Introduction   87
    4.2. On Well-Being   89
    4.3. Carefreeness and Adulthood   92
    4.4. Carefreeness and a Good Childhood   98
    4.5. Implications   105
    4.6. Conclusion   107

5. Achievement   108
    5.1. Introduction   108
    5.2. Achievement and Well-Being   109
    5.3. Achievement in Adulthood   113
    5.4. Achievement in Childhood   116
    5.5. Implications   124
    5.6. Conclusion   126

6. Friendship   127
    6.1. Introduction   127
    6.2. Friendship and Well-Being   129
    6.3. Friendship in Adulthood   136
    6.4. Friendship in Childhood   139
    6.5. Implications   143
    6.6. Conclusion   147

Notes   149
Bibliography   183
Index   193

Acknowledgments

This book was made possible by the generous support of Princeton University's Center for Human Values, where I held a remote Laurance S. Rockefeller Visiting Fellowship in the 2021–22 academic year. I am tremendously grateful for the many opportunities to discuss my work with Princeton colleagues, students, and visitors, and for the broader research support provided by the Center. I am also very grateful to the University of Sydney for additional research support both before and during the fellowship.

Researchers from all around the world have given me feedback on different chapters of this book. Special thanks to Ed Barring, Christian Barry, Millie Churcher, Elizabeth Cohen, Stephanie Collins, Ryan Cox, Annelien De Dijn, Emily Foster-Hanson, Andrew Franklin-Hall, Joe Galeosi, Melissa Ganz, Anca Gheaus, Paul Griffiths, Daniel Halliday, Matthew Hammerton, Liz Harman, Brian Hedden, Colin Hickey, Emily Hulme, Thomas Hurka, Jessica Isserow, Kathryn Joyce, Simon Keller, Suzie Killmister, David Kinney, Melissa Lane, R. J. Leland, Desiree Lim, Errol Lord, Terry MacDonald, Steve Macedo, David Miller, Daniel Muñoz, Ralph Nanan, Mike Ridge, Emily Rotzioskos, Tina Rulli, Eric Schliesser, Liam Shields, Sam Shpall, Michael Smith, Annie Stilz, Christine Straehle, Gavin Sullivan, Sergio Tenenbaum, Rosa Terlazzo, Hannah Tierney, Suzanne Uniack, Thalia Vrantsidis, Rivka Weinberg, Caroline West, and Daniel Wodak.

I am particularly grateful to Emily Rose Baird, Teresa Baron, Duncan Ivison, Holly Lawford-Smith, and Alex Lefebvre for reading the entire manuscript and providing me with helpful and insightful feedback. I am also grateful to everyone who participated in the book review I held in Sydney in April 2022.

The book benefited enormously from discussions with audiences at the University of Toronto, the University of Amsterdam, the Australian National University, Monash University, Sydney Health Ethics,

Murdoch University, the Australian Political Theory and Philosophy Conference, the University of Sydney, the University of New South Wales, Princeton University, the Kioloa Philosophy Workshop, the University of California–Davis, and Stanford University. Many thanks to everyone who took part in these discussions.

Lucy Randall has been a wonderful editor during the entire process of writing this book. I am very grateful for her encouragement and support. Thanks also to two referees for their excellent comments and suggestions, and to everyone involved in the book's production.

Finally, thanks to my colleagues, mentors, family, and friends for their support, as well as to everyone who makes it possible for me to combine full-time work with parenting. A special note of love and gratitude to my partner Ryan Cox for all the intellectual and emotional support over the years.

This book is dedicated to my three children Valentina, Octavian, and Julius, who bring so much joy to my life and always focus my attention on what matters.

PART I
PROCREATION, ADOPTION, AND PARENTING

Introduction

Is there a moral duty to adopt? Can procreation be justified? Who counts as the moral parent of a child? Should the liberal state create opportunities for citizens to embark on the lifelong project of being a parent? And, if so, should these be opportunities for procreative assistance or for adoption? These are the questions I focus on in this first part of the book.

There are two reasons why I examine the ethics of parenting before turning to the question of what a good childhood looks like. First, addressing fundamental questions around procreation, adoption, and parenting is important because it gives us the foundations on which to base a robust theory of moral parenthood—that is, a theory of who counts as a parent to a child from a moral point of view, and what implications this has for society at large. Second, this book focuses precisely on the interests that children have which are best advanced in the context of a parent-child relationship. So it is helpful to know who are the agents morally responsible for fostering the childhood goods in question, before exploring in depth what these goods amount to and why they are so important.

The connection between the two parts of the book is tighter than it may appear on the surface. My answer to the question of who counts as a moral parent partly appeals to the role that moral parents play in creating the conditions for children to lead good lives qua children. This means that being a moral parent is partly about ensuring that one's child is able to enjoy the childhood goods that moral parents are particularly well placed to foster. These are the goods of carefreeness, friendship, and achievement.

As I go about developing the core arguments of this book, I will remain agnostic on the correct position in normative ethics, but will embrace liberalism as the doctrine that should guide the use of coercive power in modern societies, thereby making two liberal assumptions throughout the discussion.[1] One key assumption is that although children cannot yet enjoy full autonomy in their lives, they should nonetheless be treated as creatures with equal and independent moral status by their parents, their fellow citizens, and state authorities. Another assumption is that resources are always limited in a liberal society, and the state should therefore focus on fairly distributing the burdens and benefits of collective life. One implication of this is that the liberal state should be securing core interests, not individual preferences. Most importantly, given children's vulnerability and their utter dependence on other parties for the enjoyment of a good childhood, special attention ought to be paid to what is in their best interests, while ensuring that their best interests are taken seriously when it comes to the state deciding how best to allocate its limited resources.

Apart from taking a broadly liberal framework for granted, the book also offers only a partial theory of child-rearing. I don't say very much about the more familiar interests of children. Indeed, I assume that many of children's core interests should be secured by the liberal state, either because the state will be better placed than the parent to secure a certain good (given its ability to coerce adults to comply with its directives) or because fair equality of opportunity requires that the state secure a given interest to roughly the same degree for all children so that they can stand as equals, both in childhood and in adulthood. I therefore assume that children's interests in health and education are better secured by the liberal state, even though parents ought to play an important auxiliary role in those enterprises. Throughout this book, I assume that the state and the moral parents are jointly responsible for children's well-being, and that they must work in tandem, each focusing on the interests they are particularly well placed to secure.[2]

Finally, it is important to note that this is a philosophical book in the field of family justice. Accordingly, I will be asking philosophical questions that many people may find odd. One of these questions is whether it is morally permissible to procreate in order to parent. Another question is whether the liberal state should play any role in the creation of children. Given that procreative parenting is a project that most citizens in liberal societies engage in with virtually no pushback by friends, family members, and fellow citizens, it may seem as if I am asking a question analogous to the question of whether it is morally permissible to cut one's hair or get a tattoo. But that is precisely why the topic of this book is so important. For there is no other activity that has so much potential for ending badly which receives so little scrutiny at the societal level. If we think of fetuses being exposed to drugs in pregnancy, or children being physically, sexually, and psychologically abused in the course of their childhoods, or if we think of children being left to their own devices with no one to give them love and attention, then perhaps it becomes clear that many citizens in liberal societies are not sufficiently attentive to the moral dimension of procreation, adoption, and parenting. Or, at least, they are not sufficiently attentive to the moral dimension of these projects before deciding whether to embark on them.

But it is not just questions around the treatment of specific children that warrant philosophical investigation. The creation of new human beings can potentially have negative effects on the environment; and our financial support for fertility treatments takes away resources that could be spent on life-saving medical research and procedures. Even more importantly, the way we treat parentless children, and how hard we work to ensure that they are adopted, say a lot about our priorities as a society and a lot about whether we care enough about what really matters. And so, even if the philosophical questions in this book may strike some as odd or uncomfortable, we owe it to future and existing children to answer them carefully and methodically.

1
Justifying Procreative Parenting

1.1. Introduction

What makes the combination of creating *and* parenting a child valuable for a person?[1] On the one hand, the activity of creating *on its own* can be meaningless for the person who does it. Think of an anonymous sperm donor who never even meets the child he helps to create. On the other hand, the activity of parenting *on its own* seems quite meaningful. Think of a stepfather who feels profound love toward a child he helps to raise. On the face of it, it is hard to see how there could be any value in the combination of creating *and* parenting a child over and above the value of parenting itself. This is a problem for those who believe that *procreative parenting* uniquely contributes to the pursuit of a meaningful life.

But the difficulty in locating the value of *procreation* in procreative parenting is not the only problem facing those who believe that there is something special about the bond parents enjoy with the children they have a genetic and/or gestational connection to. Another problem they face is to show that this value is significant enough to give them the theoretical resources to address two pressing moral challenges to the practice of procreative parenting.

The first challenge relates to the moral decision of *whether or not* to procreate given the significant environmental and opportunity costs involved in bringing a new person into the world. Procreation puts a great deal of pressure on our already overburdened natural environment, and it also takes away emotional and financial resources that could be otherwise spent on adopting a child in need. The moral insight driving this challenge is that the enterprise of procreative parenting cannot be justified in light of the much better consequences that prospective parents can bring about by engaging in *adoptive* parenting instead.

Parenting and the Goods of Childhood. Luara Ferracioli, Oxford University Press.
© Oxford University Press 2024. DOI: 10.1093/oso/9780197612705.003.0002

The second challenge to procreative parenting takes place *after* procreation; it involves the state's role in deciding how to arrange custodial rights over children given that not all procreative parents are the best available parents for the child they have created. Given the extreme vulnerability of children and the tremendous effect that the family has on how well their lives go as a whole, there is a moral case in favor of a state-run redistributive scheme whereby children are taken away from their procreative parents and brought up by whichever adult(s) can do the best job of raising them.

In this chapter, I provide an account of the value of procreative parenting that can resist these two challenges. It explains why prospective parents are morally permitted to procreate despite the environmental harms and opportunity costs involved, and it explains why (competent) procreative parents are morally permitted to parent their biological children despite the fact that the particular needs of their children might be better aligned with the parental skills of other prospective parents. More specifically, my account locates the value of parenting in the depth and robustness of the loving bond between parents and children, while simultaneously holding that the *mere* fact of intentional procreation for the purposes of parenting provides a *weighty pro tanto* reason for love of this kind.

The discussion is structured as follows. In Section 1.2, I lay out the two challenges that must be met by a successful theory of the value of procreative parenting. In Sections 1.3 and 1.4, I defend my account of the value of procreative parenting. In Section 1.5, I explain how my account meets both these challenges. In Section 1.6, I engage with the work of Christine Overall and Anca Gheaus and, in so doing, argue that my account does a better job than their accounts in explaining why procreation for competent parents is permissible and why redistribution away from competent procreative parents is not.

1.2. Two Challenges

The practice of procreative parenting can be defined in several ways. Here I understand a procreative parent as an agent who conceives a child and/or carries a pregnancy to term, and intends *to enjoy a parent-child relationship with the resulting child*. Hence, a procreative parent is someone who has gestated her child and/or shares a genetic relation to her child. By contrast, an adoptive-parent or stepparent is someone who has neither gestated her child nor shares a genetic connection to her.

This definition has a couple of implications. First, it leaves out procreators who have *not* engaged in procreation with the purpose of parenting the child, such as sperm, egg, and mitochondria donors.[2] Second, it leaves out agents who have played no genetic or gestational role in the creation of a child, but who can be said to have enabled her existence. This will be true of doctors in fertility clinics, matchmakers, and prospective parents who contract out all of the procreative work to gamete donors and surrogates.[3]

With this definition of procreative parenting in mind, we are now in a better position to assess the first challenge to procreative parenting, which I will refer to as the procreation challenge. The moral case against procreation in procreative parenting is both simple and prima facie compelling. It states that procreative parenting is morally wrong under current *nonideal* sociopolitical conditions, because prospective parents can do much more good in the world by adopting an existing child instead of creating a new person, thereby contributing to significantly fewer carbon emissions overall, as well as providing a loving home to a child who already exists.[4]

There are two distinct concerns driving this challenge. The first is that procreation, at least by citizens of affluent countries, has an environmental impact that increases what environmentalists already consider to be unacceptable levels of consumption and resource degradation.[5] The second concern is driven by the claims that children in state care already have an interest in entering into a parent-child relationship and that there is no additional value in creating a person. As Tina Rulli puts it,

> absent parents' lives are not more valuable for having merely participated in the creation of another human being. We would not give the slightest praise to the father who bragged about having many offspring if he had never actually met or cared for any of them. *It is raising the child ... that has value for a person*.[6]

So what theoretical bar must be met in order for an account to succeed in doing its job of adequately justifying procreative parenting? First, given that the procreation challenge questions the permissibility of procreation in light of pressing environmental and social concerns, we can meet it by showing that prospective parents have a compelling interest in procreation due to some good-making feature of creating the child they intend to have a parent-child relationship with. Note, however, that such an interest *need not* be more important or pressing than all the other interests at stake, including the interest of future generations in not being negatively affected by climate change, and the interest of children in care in entering into a parent-child relationship.[7] The reason for setting the bar at this level is that I assume that individuals qua pursuers of the good are in fact allowed to give *some* priority to their own projects and relationships when faced with the conflicting demands of morality, *so long as* such projects and relationships are an important ingredient of their conception of the good and have nontrivial value—that is, are of the kind that contributes to their leading a meaningful life without violating other people's basic interests.[8]

We now turn to the second challenge to procreative parenting, the redistribution challenge. The concern here is that even when parents ignore the compelling moral case against procreation and decide to engage in procreative parenting, they still don't seem to acquire a moral right to parent that child simply due to the gestational or genetic connection they share. To see why, consider the implications of a world where rights-respecting states have the technology to scan the genes of newborns in order to foresee what sort of health, educational, and psychological needs each is likely to have in the course of her life. Imagine also that a related technology allows government officials to accurately describe the profile of adults who have just given birth to a child by combining their genetic information with information about their social network, hobbies, professional aptitudes, financial circumstances, and core psychological traits. Finally, imagine that due to this information, government officials are able to accurately shift each newborn to parents who are in the best position to meet the newborn's individual needs—which rarely turns out to be the procreative parents themselves.[9]

I take it that this case supports what Liam Shields has called a "dual comparative" view of child redistribution.[10] In his discussion of whether the state has reasons to take children away from decent procreative parents, Shields argues that both the interests of the child and the interests of parents should count when deciding who should exercise custody rights over children, and that, at times, redistribution should take place precisely so that the interests of children are promoted to a greater extent than they would have been otherwise, while still ensuring that the interests of decent parents are taken into account. This is precisely what takes place in the case above. By distributing children away from their procreative parents at birth, the state secures the interest of children in being in a parent-child relationship where their interests are furthered to the greatest extent possible, while simultaneously securing the interest of decent parents in parenting.

To be sure, the putative interest in parenting one's own *biological* (that is, *gestational or genetic*) child will not be secured by an arrangement of child redistribution. But this is precisely what is at stake here. Until we can show that there is such an interest, it looks as if the state would be justified in redistributing children if that would produce better consequences overall. As Shields explains,

> [Decent biological parents] may justifiably be denied custody where alternative arrangements promote the justice-salient interests of the child in ways that are more significant than the costs to the current parents, taking into account the parents' interests and the costs of transition to the child.[11]

Note, though, that in order to block the desirability of child redistribution by the state, a defender of procreative parenting needs to do more than simply show that persons have an interest in procreation. After all, prospective parents can easily experience the value of procreation by begetting child A, and then experience the value of parenting by raising child B. If there is a compelling interest in procreative parenting, then, it is the interest in parenting the exact same child one has created, irrespective of how well one could parent other children, and irrespective of how well others could parent one's own biological child. Moreover, given that both children and adults are persons who enjoy full and equal moral status, this challenge will be best met by showing that children also have a compelling interest in developing a relationship with their (competent) procreative parents.

Both the procreation challenge and the redistribution challenge are hard to meet. The procreation challenge raises the question of why prospective parents should feel entitled to first create a child when there are existing children who already have needs and who already count as "burdens" on the natural environment. The redistribution challenge raises the question of why the value of a biological tie between parent and child should be allowed to outweigh the instrumental interest that the child has in having her interests promoted and protected to the greatest extent possible. To succeed in justifying procreative parenting, then, one must show that the biological connection between parent and child has nontrivial value and that it can contribute to the pursuit of a meaningful life by both parties to the relationship.[12]

Before concluding this section, let me briefly note that procreative parenting also faces two indirect challenges. First, it faces the antinatalist challenge that takes existence to be a net harm over nonexistence.[13] Second, it faces the antiparenting challenge of denying that one should ever parent in a world where one could better spend one's discretionary time and resources volunteering or contributing to charities aimed at meeting the basic needs of existing people (adequate nutrition, basic healthcare, and so on).[14] I do not attempt to meet these challenges in detail in this chapter, because they are not directly aimed at procreative parenting, but at procreation and parenting when carried out independently. In this book, I assume that a life worth living is a benefit to the recipient and will not address the antinatalist challenge. However, one of the aims of this book is precisely to mount a case against the antiparenting challenge by showing that parenting is in fact quite valuable to both parents and children, and it is just the sort of self-regarding project that morality must carve out some space for.

1.3. On the Value of Procreative Parenting

So where does the nontrivial value of procreative parenting lie? In this section, I argue that the value of parenting consists in a deep and robust loving bond between the child and her parent. Later, I will argue that the fact of procreation in procreative parenting provides a weighty pro tanto reason for love of this kind.

Let me start by noting that parenting can bring with it all sorts of experiences that can be valuable for particular persons, depending on their own dispositions and on how parenting fits within their overall conception of a life well lived. For instance, some enjoy the fiduciary role they play in the lives of their children, whereas others enjoy the special type of intimacy and affection they can experience in the context of family life.[15] Still, I take it that what is necessarily present in valuable tokens of parent-child relationships is what is often, but mistakenly, referred to as unconditional love (strictly speaking, unconditional love is neither typically accessible to people nor desirable, since when love is reciprocated with egregious forms of violence or abuse, it becomes hard to sustain—and rightly so).[16] This type of love—call it parental love—gives rise to a deep and robust form of caring on the part of parents, which, in turn, plays a central role in creating the conditions for children to create and experience value in the course of their lives.[17]

Consider first the *deepness* of the concern tied to parental love. As is well known, parents are typically disposed to take on a great deal of cost and make significant sacrifices on behalf of their children. Such cost-taking and sacrificing might include the ordinary giving up of most of one's discretionary time on a daily basis, so as to ensure that the child accesses good nutrition, can satisfy her curiosity and aesthetic sense through music, books, and stories, and can enjoy a sympathetic ear so as to voice her fears and concerns. But the sacrifices and cost-taking motivated by parental love can be much more extreme. For example, parents might walk away from a fulfilling but demanding career so as to be more present in a child's life, or move away from a country they love so as to ensure the child has access to better socioeconomic opportunities.

Consider next the *robustness* of the concern tied to parental love. Parents are typically disposed to continue loving their child, and so to invest in the parent-child relationship despite significant changes in their values, ambitions, and life circumstances.[18] This explains why parents continue advancing the good of their child even when faced with life's greatest challenges, such as poverty, terminal illness, divorce, or the death of a loved one. Parental love thereby sustains a loving relationship that is highly resilient, despite significant changes in the parent's circumstances and despite the passage of time.

So far I have only noted that parents are typically disposed to care deeply about the good of their child, and to do so even when their personal circumstances make such deep caring less subjectively desirable. However, to show that parental love is special, and so show that parties have an interest in participating in a parent-child relationship, it pays to compare parental love with other types of love. To begin with, compare the robustness of parental love and friendship love. First, friends are significantly less likely than parents to continue investing in the relationship when parties cease to have shared interests, when they fall out, or when they move town or country and can no longer enjoy territorially located activities. Second, friends are significantly less disposed to sacrifice core life projects for the sake of the other person in the relationship. Indeed, while some extraordinary individuals might (say) sacrifice their career in order to move their residence and care for a friend with a disability, parents typically find such sacrificing irresistible and unavoidable.

Similar results can be found when we compare parental love and romantic love. Unlike parental love, the depth and robustness of romantic love seem to be contingent on the endurance of some facts about the beloved (moral values, desirable personality traits, and so on), as well as on the subjective attribution of value to the historical-relational properties that arise within the context of the relationship (e.g., sentimental events, joint achievements, and other salient facts about the past).[19] The depth and presence of parental love, on the other hand, do not seem similarly contingent on the endurance of some facts about the child. This explains why we wouldn't be morally outraged if a married couple of 10 years separated due to one party's (say) severe depression or newly acquired physical deformation, but would find it very hard to make sense of a parent who is no longer willing to enjoy a relationship with her severely depressed or disfigured adult child.

I hope the points above suffice to render intuitive the claim that persons have an interest in participating in a parent-child relationship because they have an interest in being at either the giving or the receiving end of the deepest and most robust mode of human caring. However, to further motivate this claim, consider the likely consequences of a social arrangement whereby children were denied the opportunity to participate in a parent-child relationship and were instead cared for by well-motivated and well-trained child social workers. First, even in adequate children's homes, children would not typically enjoy a relationship with an adult who cares about their good in a deep and robust way.[20] For instance, staff might end the relationship with the child at any time by changing career or site of employment. They might also fail to make significant sacrifices for the good of the child, which would be regrettable in cases where the child needed more from the relationship than simply having her basic needs met. The thought here is that a social worker in a children's home would be justifiably unwilling to spend her discretionary time and personal savings so that a child under her care could attend a good out-of-state school or access high-quality health treatment. And even in rare cases where a member of staff stayed in the child's life for a significant period of time and bore significant burdens for her benefit, things could easily change once the child ceased to be the institution's legal responsibility.

Consider now the consequences for adults in a world where they are not allowed to participate in a parent-child relationship. If I am right that parental love renders moral actions of sacrifice and cost-taking irresistible and unavoidable across a lifetime, then in a world without families, adults would miss out on the enriching moral experience of feeling significantly compelled to create the conditions for someone else to lead a good life.[21] That is, in a world without parent-child relationships, adults would miss out on the opportunity of taking on significant costs over a lifetime in order to assist another human being to overcome the challenges and difficulties associated with both childhood (for example, inability to identify and autonomously pursue the good) and adulthood (for example, heartbreak, illness, financial stress). An important upshot of appealing to what both the parent and their child have to gain in the relationship is that my justification of the family will count as a "dual interest" one, and will therefore take seriously the independent and equal moral status of both parents and children.[22] This will become important later when we return to the challenges mentioned in the previous section.

Before I conclude this section, let me briefly dispel some potential worries about the value of parental and other types of love. First, I have not argued that all parents care deeply or robustly for their child, nor that parents are always right about what the good of their child consists in. Parent-child relationships where parents either do not care about their child, or have false beliefs about what her good consists in, do not pose a problem for my account, because they lack the value that justifies parties having a compelling interest in participating in such relationships in the first place.[23] A child who is in a relationship with a parent who does not care for her deeply and robustly, or who holds false beliefs about what she is morally entitled to, would be better off in an adequate children's home.

Second, I have not suggested that *only* parental love gives rise to deep and robust modes of caring. What I have suggested is that other valuable loving relationships are typically less likely to reach the same levels of deepness and robustness. Indeed, for my purposes here, it suffices to highlight the fact that *valuable* tokens of other loving relationships seem to be valuable even in the absence of resilience and significant personal sacrifices. For instance, we might think that a romantic relationship where parties teach each other important life lessons still gives rise to a valuable loving relationship, even if the relationship is not very resilient, and both parties will eventually part ways.[24] We might also think that a friendship where parties play the role of primary confidant in each other's life is still valuable even if they are not disposed to make significant sacrifices for each other's sake. The point here is simply that parental love is valuable because of its role in motivating a deep form of caring across time and alternative circumstances, whereas other types of love seem to be valuable even when the caring they give rise to is not very resilient, and even when it fails to motivate parties to place the good of their beloved on a footing equal to or even higher than their own.

1.4. Procreation and Reasons for Love

In the previous section, I argued that parental love is valuable for the role it plays in sustaining a robust relationship of loving sacrifice between parent and child. But an important question that helps us think through the value of procreative parenting is: What renders this type of parental love *justified*? Note that whatever the answer to this question may be (and assuming that the answer is not "nothing"), it will have to appeal to facts that make sense from both a first- and a third-person perspective.[25] An appeal to subjectively valuable properties will only go as far as *explaining* parental love in some circumstances. For instance, we might be able to explain why a macho father of three only loves his equally hypermasculine son without endorsing the position that masculinity gives parents normative reasons for love.

Now, for those who believe that there are normative reasons for love, there are three main answers in the literature: love results from lovable facts about the person (the property view), from loving-conducive facts about the relationship (the relationship view), or from a combination of these.[26] If we apply these accounts to the case of parent-child relationships, we arrive at the following possibilities.

The first is that parental love is justified by the intrinsic qualities of the child. A parent who loves her child does so for properties like playfulness and curiosity, according to this view. The second possibility is that parental love is justified by the fact that parent and child stand in an intimate relationship. Here what justifies love on the part of the parent is precisely the fact that the parties interact with one another intimately and share a great number of valuable projects and activities across a lifetime. A final possibility is that parental love is justified by the fact that the intrinsic qualities of the child are themselves *shaped* by the mutual interactions between parent and child in the course of the relationship—that is, love is justified by historical-relational properties. Such a hybrid account has the resources to explain why love is not easily transferable or lost. Indeed, were the parents to meet another child who is equally (or perhaps even more) playful and curious, they would not have a reason to adopt this other child instead, because their own child's curiosity and playfulness have themselves been shaped by their intimate relationship (that is, by hours of playing and reading together), and have acquired even greater value as a result. If this view is correct, then parents should love their child not only because she is playful and curious, but partly because these qualities have developed in particular ways due to their numerous interactions.[27]

So which of these theories is correct? As far as I can see, property accounts that appeal to relationality and historicity (that is, accounts that combine the property and the relationship views) seem quite plausible when attempting to justify the love we find in romantic relationships and friendships. However, consider the following two cases:

1. Bia loves her 12-month-old child Charlie, even though Charlie is extremely demanding and difficult. Charlie is always irritable, unwilling to play, reluctant to eat, have his nappies changed, have a bath. As a result, all caring and playing activities demand a high degree of effort and patience on the part of Bia. Despite Charlie lacking properties that are lovable from an objective point of view, Bia loves him deeply and robustly.
2. Billy loves his 12-month-old child Chad, even though Billy has never met Chad. Billy and Chad's mother separated after conception, and she has denied Billy access to the child. In fact, Billy only knows Chad's most basic information and has seen some of his photos. Despite the absence of a relationship, Billy loves Chad deeply and robustly, and is involved in a legal battle with Chad's mother in order to co-parent him.

Are Bia and Billy making a mistake? Or is there something about procreation that renders their love for their children wholly *justified*? I take it that having intentionally brought a vulnerable child into the world for the purposes of parenting will give an agent a weighty pro tanto reason for loving the child deeply and robustly, and that such a reason for love will win out against a number of potential pro tanto reasons against love, such as the fact that a particular child lacks lovable intrinsic properties, or the absence of an intimate relationship between procreator and progeny.

Indeed, it seems to me that procreation, when intentionally undertaken for the purposes of parenting, gives rise to a weighty pro tanto reason for love even in circumstances like case 1 and case 2, where facts about the child do not justify love or when a parent-child relationship has not yet developed. And one reason this matters morally is that some children lack lovable intrinsic qualities; and, at times, what children need the most is someone deeply motivated by love to *enter* into a relationship with them. The core idea here is that the procreative aspect of procreative parenting justifies love in the most difficult of circumstances and that, in so doing, it is the closest we get to unconditional love. It justifies love even when neither the intrinsic qualities of the beloved nor facts about the relationship can do the trick.

Of course, this is not to deny that there can be additional normative reasons for parental love. In the course of the parent-child relationship, children typically present a set of intrinsic qualities, and parents and children go through a number of events and interactions that can have a great deal of value. But what makes procreation special is that "being one's progeny" is a relational fact that obtains prior to the establishment of a parent-child relationship and cannot be lost by the child nor possessed in greater degree by anyone else. Indeed, the fact that the parent has intentionally brought their child into the world in order to parent her is a fact that remains true for the rest of her life, and it is a fact that only obtains for the parent's other biological children (if there are any), who should be loved for the same reason.

At this juncture, one might insist that a similar story applies to adoption and that I have not yet established that procreative parenting enjoys nontrivial value. After all, adoptive parents do say something intelligible when they say that they love their adopted child *because* she is their child.

I certainly believe that adoptive parents are typically presented with several reasons for love once they are in an intimate relationship with their child. However, I still hold that such love will be justified by an appeal to facts about the child and/or facts about the relationship, and not by an appeal to the fact of adoption. Contrary to what takes place in procreation, the mere fact of adoption cannot be a weighty pro tanto reason for love. To see why, consider the following case.

> 3. Ada has been on the waiting list for adoption for nine months and has finally been assigned a 12-month-old child, Chelsea, whom she can take home after signing the adoption papers.

However, after the final legal document has been signed, an official rushes in and lets Ada know that a different child of a similar age, Cheryl, would be a much better fit for Ada (Ada's native language is French and Cheryl was cared for by a French-speaking mother before becoming an orphan). The official therefore suggests revoking Chelsea's adoption so that Ada can take Cheryl home instead.

As this case illustrates, adoption on its own does not justify love. It would be very strange if Ada responded to the official's offer by saying that in signing the adoption documents, she was *justified* in loving *Chelsea* deeply and robustly. And the strangeness of such a response can be explained by the fact that in adoptive parenting, love is justified by an appeal to facts about the child, facts about the relationship, or (most plausibly) a combination of both. Love is not justified by coming to sign a set of legal documents.

This nontrivial distinction between reasons for love in procreation and adoption explains why a procreative parent would be justified in wanting to parent her biological child even when she could have a much better relationship with another child. It also explains why we typically find understandable the behavior of procreative parents who spend much of their lives trying to find a child who has been kidnapped or accidentally swapped for another child after birth. And here, again, there is a relevant difference between procreation and adoption, which can be captured by a modified version of case 3.

4. Ada has been on the waiting list for adoption for nine months and has finally been assigned a 12-month-old child, Chelsea, whom she can take home after signing the adoption papers. However, after the final legal document has been signed, an official rushes in and lets Ada know that there has been a bureaucratic mistake and that a competent foreign couple has already taken Chelsea overseas. The official therefore suggests that Ada adopt another child instead.

With regard to case 4, I think it would be very strange if Ada responded to this bureaucratic mistake by refusing to adopt another child in need and choosing instead to spend time and resources trying to track down the couple who took Chelsea away from her. I believe we would find such behavior inappropriate because, at that stage, Ada's love for Chelsea was not yet justified.[28]

1.5. Back to the Challenges

We are finally in a position to see why procreative parenting has the sort of nontrivial value that explains why competent prospective parents are justified in having a biological child even in light of the moral reasons that count against it. Procreative parenting justifies love irrespective of facts about the child or facts about the relationship. The love of procreative parenting is therefore the closest we can get to unconditional love: the mere fact that parents have intentionally created their child gives them a weighty pro tanto reason for loving the child deeply and robustly. This, in turn, gives parents reasons to take on costs and make sacrifices for the good of their child across a lifetime. It is therefore not surprising that so many prospective parents are subjectively attracted to procreative parenting, and see it as an important ingredient of their conception of what it means for their lives to go well. They want to experience precisely this form of love and, in so doing, to care deeply and robustly about someone else's good, irrespective of her intrinsic qualities and irrespective of facts about their mutual interactions over the course of an intimate relationship.

Note, though, that the argument here does not imply that there is a duty to procreate rather than adopt. Adoption retains a number of important moral features that will be considered quite attractive to a number of people. For those who are subjectively attracted to entering into a relationship with a child who already exists and who is already in need of their love, adoption will be preferable to procreation. The same is true of those who want to become parents but want to minimize, as much as possible, their carbon footprint.

Still, one might think that although my account does not support a duty to procreate, it might still show that the relationship one enjoys with one's biological child is in some sense superior to the relationship one enjoys with one's adopted or stepchild.[29]

I think this is a valid concern, but it can be resisted. At no stage in the discussion have I argued that procreative parenting is, all things considered, *superior* to other forms of parenting. There is no denying that in the case of adoption, there is a great deal of moral value in first assisting a child in need and then parenting her.[30] Indeed, all I have said is that procreative parenting is distinctively valuable; but that is wholly compatible with adoption being distinctively valuable in its own right. Second, I have only argued that the procreative aspect of procreative parenting has nontrivial value; I have not in any way suggested that much of the value of procreative parenting derives from procreation. Quite the contrary: much of the value of procreative parenting comes from parenting. Procreation simply gives parents a weighty pro tanto reason for love, and this is neither trivial nor earth-shattering.

There is, however, a second concern in the vicinity. The worry here is that if parental love enjoys somewhat distinct justifications in cases of adoption and procreation, then parents in mixed families have a moral reason to treat their biological and adoptive children differently, which would be quite a problematic result.[31]

It is true that parents in mixed families will have a normative reason for loving the child they have created that is not there for the child they have adopted. But recall that there are other normative reasons for love that do not refer to procreation. Moreover, reasons for love, whatever they may be, will still be outweighed by the stringent duty of justice that parents have to fairly distribute the benefits and burdens of family life.

To better see how reasons for love do not block the demands of justice in a mixed family arrangement, think of a mother who loves both her biological and her adopted child deeply and robustly, but who is in deep awe of the latter's extraordinary moral character. In that case, we might say that the adopted child's unusual disposition for doing good gives the mother an additional reason for love, but that it would still be deeply problematic for her to provide additional benefits for that child. This is because the duties of justice that apply to the family make any form of favoritism unjustified, even when motivated by love.

I hope I have done enough to show that procreative parenting can in fact withstand the procreative challenge. I now turn to showing that my account also has the resources to resist the redistribution challenge.

From the perspective of the parent, it is now (I hope) easy to see how distribution fails to secure her interest in procreative parenting. This is because the interest in procreative parenting is not the interest in procreation and parenting, but the interest in parenting one's own biological child. An arrangement of child redistribution by the state will therefore completely disregard the compelling interest of a competent procreative parent in raising a child she already has a weighty pro tanto reason for loving deeply and robustly.

To be sure, one could argue that what children have to gain from redistribution justifies disregarding the interest of procreative parents in parenting their biological child. After all, children have an instrumental interest in having their interests protected and promoted to the greatest extent possible, and the parent-child relationship is a mere means of achieving that end. In cases where biological parents are not in a position to further the child's interests to the greatest extent possible, it is the interest of the procreative parent that should give way, not the interest of the child. The case in favor of child redistribution would thereby settle the issue of whether the justification of the family should appeal to the interests of both parents and children, or of children only.

I think that there are good reasons to stick with a dual-interest theory of the family since we should treat neither adults nor children as creatures whose interests count for less.[32] Still, one might insist that because a dual-interest theory is unable to give the correct verdict with regard to the desirability of child redistribution, we should conclude that, in the end, procreative parenting is often impermissible, since it makes it hard for the interests of both parent and child to be jointly secured.

I resist this pessimistic result. First, I believe we must have a capacious understanding of parental competency, one that goes beyond avoidance of abuse and neglect and ensures the sufficient protection of all the core interests of the child. After all, children don't only have a compelling interest in not suffering abuse or neglect. They also have core interests in education, health, leisure, friendship, self-expression, access to meaningful projects, and everything else we believe is a necessary ingredient of a good life.[33] In the next chapter, I will spell out what parental competency entails by discussing the conditions under which adults acquire and retain a moral right to parent. Incompetent procreative parents are therefore those who lack the moral right to parent, and for that reason, lack a moral claim against redistribution.

Second, because parental love creates the best conditions for children to have a good childhood, I contend that children also have an additional interest in being parented by someone who has reason to love them irrespective of their intrinsic qualities and irrespective of facts about the relationship. The claim here is that children also have an interest in being at the receiving end of a type of love that is almost unconditional (that is, conditional only on the child not being a moral monster). Were the child, and by implication the relationship, to become extremely difficult, parents would still have a weighty pro tanto reason for loving her. This explains why a competent biological parent still has a stronger claim than the better parent to enter into a relationship with the child.

But what about the brilliant nonbiological parent? Don't outstanding parental skills count more for the child than being at the receiving end of a form of love that is almost unconditional? Perhaps. But we cannot conclusively settle this question until we are confident that there is such a thing as brilliance in parenting, and that such brilliance leads to a significant increase in value for the child. While the difference in value for the child between bad and competent parents is significant (especially after we set the bar for competency at a high level), the difference in value for the child between competent and brilliant parents could be marginal. In fact, in Part II of this book, I will lend support to the plausible position that there is no brilliant parent, since once parents succeed in supporting their children in being carefree, and pursuing meaningful relationships and projects, there is very little scope for doing significantly more in terms of creating the conditions for children to lead good lives.

But suppose that there is a parental analogue of Shakespeare or Leonardo, and that such brilliance would lead to a *significant* increase in value for the child. Like other high-stakes scenarios, it seems that here children would in fact have a stronger interest in being in a parent-child relationship with the brilliant parent than being in one with a competent biological parent. This, however, does not entail redistribution from the biological to the better parent (as is the case for accounts that fail to locate the nontrivial value of procreative parenting). Rather, it would only entail redistribution from the competent to the *brilliant* parent.

1.6. Alternative Responses

I now discuss how other theorists have responded to the two challenges raised earlier, and show why my account is more adequate or complete than theirs. In particular, I discuss how Christine Overall addresses the procreation challenge, and how Anca Gheaus addresses the redistribution challenge.[34] I take each in turn.

In response to the procreation challenge, Overall argues that the interest in procreation is an interest in creating a party to a relationship, where the parent loves the child "deeply and madly." As she explains: "The difference in procreation is that the parents not only start to build a relationship with the child but actually *create* the person with whom they have the relationship. They choose to have *their child*."[35] She also concedes that unconditional love is neither feasible nor desirable, and goes on to say that the conditional love we find present in the parent-child relationship is the kind that is conditional "on who the child is; it values the child for what he chooses to be."[36]

As becomes clear, my account is not in opposition to Overall's but fills some of the gaps she leaves open. For instance, Overall does not tell us why creating the other party to a relationship is of value, nor does she explain how such deep and mad love for a child is distinct from the love of other relationships. However, my main concern with Overall's account is that she appeals to the intrinsic qualities of the child when discussing the reason parents have for loving their biological child, and, as we have just seen, this is a mistake. As I have shown in the previous section, procreative parents are justified in loving their child *irrespective* of who their child is—unless of course she is a moral monster. The mere fact of intentional procreation is a weighty pro tanto reason for parental love.

Let us now turn to Gheaus's response to the redistribution challenge. Gheaus argues that (competent) biological parents have a right to parent their biological child because biological parents have already started the relationship with the child in pregnancy.[37] As she explains,

[The relationship] starts even before the baby is born, partly *because* birth parents devote significant resources to pregnancy and support the many kinds of costs it entails. Thus, to shuffle babies between all people that are willing and able to parent would be unfair to birth parents and would destroy already formed parent-baby relationships.[38]

There is much to say in favor of this response to the redistribution problem, and I do not deny that couples typically take on a great many costs in pregnancy, and often feel that the relationship they have with their infant is one that started some time before the birth. However, I believe that Gheaus's response to the redistribution problem has two failings. First, it fails to locate the value of *procreation* in a way that it remains neutral among the different and morally relevant causal roles one can intentionally play in procreative parenting.[39] Second, it relies on an unduly expansive understanding of what a relationship is.[40] Let me tackle each of these concerns in turn.

Consider first the implications of Gheaus's account for Billy's case above. Because Gheaus does not attribute any value to the genetic connection between procreative father and child, her account delivers the result that Billy has no compelling interest in parenting Chad simply because he was prevented from supporting the gestating mother during pregnancy. This is counterintuitive. A competent and willing procreative father, such as Billy, seems to have a strong claim to parent his genetic child, even if prevented from supporting Chad's mother with the financial and emotional costs of pregnancy. What matters here is that he has engaged in procreation with the intention of entering into a parent-child relationship with the resulting child, and would have helped with the costs of pregnancy if given a chance. Once we remember that pregnancy is not overly costly for all persons, and that some women (and trans men) are not emotionally attached to the child until birth, it becomes hard to believe that Billy's lack of interaction with the gestating mother during pregnancy did in fact remove his claim to enjoy a parent-child relationship with Chad.

A second problem with Gheaus's account comes from her conception of what a relationship is. For Gheaus, the fact that a gestating parent (and supporting partner, if there is one) eagerly anticipates the arrival of the child, combined with the fact that the gestating parent cannot help but bestow a number of benefits on the fetus, makes it the case that there is already a *relationship* between them in pregnancy. But the problem here is that we don't typically think that loving actions and emotions, as well as the bestowal of benefits, are sufficient for the existence of a relationship.

To see the point, consider the case of unrequited love on the part of a singer in a bar toward a regular customer she has never exchanged a word with. It is certainly true that there is a lot of anticipation and fantasy on the part of the singer in relation to her beloved. It is also true that her beloved feels a sense of security and warmth when listening to the singer's angelic voice. Still, it is a stretch to claim that these two enjoy a relationship.[41] Although we speak loosely of a relationship between people who share blood ties, a common ancestry, or an affiliation, the kind of relationship that could block the desirability of child redistribution would have to entail more than a mere connection. This is not to deny that some biological parents (especially those doing the gestating) feel as though there is already a relationship. The point here is that this is a subjective experience that cannot be generalized to everyone who engages in procreative parenting. As Margaret Olivia Little notes, "With gestation . . . there is little to the relationship, as a relationship, other than the biological substrate and the *woman's experience and conception of it.*"[42] My own account of the value of procreative parenting explains why competent biological parents have a claim against redistribution that is independent of whether procreator-to-fetus relations count as a relationship proper and independent of whether procreators indeed experience their connection to the fetus in pregnancy as a form of relationship.

1.7. Conclusion

Let me conclude the discussion by once again emphasizing that I have not denied that adoption is an extremely valuable social practice and that there are normative reasons for love that apply for parents irrespective of the existence of a biological connection between them and their child. In fact, in the next two chapters, I explain why adoptive parents have a moral right to parent that is as weighty as the moral right of procreative parents. I also show that the liberal state should render adoption more feasible and desirable for its citizens.

What I have denied in this chapter is that adoptive parents have a *weighty pro tanto* reason for love merely due to the legal status of adoption. Like a married person who might respond to the question "Why do you love X?" by saying that she loves X "because X is her spouse," adoptive parents do say something intelligible when they claim that they love their adopted child because she is their child. However, it is precisely here that we must tread carefully. If there are reasons for love, what these parties mean is that there are facts about X and/or facts about the relationship with X that justify their love for X. They cannot possibly justify their love by appealing to the legal status enjoyed by X.

Instead of denying that adoption has significant moral value, I have instead focused on showing that intentionally creating a person for the purposes of having a relationship with her gives parents a weighty pro tanto reason for love that remains salient for the entirety of the parent-child relationship. If this argument is sound, then the main contribution here is to locate the nontrivial value of procreative parenting so that competent prospective parents are morally entitled to procreate and parent their biological child (and so entitled to function as moral parents to their biological child). Of course, some prospective parents might know that they would not be moved by such pro tanto reason for love, and so in such cases, they would not be justified in procreating, and should choose to adopt instead.[43]

Despite the progress we have made in this chapter, more work on the ethics of parenting is needed. Indeed, even if the arguments in this chapter are sound, we are not thereby entitled to assume that all adjacent moral questions about parent-child relationships have been settled. In the next two chapters I will say more about the limits of the moral right to engage in procreation in particular, and parenting more generally. For now, I hope the discussion in this chapter will go some way toward tackling the gap between the philosophical jury on the triviality of procreative parenting and the overwhelming support for it at the societal level. Although it is not typically the job of philosophy to vindicate the status quo, I hope my account has explained why many people are right in thinking that procreative parenting is a special type of project which has the potential of adding a great deal of meaning and purpose to their lives.

2
The Right to Parent and Moral Commitment

2.1. Introduction

In the movie and novel *A Light between Oceans*, a lighthouse keeper and his wife live on an isolated Australian island in the interwar period. The couple tries desperately to conceive a child, only to be confronted with a series of miscarriages. One day a boat washes ashore, carrying a dead man and an infant who is still alive. Instead of alerting the authorities on the mainland, they bury the man's body on the island and take on the role of loving parents to the child. Some years later, the police locate the child, reunite her with the biological mother, and prevent the couple from continuing their own relationship with the child.

As to be expected, everyone involved is left scarred by this experience. The child is left longing for the two people she is already attached to. The couple is left longing for a child they have loved as their own for quite some time. The biological mother is left parenting a child who does not initially acknowledge her as a parent, as well as feeling great sympathy for the couple's predicament. Yet it is hard to deny that a continuing relationship between child and her former carers would make it very hard for the biological mother to adequately resume her parental role.

Such tragic cases of custodial disputes are not confined to fiction. Cases where prospective parents claim custody over a child to the exclusion of others are abundant in family courts in all liberal-democratic societies. Yet, before the legal systems of these societies can be well equipped to determine who should parent a given child in any particular case, we need to adequately answer a prior philosophical

Parenting and the Goods of Childhood. Luara Ferracioli, Oxford University Press.
© Oxford University Press 2024. DOI: 10.1093/oso/9780197612705.003.0003

question: What in fact determines moral parenthood? Or, more explicitly, who counts as the *moral* parent of a child?

Before I can defend my own account of moral parenthood, let me explain what philosophers typically understand the moral parent to be. A moral parent is an adult who has the moral right to be in an intimate paternalistic relationship with a particular child. This moral right explains why the child (who is subjected to ongoing paternalistic treatment by the moral parent) lacks grounds for complaint. This moral right also explains why other nonstate agents have a moral duty of noninterference and must respect the decisions undertaken by the moral parent. Note, however, that moral parenthood is not only about rights. After all, a moral parent acquires a number of moral duties by virtue of exercising the parental role, such as a duty to educate the child for moral life and to consult with her when appropriate.[1]

In this chapter I argue that the parental role is best undertaken by those who *morally* commit to pursuing a parent-child relationship with a particular child, and that moral commitment can arise without any form of causal connection between the parent's actions and the existence of the child, and that it goes well beyond merely consenting to the parental role. I show that my commitment account of moral parenthood has several advantages over its competitors. It does not privilege procreative parents over adoptive parents, it takes the interests of children seriously, and it makes sense of the entirety of the parent-child relationship. If I am right that the moral right to parent follows from a moral commitment to a particular child, as opposed to a causal relationship or an act of consent, then this will place us in a good position to establish who are the agents responsible for working alongside the liberal state in ensuring that children can lead good lives qua children.

The discussion to follow proceeds in five parts. In Section 2.2, I make some important preliminary points. In Section 2.3, I set up the desiderata for a correct theory of moral parenthood, and show that the two most prominent accounts—the causal and the voluntarist accounts of moral parenthood—fail to meet all of the desiderata. In Sections 2.4 and 2.5, I argue in favor of the commitment account of moral parenthood. In Section 2.6, I respond to objections against it.

2.2. On Procreation and Parenthood

Before I discuss the desiderata for a correct theory of moral parenthood, it is important to make some distinctions clear, as well as to describe what I take to be the default position in the debate pertaining to the essential feature(s) of moral parenthood.

As already hinted at in the previous chapter, parents who procreate are also referred to as biological parents in the literature. In this chapter, I will refer to procreative parents and biological parents interchangeably. Note, though, that there is an important distinction between procreative (or biological) parents on the one hand, and *causal* parents on the other hand. A person who intentionally contracts the service of a surrogate and of gamete donors for all the genetic material required for procreation might be considered a causal parent but not a procreative or biological parent.[2]

Another important distinction is the one between moral, social, and legal parenthood.[3] The idea here is that the question "Who is C's parent?" allows for different answers in different domains. A legal parent is the parent dictated by law. A social parent is the parent dictated by societal norms. A moral parent is the parent dictated by morality. Often there is an overlap between all forms of parenthood, but at times they can come apart. We can think of a lesbian couple in a society where the legal code privileges the genetic connection between child and biological mother, as opposed to the gestational connection, which is deemed to be the most relevant one by society at large. Let's imagine that in this scenario, one of the biological mothers gestates the child, the other provides for her genetic material (together with a sperm donor), but that, unfortunately, both of them fail to promote and protect the child's interests up to the morally relevant threshold, which happens to be higher than what social and legal norms deem acceptable. In this case, society will acknowledge the gestating parent as a parent, the law will recognize the genetic parent as a parent, and, morality will fail to recognize both as parents.

Because in this chapter I am primarily interested in the question of *moral* parenthood, I will focus on the question of which individual or group of individuals has *a moral right to parent* a particular child. But unlike many philosophers who have tackled this question in the past,

I do not start with the question of who is morally *required* to enter into a parent-child relationship with a particular child.[4] Instead, I start with the question of who is morally *permitted* to pursue such relationship. The reason for this is simple: there is significant disagreement among philosophers over whether moral parenthood could ever be a matter of duty. Indeed, while many causal theorists insist that there is a duty to become the parent of a particular child, and that this duty falls on the person who shares some relevant causal connection with her existence, many voluntarist or consent theorists deny that agents could ever be under a *moral duty* to parent a particular child, and that consent is required for incurring the parental role.[5] At the same time, however, everyone agrees that moral parents have a moral right to engage in an array of paternalist actions within the realm of an intimate parent-child relationship. Focusing on the question of permissibility, without simultaneously arguing against the existence of a duty to become someone's parent, does not then privilege any side of the debate, since everyone agrees that moral parents are those who have a moral right to parent a particular child. (The disagreement is only over whether this moral right "piggybacks" on a prior moral *duty* to become a child's parent.)

Let me now conclude this section by explaining where my discussion fits in the broader debate between monist and pluralist theories of moral parenthood. As is to be expected, monist theories are those that locate the grounds of moral parenthood in only one essential feature, such as consent. Pluralist theories, on the other hand, locate the grounds of moral parenthood in a plurality of factors. Pluralists usually arrive at their conclusion by noting that distinct factors such as genetic connection, gestation, and consent (as in the case of adoption) all seem relevant for determining who counts as a moral parent.[6]

There are certainly good reasons for taking pluralist accounts to be the default position in the debate over moral parenthood, for it seems that we are better off accepting multiple grounds of moral parenthood—that is, accepting multiple sufficient conditions for the enjoyment of a moral right to parent a particular child—rather than excluding obvious cases simply because they do not fit our theory. For instance, it seems that we are better off going pluralist than denying moral parenthood in the case of adoptive parents, because adoption is not covered by a causal theory.[7] Indeed, once we compare a biological and an adoptive parent who are equally excellent parents, it seems preferable to give up on the quest for a monist theory of moral parenthood over asserting that the adoptive parent in question is not a *moral* parent, but merely a social or legal parent.

Having said that, if we develop a monist theory of moral parenthood that is extensionally adequate and well motivated, then we will have good reasons for thinking that the pluralist has not gone deep enough in her inquiry and has failed to recognize that there is in fact something that is essential to all morally valid parent-child relationships. In other words, the best way to argue for monism over pluralism in this debate is to successfully unify cases that pluralists have seen as lacking unity. In the remainder of this chapter, I hope to develop a theory which does just that.

2.3. Three Desiderata for a Correct Theory of Moral Parenthood

Before I can explain how moral commitment is at the core of all morally legitimate parent-child relationships, it pays to defend a set of desiderata for a correct monist theory of moral parenthood, while simultaneously discussing how two preeminent monist accounts—the causal and the voluntarist accounts—fail to meet (some of) them.

Let me start by emphasizing that the desiderata I have in mind are not meant to be exhaustive. Rather, they strike me as the most important and central ones, and so give us solid resources to construct a monist account of moral parenthood that is successful. The desiderata are as follows. First, a correct theory of moral parenthood should be attentive to the interests of both parties in a parent-child relationship. Call this the dual-interest desideratum. Second, a correct theory of moral parenthood should be able to identify an essential feature of parenting that is true of both adoptive and procreative parenting. Call this the inclusion desideratum. And third, a correct theory of moral parenthood should identify an essential feature of moral parenthood that obtains both at the time at which the parent-child relationship is formed, and later in time. Call this the relationship desideratum. Let me motivate each in detail.

2.3.1. Dual Interest

As I alluded to in the previous chapter, one finds three general approaches to the justification of the family qua institution in the literature on family ethics.

One approach requires that the justification of the parent-child relationship be one that appeals to the interests of the child only.[8] Such child-centered accounts will only accept parent-child relationships in a world in which families are indeed better than actual and conceivable alternative arrangements at promoting and protecting the interests of children.

A second approach, which comes from the opposite direction, has it that parent-child relationships can be justified solely by an appeal to the interests of parents.[9] For those who buy into this approach, it does not matter which arrangement actually does well at promoting and protecting the interests of children, since it is the interests of the parents that count when we get into the business of justifying the family.

A final approach requires that we identify the pressing interests of both children in having parents and of parents in having children.[10] The dual-interest account can avoid the counterintuitive implications of a world where state-run institutions of child-rearing are truly excellent. After all, it can explain why children should still be parented by *good* parents despite the *excellence* of state-run institutions, as well as why they should be under the care of the state in cases of parental incompetency (where the bar for competency is placed moderately high). Note, though, that none of these theories can answer the question of which child should be paired with which parent, which is the question we are pursuing in this chapter. All they can do is answer the broader question of why we should have families in the first place.

Given that the dual-interest account of the family does a much better job than the alternatives in acknowledging the equal and independent moral status of both parents and children, we should theorize about moral parenthood under the assumption that a successful account of moral parenthood is one that takes the interests of both parents and children seriously.[11] Of course, theorists disagree about how to best cash out a dual-interest account, with some arguing that children have an interest in being treated paternalistically by loving parents, who, in turn, have an interest in exercising a fiduciary role in the lives of their children, with others calling attention to the central role of intimacy and affection within the family.[12] And, as I argued in the previous chapter, what seems to be at the core of valuable parent-child relationships is the fact that loving parents are robustly disposed to protect and promote the interests of their children up to a high level, and that the ability to act on such disposition also enriches the lives of parents.[13]

So how do the causal and voluntarist accounts mentioned earlier fare with regard to this desideratum? It is clear that neither of them takes the interests of children sufficiently seriously, for neither account guarantees that children will indeed be parented by people who are in fact robustly disposed to protect and promote the interests of their children up to a high level. Consider the causal account first. There is no necessary connection between being a procreator and being disposed to do a good job at parenting. Indeed, family courts around the world are all too familiar with procreators who turned out to be unwilling to respect the most basic rights of their biological children, let alone create the conditions for their lives to go well.

The same is true of voluntarist accounts, which focus on the fact of consent to the parental role. One can consent to being a parent and yet be quite bad at it. There is nothing about consenting to an activity or project that implies having the dispositions required for doing a good job at it. Consider the following case.

> **Guardian:** Mary receives an email from a couple of friends sharing their news that they are expecting their first child, and letting her know that they would like her to be the legal guardian should the child be orphaned. Mary knows that she lacks the relevant disposition for adequate parenting, but does not take seriously the possibility that they could both die and that in this event, she would be expected to become the child's parent. Mary decides to accept

the invitation, only to find herself, a few years later, parenting the orphaned child in a less than satisfactory manner.

As is clear, Mary has consented to the parental role, but her consent neither follows from her having the relevant dispositions for adequate parenting, nor ensures that the relevant dispositions will eventually be formed. And as the case makes clear, consent without the relevant disposition to act as a good parent does not take the child's interests sufficiently seriously.[14]

It is important to emphasize that both causal and voluntarist accounts can, and often do, make the moral right to parent conditional on competency. That is, they can accept that an incompetent social or legal parent will, at some point, stop counting as a moral parent. But this move raises an interesting question. If being a competent parent is so important for moral parenthood, then why wouldn't competency already be part of the story that grounds it? As we will see later, one can tell a story about the grounds of moral parenthood that is already sensitive to an individual's capacity and willingness to parent well.

2.3.2. Inclusion

A second and related desideratum is that a successful theory of moral parenthood should be capable of acknowledging (some) adoptive parents as proper moral parents. As we have already seen, what is distinctively valuable about parent-child relationships is the motivational role of parental love, and the fact that loving parents are robustly disposed to protect and promote the interests of their children up to a high level. And, of course, there is simply no reason to think that adoptive parents are less motivated than procreative parents to protect their child's interests. Given that a monist account of moral parenthood will appeal to only *one* essential feature of the parent-child relationship, it had better be a feature that does not relegate adoptive parents to the role of mere social and legal parents.

So how do the standard views fare here? Although we can certainly make sense of the idea that both adoptive and procreative parents consent to being parents by in the first instance signing a legal document, and in the second instance deciding not to abort or put the child up for adoption, it is well known that causal theories are unable to adequately acknowledge adoptive parents as moral parents. After all, adoptive parents are not causally implicated in the existence of the child they have adopted, no matter what procreative acts one takes to be morally relevant. Whether we are talking about a causal account that focuses on the intention to create, provision of genetic material, and/or gestation, adoptive parents necessarily fail to meet all of them.[15] Yet it seems shortsighted to focus on the creation of a person, and the alleged compensatory obligations that follow from it, over all the other morally salient features of a parent-child relationship. The fact that loving parents spend the entire relationship assisting the child to lead a good life seems far more morally significant than the fact that they sometimes also bring them into existence.[16]

To be sure, this is not to deny that procreation has moral value and that procreative parents may have an interest in parenting their own biological child.[17] A theory of moral parenthood that is completely dismissive of the interest that many persons have in engaging in procreation, or that cannot explain why procreators are wronged if there is a baby swap at the hospital, is in serious trouble. But we can certainly accommodate the moral weight of procreative parenting without making it the grounds of moral parenthood. This can be done by showing that moral parenthood is grounded in a property that can be instantiated even before birth. I will return to this point later.

2.3.3. Relationship

A final desideratum for a successful theory of moral parenthood is that it should allow us to identify not only who is allowed to enter into a parent-child relationship, but also who is allowed to *stay* in that relationship after it has already developed a history. That is, we want to be able to say that a moral parent is someone entitled to develop a loving relationship with a child, and then continue participating in that relationship across time. But, most importantly, a monist theorist should appeal to the very same property when assessing whether a prospective parent is entitled to enter into a relationship with a child, and whether she is entitled to maintain it. After all, a monist theory of moral parenthood is in the business of answering the question of who has a moral right to parent a particular child, and that question can arise at any moment of a child's life (as the story in *A Light between Oceans* makes clear).

With regard to this desideratum, it looks like both voluntarist and causal accounts run into trouble.[18] Although it is not strange to appeal to a causal connection between the parent's actions and the existence of the child, or the fact of consent to the parental role prior to the establishment of the relationship, it seems odd to appeal to these features once the relationship has already developed over the years. In fact, to do so would seem to express an utter underappreciation of the morally salient features of the parent-child relationship. To see this point, imagine the following case:

> **Surrogate:** Jane, a gestating parent in a surrogate arrangement, agrees to parent the resulting child after the commissioning parents have a bitter divorce and decide against forming a family. Jane's husband, John, also agrees to the arrangement. After five years, they receive a letter from the government saying that there was a miscarriage of justice, and that in such cases, the child should be parented by their genetic kin, not individuals who are genetically unrelated to the child. Jane responds to this custody challenge by pointing to the fact of gestation on her part, and of consent on John's part.

I take it that it is odd for Jane to respond to this legal challenge by claiming that the reason *she* should continue to parent her child is because she gestated and gave birth to the child five years ago. Similarly, it is odd for her husband to appeal to the fact of consent at the time of birth. And the reason why it is odd to appeal to these facts after many years of parenting comes down to the fact that they seem somewhat trivial in a context of a loving parent-child relationship. That is to say, once the parent-child relationship is under way, the moral significance of consent and procreation fades away, and so it cannot be the case that the relationship continues to be grounded in any of these properties. The thought here is that for an essential property P to continue grounding a relationship R across its history, P's moral significance cannot evaporate with the passage of time. Rather, P must continue to do the relevant foundational work, whereby it makes sense for the agent to continuously appeal to P when explaining why she is morally entitled to continue investing and participating in R.[19]

2.4. On Moral Commitment

In the previous section, I defended three desiderata for a successful monist theory of moral parenthood. In this section, I defend a novel theory of moral parenthood that meets all of them: the commitment theory.

Let me start by pointing to an important phenomenon in moral practice that has unfortunately not yet received a great deal of attention from philosophers: the phenomenon of moral commitment.[20] Moral commitment, as we will see later, can adequately explain what grounds moral parenthood, because it provides us with a property that takes the interests of parent and child seriously, that does not privilege biological parents over adoptive parents, and that extends across the entirety of the parent-child relationship. But what exactly counts as a moral commitment?

As I understand it, moral commitments are commitments that persons make to morally valuable projects and relationships partly due to their recognition that such projects and relationships are of great value. Moreover, moral commitments are moral not only due to their *promotion* of moral value, but also because of the fact that they are carried out by agents who are also in the business of *respecting* value, and so acting within the constraints of morality. A paradigmatic example of a moral commitment can be seen in the work of professionals behind Médecins Sans Frontières (MSF). These are individuals who are devoted to saving the lives of civilians in military conflict around the world, and who are inspired by the fact that their humanitarian work can be carried out without the use of violence. Indeed, the work of those involved with MSF counts as a moral commitment not only because saving the lives of innocent people is an exceptionally valuable activity to engage in, but also because it is an activity pursued without recourse to gross human rights violation. It is therefore not surprising that this organization is widely seen by members of the public as an exemplar of humanitarianism.

To better understand what moral commitments are, let us look more closely at the three aspects of moral commitments I have just alluded to. First, moral commitments are motivated by value recognition.[21] Second, moral commitments are adequately expressed in moral actions.[22] Third, moral commitments cannot be founded on, or expressed via, the violation of stringent moral requirements.

The first important dimension of moral commitments is that they are sufficiently motivated by a recognition on the part of the committed agent that a project (which can include both impersonal projects and relationships) that she intends to pursue, or that she is already pursuing, is morally valuable. To see the importance of value recognition, consider a marriage. Whereas Mary doesn't *morally* commit to a marriage with Jay when she enters into it so as to escape poverty or because she made a promise to her grandmother that she would marry by the age of 30, she certainly commits morally to a marriage when she enters into it for reasons having to do with her love and concern for Jay.

Now it is certainly true that often we are attracted to a project for a number of reasons, and many such reasons make no reference to the moral value of the project itself. Apart from valuing the relationship with Jay, Mary might be attracted to the financial security that comes with signing a marriage certificate. The same rationale might be at play with those actively involved with the work of MSF. A doctor who joins this organization to provide emergency health treatments in conflict areas might value many aspects of the job, such as the financial security and the ability to travel. But if she is not at all moved by the fact that the work itself is morally good, then her humanitarian work does not rise to the level of a moral commitment. The thought here is not that morally committed agents are immune to nonmoral considerations, but rather that they will not be morally committed to a valuable project if they do not actually appreciate its moral dimension.[23]

One could, of course, try to put pressure on the necessity of value recognition for moral commitments. For instance, Mike, the CEO of a mining company, might be a closeted environmentalist and yet be great at his job. We might therefore say that he is committed to his job despite finding it morally reprehensible. Although it is certainly true that we often speak of persons as being committed to something merely because they are good at it, it is actually premature to refer to it as a *moral* commitment. This is simply because being good at something does not suffice for moral commitments, even if it suffices for commitments more generally. Consider again Jay's marriage proposal. Mary might marry Jay just for his money or to keep up a promise she made years ago, and yet turn out to be a good spouse.[24] So in Mike's case, it is just not true that he is *morally* committed to his job. Rather, his great performance might be a result of other reasons, such as his desire to maintain his current standard of living. But because he is aware of the fact that polluting activities have no moral value in the first place (and so no moral value to be recognized), he is not in fact morally committed to his job.

Now, we have already alluded to the fact that excellence tends to indicate commitment. This is because typically when someone values a worthwhile project, she takes it very seriously. But, again, this is not always the case. Sometimes individuals genuinely value a given project, but choose to prioritize other aspects of their lives.[25] Paul might genuinely value the lives of poor people in the developing world, and yet end up failing to donate to charity because he is too busy with his other projects. But irrespective of why he fails to express his moral values in his actions, he simply does not count as being morally committed to humanitarianism when he fails to act in ways that clearly express recognition of its value.

It is perhaps easier to see the point by returning to the marriage analogy. Suppose Jay can recognize that his romantic relationship with Mary as something that makes his life meaningful. (So he is radically different from the spouse who married for financial reasons or to keep up a promise.) Yet, he puts a number of other projects ahead of his marriage and so ends up being a pretty lousy spouse. He is not there for Mary when she needs him. He gets distracted when she is telling him about her day. He avoids spending time together. In such cases, he values his relationship, and continues to consent to it, but he is not committed to it to a sufficient degree for it to count as a moral commitment.

It is certainly tempting to resist the cases above by claiming that Paul simply doesn't value the lives of poor people, or that Jay doesn't value his relationship after all. But I think it would be a mistake to insist that when one values a worthwhile project, one is necessarily motivated to do a good job at engaging with it.[26] The problem here is not that these characters fail to recognize the importance of eradicating poverty, or of their intimate relationships, but it is just that they don't act in ways that adequately express such recognition. The problem is precisely that they choose not to bear the relevant burdens or incur the relevant opportunity costs despite being aware that doing so is typically required for *adequately* expressing the recognition of the moral value in place.

Before we can discuss what this means for parent-child relationships, let me briefly mention one final aspect of moral commitments that is necessary for aligning this particular theory of the nature of moral commitments with a plausible picture of morality. This is that they can only be pursued in ways that do not violate the most basic moral demands that bind us. If MSF starts killing some civilians in order to make their job of saving thousands of lives easier (by, say, making use of drones to distract combatants), a moral commitment would no longer be in place. If Paul steals the decently earned money from his friends to give to charity, he won't count as being morally committed to humanitarianism, even if the money saves lives. This is because the violation of basic moral requirements for the pursuit of a project disqualifies that project from counting as a *moral* commitment.[27] The result here is that moral commitments are not only the result of value recognition and the performance of actions that adequately express such recognition, but they are also the result of pursuing valuable projects while still firmly remaining within the strictest bounds of morality.

2.5. Committing to a Child

Now that we know that moral commitments entail taking adequate and morally permissible means to ends one rightly recognizes as valuable, we can answer the following question: What does it mean to be morally committed to the parental role? As should be clear by now, when adults morally commit to a parent-child relationship with a particular child, they do so at least partly because they recognize the moral value of taking up the parental role, and not for unrelated reasons, such as wanting to please family members or being concerned about the stigma that attaches to not caring for a child that they have created. Again, I do not mean to deny that such reasons can be quite salient for many individuals. Nor do I mean to suggest that it is morally problematic to be partly moved by nonmoral considerations. The point here is simply that for a moral commitment to a particular parent-child relationship to arise, parents have to actually recognize the moral value of their unique paternalistic relationship with a particular child, and be sufficiently moved by *that* reason.

In addition to recognizing the moral value of the parent-child relationship, moral parents are those who act in ways that *adequately* express such recognition. This means that they adequately promote and protect the interests of their children up to a moderately high level, and create the conditions for their lives to go well. A parent who recognizes the value of his paternalistic relationship with his child, but reliably fails to pay adequate attention to her interests, is not morally committed to the parental role, even though he might be fully aware of the fact that the child enriches his life significantly.

Finally, a moral commitment to a child cannot arise as a result of, or be expressed via, immoral actions. This is why rapists and child kidnappers do not count as moral parents even when they have done a great job at parenting the child they have created or kidnapped. There is simply no moral commitment to a child when the agent pursues the parent-child relationship via morally impermissible actions.[28]

So far, so good; but why should the moral right to parent attach to the morally committed parent? The reason is simple: a morally committed parent is necessarily a good parent, and that is not true of those who merely consent to being in a parent-child relationship, or of those who merely played a causal role in the child's existence. This is because a morally committed parent is necessarily robustly disposed to take on the steps required for her child's life to go well. For one, she can recognize the moral privilege of participating in a parent-child relationship and the ways in which such a unique paternalistic relationship can significantly enrich her life and the life of the child. But, most importantly, the morally committed parent is disposed to act in ways that adequately express such recognition by engaging in all sorts of actions that create the conditions for the child's life to go well. This is why a morally committed parent is reliably there in the middle of the night soothing a baby who is ill or a child who is scared of the dark. I complained earlier that other accounts were not naturally capable of matching children to parents who would in fact be good at parenting. The moral commitment theory does not have this problem since it builds competency into its internal logic. An incompetent parent does not act in ways that *adequately* express recognition of the moral value of the parent-child relationship; quite the opposite.

It should therefore be clear that a theory of moral parenthood that appeals to moral commitment will be quite well placed to comply with the aims of a dual-interest theory of the family, and so meet the first of our desiderata. Indeed, it is certainly in the interest of children to be parented by adults who recognize the value of the parent-child relationship and who act in ways that adequately express such recognition. But it is also in the interest of *parents* to be morally committed to the projects that they participate in. This is true not only because the parents are more likely to enjoy a relationship that they in fact recognize as worthwhile, but also because it is easier to discharge the paternalistic duties associated with the parental role when one is already disposed to act in ways that express the value of that role (and this is true irrespective of whether or not the parent has other motives for doing so).

But the commitment theory has further advantages. It is capable of recognizing both adoptive and procreative parents as moral parents, and so capable of meeting our second desideratum. The reason for this should be clear: the capacity to morally commit to a child does not depend on one's previous causal connection to her existence.[29] An adoptive parent can easily act in ways that adequately express recognition of the value of the paternalistic relationship he has with an adopted child, while still remaining within the strictest bounds of morality.

Despite not privileging procreative parenting over adoptive parenting, the commitment theory can still explain why we think that many procreative parents should count as the moral parents even before their child's birth. This is because many gestating parents act in ways that already express recognition of the value of the future child. They choose not to have an abortion, decide not to take active steps to harm the fetus, and seek medical treatment and support during pregnancy.[30] And even gestating parents who are somewhat ambivalent about becoming parents can count as morally committed if, by the time the child is born, they have come to value the relationship with their newborn and want to maintain that relationship. After all, the mere act of gestation will be considered a form of recognition of the value of the future child, so long as the gestating parent does not actively harm the fetus by engaging in behavior that is clearly detrimental to its healthy development.

Another advantage of the commitment account is that even nongestating moral parents can show commitment even before the birth. Commitment can be expressed by supporting the gestating parent with the costs and hardships of pregnancy, but it can also be evidenced by preparation for taking up the parental role after birth—by, for instance, seeking joint custody and/or negotiating more flexible hours at work.[31]

Most importantly, the moral commitment theory is compatible with the claim advanced in the previous chapter that procreative parenting is a distinctively valuable activity, and that agents are morally permitted to create and parent their own biological child if they are capable and willing to morally commit to the parental role.[32] In a sense, procreation then gives some prospective parents a unique opportunity to morally commit to a child at the expense of other willing agents. This would explain why it is impermissible for other agents to deceive a biological parent so that he is not aware of a pregnancy or his genetic connection to a child. This does not mean that causation is grounding moral parenthood, however, since one can have an interest in pursuing a relationship R that contains a property P without P itself explaining why one is entitled to continue investing and participating in R. We can concede, for instance, that some adults have an interest in an egalitarian romantic relationship without egalitarianism being the property that makes all romantic relationships morally valuable.

Finally, the moral commitment theory can identify an essential feature of moral parenthood that obtains both at the time the parent-child relationship is formed, as well as later on. For there is no denying that moral commitment is already there on the part of those procreators who provide the fetus with a hospitable womb, and on the part of adoptive parents who have taken a child home and introduced her to relatives as a new member of the family. But most importantly, moral commitment will continue grounding moral parenthood throughout the whole childhood, and beyond. A morally committed parent, whether adoptive or procreative, will continue valuing the parent-child relationship and engaging in actions that are expressive of this fact. So long as the parent continues creating the conditions for the child's life to go well, she will continue to count as a *moral* parent.[33]

2.6. Objections

At this stage, a critic might respond to this discussion with a couple of observations. She might call attention to the fact that, at times, no one is willing to morally commit to a child, and that my account legitimizes a world where many children are parentless (they have no moral parents). Call this the problem of *parental scarcity*. Alternatively, she might point to the opposite problem and insist that, at least on the face of it, it appears that a large number of prospective parents can morally commit to being in a parent-child relationship with a particular child. Call this the problem of *parental proliferation*. I will respond to each of these concerns in turn.

It should be clear by now that a moral commitment account is not committed to the claim that a moral right to parent piggybacks on a prior *duty* to enter into a parent-child relationship with a particular child. The reason for this is that a moral right to parent follows from a moral commitment to a particular child, and not an alleged compensatory obligation that arises when one engages in procreation or orchestrates the existence of a child. The problem is that this leads to a situation where, in some cases, no one counts as a moral parent because no one has morally committed to a particular child. This is troubling.

There are actually two concerns behind the parental scarcity problem. One is that we want children to have at least one moral parent. Another concern is that we want procreators to take their procreative responsibilities seriously. A moral commitment theory, so the objection goes, neither guarantees that every child will have a moral parent, nor that procreators will refrain from engaging in procreation willy-nilly, since they can always choose not to morally commit to the child after procreation.

It is certainly true that a commitment theory delivers the result that at times there is no moral parent for a particular child, but I take this fact to be symptomatic of a larger problem which also plagues the causal and the voluntarist accounts of moral parenthood: the fact that sometimes people are either unable or unwilling to parent well. Consider the voluntarist account first. In the same way that, at times, no one commits to a child, sometimes no one volunteers to take up the parental role.[34]

What about casual theories? Shouldn't we acknowledge that they do much better than their alternatives when it comes to avoiding the problem of scarcity? I certainly think it would be disingenuous to deny that this is something that causal theories have going for them. After all, causal theories do not rely on willingness when it comes to matching parents and children, and so are in a better position to avoid situations where children end up parentless (although, of course, they cannot altogether avoid parental death). But it is important to emphasize that, by minimizing scarcity, a causal theory introduces a problem that is just as serious as the problem of parental scarcity: the problem of temporary parental abuse and neglect. After all, many procreators don't want to become parents precisely because they know that they wouldn't do an adequate job. Whereas the commitment theory won't affirm a moral right to parent on the part of such persons, a causal theory will assign them a moral duty to parent, which will be taken away only after some damage to the child has already been inflicted. By attaching a duty to parent to procreators merely on the basis of their causal role in the child's existence, and by making the maintenance of that duty conditional on the avoidance of abuse and neglect, a causal theory legitimizes a world of temporary bad parenting.[35]

Now, does that mean that all accounts fail to take the interests of children seriously? I believe not. The commitment theory can, for instance, appeal to the existence of *adequate* children's homes, and of staff who are actually willing and trained to do their job well, and to claim that life in such homes is superior to life under abusive and neglectful parents, even if the stigma attached to being in care deceives us into thinking that the situations are in fact comparable.

This is not to deny that adequate children's homes are quite hard to come by in many sociopolitical contexts (especially in poor countries). In fact, when adequate children's homes are not an option, it is not clear that it is better for children to be raised in inadequate ones rather than by bad parents. This does not mean that we should count the bad parent as a moral parent. In such cases, we might want to assign legal parenthood solely on the basis of what is less bad for children under nonideal circumstances, and still deny that bad parents count as *moral* parents.

But what about parents who are not abusive or neglectful, but do not count as morally committed? That is, what about mediocre parents who do not violate the most basic rights of their children, but still fail to create the conditions for their lives to go well? Isn't it better that children are raised by such persons as opposed to being raised by child social workers willing to do their job well?

First, it is important to be clear about the omissions of the mediocre parent: mediocre parents may not violate the basic rights of their child, but neither do they create the conditions for the child to flourish. Going back to some of the cases I mentioned earlier, we would have to say that the mediocre parent is *not* typically there adequately attending to a sick baby or scared child.[36] With that in mind, I think the problem of thinking that mediocre parents can be moral parents is that although some very independent children might manage to lead good lives under such arrangements, I suspect that most children would be better off in the care of child social workers who adequately attend to their well-being.

A theory of moral parenthood should insist on grounding moral parenthood in a property that is typically to the benefit of children, even if it is true that some exceptional children can still flourish without it. (In the same way, we might want to argue that only liberal-democratic states are legitimate, even if it is true that under nonideal conditions some individuals will still flourish in a dictatorship.) The way to deal with mediocre parents is therefore to claim that, under sociopolitical conditions where the stigma of being raised in care is high, and where adequate children's homes fail to attract highly qualified workers, mediocre parents may prove to be acceptable legal parents. This does not mean that mediocre parents count as moral parents, however. Indeed, given the dual-interest desideratum, the relegation of mediocre parents to the role of mere legal and social parents is not problematic in the way that the relegation of *committed* adoptive parents to the role of mere legal and social parents is.[37]

Clearly, more empirical research needs to be done on what is best for children under nonideal circumstances. But whatever the results of these studies, a theory of moral parenthood can set the bar for *moral* parenthood high, and accept that parental scarcity arises as a result. Given that the same problem arises for voluntarist theories, and that causal theories can only address this problem at the expense of legitimizing temporary abuse and neglect, the moral commitment theory should not be rejected on this basis.

It is also important to add that the moral commitment theory can minimize parental scarcity by claiming that procreators who are uncommitted have stringent duties vis-à-vis their procreative choices. Indeed, their negative duty *not* to procreate when they know or suspect that they will be unable to commit once an identifiable fetus/child exists, or when they lack the ability to ensure that committed others can step in is very stringent indeed.[38] Instead of focusing on the obligation of uncommitted procreators to parent and therefore risking situations where children suffer abuse and neglect, we should instead focus on their stringent obligation not to procreate in the first place. And in cases where uncommitted agents end up procreating, they could still acquire other stringent obligations. For instance, they will certainly have an obligation to protect and promote the basic interests of the child until she is under the care of another party, and they might even have a duty to bear some of the financial costs associated with child-rearing (I am agnostic about whether procreation gives rise to financial duties of this sort).

Note, though, that while a duty to bear some of the costs of child-rearing could only attach to those causally responsible for the child's existence, a duty of care falls on anyone who ever finds herself in such a position that she is uniquely capable of meeting the basic needs of a child. Such a position of unique capacity to protect a vulnerable child from harm can follow from procreation, but it need not.[39]

Let me now turn to the problem of parental proliferation: in a nutshell, the concern that a child might end up with too many parents.

The main worry here is that if anyone can be a parent by morally committing to the parental role, we fail to treat existing parents with the respect and recognition they deserve.

To begin with, it is important to call attention to the fact that insofar as parental proliferation is a problem, it is also a problem for some versions of the causal theory (those that accept many ways of contributing to a child's existence), and for any version of the voluntarist account that understands consent as the acceptance of the parental role.[40] So there is nothing in particular about moral commitment that opens the parental floodgates, so to speak. It is also important to briefly recall the fact that morally committed agents actually stay within the strictest bounds of morality, and that someone who takes a child away from her existing moral parent will *not* count as a moral parent, no matter how good a parent she is.

But, of course, the problem of parental proliferation is different. The worry is not that the theory justifies the kidnapping of a child. It is, rather, that the theory allows for additional people to unilaterally insert themselves into the family by morally committing to the parental role.

The worry is misguided, however. This is because, as an existing moral parent, my moral commitment to my child is violated not only if someone abducts her, but also if he unilaterally inserts himself into my family life. This is because for any additional person who commits to my child without my consent, my ability to engage in actions that adequately express recognition of the value of my relationship with the child is severely compromised. Implications may include, for example, the inability to see my child as much as it is good for our relationship and the inability to forbid her to engage in what I take to be risky activities.

Whereas a child can have several parents insofar as they morally committed together at some point in time, a child cannot have several parents when some have forced themselves into a co-parenting arrangement.[41] In the former case, doing it together basically means expressing the joint commitment to *support* each other in the development of several distinct paternalistic relationships, which would, without mutual support, conflict with one another. In the latter case, there is no joint action, but instead the violation of a basic moral requirement not to significantly jeopardize the moral commitments of others.[42] The overall idea here is that a moral commitment theory does not allow for parental proliferation because it does not allow agents to morally commit to a child when that act would in fact significantly jeopardize the moral commitments that are already in place—commitments that are in the interest of both the child and her moral parent(s).[43]

Now, there are peculiar cases where the insertion of a new parent into family life *is* in the best interest of the child, while creating only a mild inconvenience to existing moral parents. Indeed, cases involving a morally committed biological parent who failed to commit in the past as a result of someone else's deceit, or a morally committed stepparent whom the child already sees as a parent would be of this sort.[44] I take it that a correct theory of moral parenthood needs to include such cases on pain of not taking children's interests sufficiently seriously.

2.7. Conclusion

In this chapter, I tackled the following question: What gives someone a moral right to parent a particular child? Unlike causal accounts, which focus on one's contribution to a child's existence, and unlike voluntarist accounts, which focus on the fact of consent to the parental role, my account focuses instead on the moral commitment on the part of the parent to a unique paternalistic relationship with a particular child. It says that a moral parent is the person who morally commits to the parental role vis-à-vis a particular child, and that moral commitment is present insofar as the parent values the child (and instrumentally values the unique paternalistic relationship which the child's wellbeing depends on), acts in ways that adequately express this fact, and does not violate basic moral requirements in order to pursue this relationship. (To be sure, the commitment account does not commit itself to the claim that there is a duty to take on the parental role, but I am indifferent as to whether it should be seen as an improved voluntarist account that meets all the desiderata or whether it should be classified as something else.)

To underline the attraction of the commitment account, let us return to *A Light between Oceans*. My verdict here should be clear. The biological mother was the moral parent all along, and it was unacceptable for the couple to take on the parental role without first checking that this child was indeed an orphan. Unlike causal accounts, however, a commitment theory explains why the original mother should resume her parental role even if she had adopted the child rather than given birth to her. And unlike standard voluntarist accounts, a commitment theory explains why she should not resume her parental role if she was not morally committed to the child, but had merely consented to the relationship for other reasons.[45]

Apart from being extensionally adequate, the moral commitment account does several other things: it does not legitimize temporarily bad parenting, and it does justice to existing moral parents, whether they have adopted or procreated the child. Finally, it gives the state a foundational story that explains why the legal right to parent should ideally be in the hands of those who are disposed to pursue the good of their children, thus creating the best conditions for children's lives to go well.

3
The Opportunity to Parent and Adoption

3.1. Introduction

A recent study on child-removal rates in Australia showed that in the period between 2019 and 2020, 30,600 Australian children were removed from their procreative parents for two years or more due to abuse and/or neglect.[1] But in the year before that, only 310 children were adopted (with adoption processes taking on average five years to be completed).[2] Almost half of all children who qualify for adoption in Australia spend their childhoods under the full authority of the state with the support of several foster families (families that care for children temporarily without counting as their legal parents).[3]

From these figures, one would think that despite adoptive and procreative parenting being morally on a par (as discussed in the previous chapter), Australians are not interested in adopting, and overwhelmingly favor procreative parenting over adoptive parenting. But, in fact, 17 percent of respondents to a survey of over 1,000 Australians were reported to have "actively looked into or given serious thought to adoption."[4] These figures suggest that policymakers in Australia are in some sense failing those who would like to become adoptive parents, as well as the children who would benefit from adoption. More importantly for our purpose, such figures raise the pressing question of what role a liberal state should play in the creation of families, be they adoptive or biological. In this chapter, I turn precisely to the question of how the liberal state should go about creating opportunities for parenting.

As is to be expected, the question of family creation becomes particularly pertinent once we have a better sense of the value of adoption, procreation, and parenting for the citizens of a liberal society. This was the focus of the previous two chapters. There I examined the following

Parenting and the Goods of Childhood. Luara Ferracioli, Oxford University Press.
© Oxford University Press 2024. DOI: 10.1093/oso/9780197612705.003.0004

philosophical questions: (1) Can procreative parenting be justified? and (2) Who counts as the moral parent for a child? I argued that procreative parenting can be sufficiently valuable for particular individuals despite not bringing about the best consequences for existing children in need of parental love, nor for future generations likely to be affected by climate change. But I also argued that when it comes to the question of moral parenthood, both procreative and adoptive parents can count as proper moral parents if they are morally committed to the parental role. Although these arguments by themselves do not settle the question of family formation by the liberal state, they do have implications for the question of what citizens owe one another when it comes to the establishment of parent-child relationships. And, as we will see, they pave the way for a *pro-adoption* take on justice in family creation.[5]

The discussion in this chapter is divided into four sections. In Section 3.2, I make a case against certain kinds of reproductive technologies and practices, showing that citizens lack a positive right against their fellow citizens to enjoy all the conditions for procreative parenting. In Section 3.3, I make a case for adoption, showing that the right of children to be loved creates a duty on the part of the state to facilitate adoptive parenting as a mode of family formation. In Section 3.4, I discuss the implications of saying that the state must make adoption more desirable and feasible, and of arguing that citizens lack a justice claim to access certain kinds of reproductive technologies and practices. In Section 3.5, I respond to a couple of objections to the arguments developed in this chapter. The upshot of my discussion is that under current sociopolitical conditions, justice tells against the provision by the liberal state of certain assisted reproductive technologies and reproductive practices, such as in vitro fertilization (IVF) and surrogacy, and that justice requires that adoption be made much more accessible and attractive to those willing to morally commit to the parental role.

3.2. The State and Procreation

When we think about the ethics of procreation, we don't often think of the liberal state playing an active role in the creation of human lives. But, of course, the state can have policies and laws in place that will indirectly encourage or discourage procreation. Some of them are policies and laws that render *parenting*, be it adoptive or procreative, more feasible for its citizens. Things like affordable housing, subsidized childcare, high-quality public education, and legislation that supports access to flexible working hours for parents all count as pro-parenting interventions by the liberal state. And the reason they should be understood primarily as pro-parenting rather than pro-procreation is straightforward: they place parents in a better position to discharge their parental duties to their children than they would be otherwise, and they do so irrespective of whether parents have procreated or have adopted the child that they now enjoy a parent-child relationship with. Moreover, such interventions can be justified by a direct appeal to children's interests, since they will increase the quality of the care received by children and will make it more likely that children will in fact enjoy all the goods that make a childhood go well.

Other policies and laws, by contrast, will uniquely encourage procreation over adoption on the part of citizens. That is, there are a number of state interventions that encourage prospective parents to choose procreation over adoption. For instance, the liberal state can indirectly encourage procreation by making the adoption process unduly burdensome for its citizens, while making contraception and abortion less easily accessible than they could be. Another way the state can encourage procreation is by providing generous paid parental leave only to procreative parents.

A particularly controversial way in which the state can encourage procreation is by legalizing the transferal of gamete material and access to surrogacy, as well as subsidizing the costs associated with assisted reproductive technologies, such as IVF. For prospective parents who have no trouble conceiving and gestating a child "naturally," such policies will make no difference as to whether or not they decide to engage in procreative parenting. But for those who cannot conceive and/or gestate a child without contribution from third parties, pro-procreation interventions by the state make a significant difference when it comes to their ability to seriously entertain the project of procreative parenting. The question for this section is: Does justice in a liberal society require such policies and laws on the part of the liberal state?

Before I argue that the answer is no, let me briefly note that the argument in this chapter is wholly compatible with other arguments against assisted reproductive technologies and practices that focus on the potential for exploitation of gamete donors and surrogates, and the right of children to know their genetic or biological origins.[6] Notwithstanding such compatibility, my own case against pro-procreation policies and laws does not rely on the validity of any of these other arguments, and so should be assessed independently.

First, let me grant that the liberal state has a stringent duty to protect the bodily integrity of its citizens, as well as to ensure that citizens who decide to procreate receive an adequate level of healthcare. These obligations on the part of the liberal state will go a long way toward ensuring that citizens are not forced to procreate against their will, are not coerced into having abortions or sterilization procedures, and are not put in a position where their choice to engage in procreative parenting leads to death or disability due to a lack of affordable and adequate pre- and postnatal care. In the context of thinking critically about what justice requires in the area of family formation, it is very important to keep in mind that many of the injustices associated with procreation are in fact a result of the violations of women's (and trans men's) bodily autonomy and right to healthcare, and not a violation of their right to procreation—or, at least, not a violation of an alleged *positive* right to procreate.

The first question I want to address in this chapter is whether the lack of genuine access to gametes and surrogates is a form of procreative injustice. In other words, apart from the familiar rights of bodily integrity and adequate healthcare, is there also a right to receive assistance in procreation, understood as having access to the materials and procedures required for the creation of new human beings?

Many philosophers have articulated compelling reasons against a positive right to procreative assistance.[7] Suzanne Uniacke, for instance, argues that

> another person's consent is crucial to the permissibility of using parts of his or her living body, in what would otherwise be highly intrusive ways, in meeting any of these ends. And one's need or desire does not itself oblige others to give such consent.[8]

In a similar vein, and in the context of an alleged positive right to surrogacy, Christine Straehle adds that "a right to assisted procreation is unintelligible because it is impossible to promise the effective protection of the interest at stake, where the protection requires the collaboration and consent of a third party."[9] The common thread here is that a positive right to something cannot require fellow members of society to provide something that they are not morally obliged to provide. This would explain why there is no positive right to someone else's spare kidney, to sex, or to close friendships.[10]

In this chapter, however, I want to go a step further than those who have pointed out that it would be impossible to guarantee that all citizens have access to gametes and gestational support without necessarily violating the bodily autonomy of their fellow citizens. In particular, I argue that not only it would be impossible to protect a positive right to procreation, but also that in many cases, third parties are actually under a moral obligation *not* to collaborate and consent to coprocreation. Let me explain.

Let me start by defining co-procreators as persons who provide the gamete or the gestational environment for the creation of a human being.[11] This means that a heterosexual couple that procreates without assistance from third parties will count as co-procreators; so too will the surrogate mother, and sperm and egg donors.[12]

Let me also note that other parties who play a significant role in the creation of a person (doctors in the fertility clinic and romantic matchmakers, for instance) will not count as co-procreators, although under some conditions they may have certain moral obligations with respect to procreation. Later I will explain why there is an important distinction between those who play a core biological causal role in procreation and those who don't. For now, it may suffice to note that the distinction is at play in other contexts where harm can take place if people act negligently when engaging in a risky enterprise, such as driving. The car dealer who sold you a car at a bargain price, the mechanic who fixed the car's engine, and the petrol station worker who sold you petrol are all part of the causal chain that may end in the death of a pedestrian; yet you are the only one who counts as a driver, and you were the one who violated a stringent duty not to consume alcohol prior to going behind the wheel.[13]

In light of this definition of co-procreators, what are the conditions under which co-procreators should not collaborate and consent to the creation of a child? One obvious condition is that they should not collaborate and consent when they know that that there would be no moral parent for the resulting child. Think of an egg donor who donates to a couple who has already lost custody of their other children due to abuse. Or think of a surrogate mother who is asked to gestate the child of two violent and sadistic male criminal offenders. It seems pretty clear in these cases that there is a stringent moral obligation not to co-procreate due to the likelihood that the child will have some of her core rights violated.

In a similar vein, I believe that anonymous egg and sperm donation (that is, when one donates or sells sperm or eggs to a bank without knowing who will make use of it), as well as commercial surrogacy (when one sells one's gestational labor to a stranger), can also be morally problematic due to a lack of knowledge as to whether or not the child will be under the care of a moral parent.[14] After all, when one donates an egg or sperm to strangers, or when one works as a commercial surrogate for them, one plays the co-procreator role without being reasonably confident that the child will be adequately cared for. Unlike the previous cases, where it is reasonable to infer that the child will not be adequately cared for, in anonymous gamete donation and commercial surrogacy one is simply not in a position to know. Although it is certainly morally permissible to co-procreate with a friend, or to function as the surrogate to a sibling or cousin when one knows such persons would be morally committed parents, it is not morally permissible to co-procreate under conditions of *care uncertainty*.[15]

To head off a possible early objection to my argument, let me explain why a potential assessment of parental competency by the fertility clinic will not let co-procreators off the hook. The concern here is that those willing to make use of the reproductive work or material of third parties have a very strong incentive to craft a false positive narrative about themselves so that they can receive the relevant assistance. This means that they are unlikely to reveal themselves in all of their shortcomings and weaknesses. Although it is true that such clinics can easily employ psychologists to try to assess the parental competencies of their clients, the assessment will typically be suboptimal.[16] That is, the assessment coming from a fertility psychologist in the space of a few meetings will never compare to the knowledge that is available to the intimates of prospective parents.[17] Only individuals who have known prospective parents for a long period of time, who have seen them act in a myriad of circumstances, with varied levels of stress and difficulties, and who know their values and their most salient dispositions and attitudes will find themselves in an adequate position to assess their parental competency.[18]

It is important to be explicit here that I am not arguing that it is always impermissible to co-procreate with others when one is unwilling to morally commit to the parental role.[19] A stronger view of this kind is suggested by James Lindemann Nelson in the following passage:

> People who make their ova or sperm available for assisted reproduction have taken up a central—indeed essential—place in the causal chain aimed at the production of these valuable, vulnerable beings, and they've hardly been invited to reflect on the moral relationship they may thereby be putting in place.[20]

But as I have explained above, when one co-procreates with people who one knows will be morally committed to the parent-child relationship, one adequately reflects on the importance of the moral relationship between child and moral parent. What one doesn't do is choose to become the moral parent oneself. The upshot here is that individuals can permissibly donate gametes or serve as surrogate mothers to someone else, but that action requires knowledge of the parental capacity of those who will parent the resulting child. Moreover, I take this to be a stringent duty that falls on all co-procreators, including those in a heterosexual relationship who need no assistance from third parties. Indeed, a woman who willingly procreates with her violent and abusive husband violates this stringent duty, no matter how much she wants a child.

Before I explain the implication of care uncertainty for the laws and policies of a liberal state, let me dispel the concern that this argument is overinclusive. The worry here is that the argument not only has the result that co-procreators should not co-procreate when they are not parties to the type of intimate relationship that allows adequate assessment of each other's parental competency, but also that fertility clinics should not be allowed to operate either. Since fertility clinics don't know their clients in an intimate way to assess if they would be morally committed parents, it looks as though they violate a stringent duty not to enable procreation under conditions of care uncertainty. How can we avoid such a counterintuitive implication?

The reason why, say, a sperm donor acts wrongly by donating sperm to people he does not know well is that procreative acts that are biological in the relevant sense serve only one moral function: the creation of a new person. Given that such biological procreative acts are *only* about creating vulnerable and needy human beings, and given that the stakes are incredibly high, one must not engage in those acts unless one is reasonably confident that the child will be cared for by moral parents.[21]

By contrast, compare the sperm donor with the romantic matchmaker. When I introduce two friends looking for love, I may start a causal process that leads to the creation of a person, or I may not. Introducing friends who later become lovers is an act that is mundane and typically morally benign. A world where people will only introduce friends and acquaintances to one another if they are reasonably confident that they would be morally committed parents is a world where many things of value are lost: our ability to enjoy time with many of our friends at the same time; our ability to create the conditions for new valuable relationships to arise; our ability to engage with others primarily as social creatures, rather than biological ones, and so on and so forth. But, most importantly, such acts on the part of matchmakers are not even necessary to avoid noncommitted parenting. After all, there are other parties on the scene—namely co-procreators—who play a much more fundamental, and therefore morally relevant, role in procreation. These are also parties who can easily stop the causal chain in case of care uncertainty without undermining a socially justified practice or institution. The thought here is that there ought to be a division of moral labor if we, as a moral community, care about other valuable things in addition to children being parented by morally committed parents. And if there ought to be a moral division of labor, the parties with a stringent duty not to procreate under morally problematic conditions should be the co-procreators themselves.

Next, compare the commercial surrogate or the gamete donors to the fertility clinic. Again, there is value in the existence of fertility clinics that would be lost should clinics be treated as co-procreators.[22] For instance, a sister would not be able to act as a surrogate to her sibling who would be a morally committed father, but who is in a gay relationship with another morally committed man. Or she might not be able to donate an egg to her sister who would be a morally committed mother, but who cannot procreate unassisted due to ovarian cancer. In other words, fertility clinics can enable procreation on the part of co-procreators who are morally committed parents, and who have adequately assessed each other's parental competency. The thought here is that there would be an important loss of value should such clinics be prevented from operating since co-procreation with the support of a fertility clinic need not be a negligent enterprise. Indeed, counting the fertility clinic as a co-procreator is not necessary to avoid noncommitted parenting since there are other parties on the scene—namely co-procreators—who play a much more morally relevant role in procreation, and who can stop the causal chain in case of care uncertainty without undermining a valuable social institution.

Now, this is not to say that friends and doctors who may play a nonbiological causal role in procreation have no moral obligations whatsoever. When their acts will *undoubtedly* lead to serious harm, they ought to refrain from acting. For instance, if I have two friends who I am confident would be terrible parents, and who I know are desperate to become parents, I should take reasonable steps not to introduce them to one another. If I am a doctor in a fertility clinic and I have two co-procreators who have a harmful genetic condition, but who want to procreate despite the serious harm to their biological child, I ought to refrain from enabling that process. In such cases, the harm is foreseeable, and I am in a position to prevent it from taking place due to the unique feature of my situation. Moreover, the children who don't get to exist as a result of my intervention are not harmed by nonexistence, since nonexistence is not harmful *to them*.[23]

Another way to explain the difference between procreators and fertility clinics at play here is to say that the stringent duty not to co-procreate under conditions of care uncertainty falls on co-procreators in the same way as the duty not to drink falls on all drivers. Given other morally valuable things we ought to care about, there cannot be a duty on everyone else that they take all available steps to prevent bad parenting and drink-driving on the part of all other moral agents. That being said, there are unusual situations where I ought to act so as prevent someone from driving while inebriated or from procreating willy-nilly, but that is not because I count as a driver or as a co-procreator, but rather because I find myself in a specific situation where harm is foreseeable, and I can prevent it without incurring significant costs to myself and without undermining a valuable social practice or institution.

So now that we know that co-procreators have a stringent moral duty not to procreate under conditions of care uncertainty, but that fertility clinics can still be justified qua social institution, what are the implications for the liberal state? As I see it, the liberal state can preserve the positive side of assisted reproductive technologies and practices while discouraging the morally problematic side by making *anonymous* gamete donation and *commercial* surrogacy illegal.[24] We may even conceive of this obligation on the part of the state as a moral duty to create morally appropriate background conditions for the creation of human beings. The idea here is that the liberal state owes it to potential children that its laws and policies encourage responsible co-procreation on the part of its citizens while discouraging co-procreation that counts as negligent if such discouragement can take place without the violation of rights to privacy and bodily integrity.[25] Such a stance by the liberal state will not only minimize the risk of exploitation that attaches to the commercialization of body parts and bodily functions, and put children in a better position to know about their biological origins, but will also place co-procreators in an adequate epistemic position when it comes to deciding whether or not to co-procreate. Instead of tempting co-procreators to procreate under inadequate epistemic conditions, thereby acting negligently, prospective parents who need assistance from third parties can always invite friends and family members to co-procreate with them or for them. For only such arrangements are not exploitative in nature, in line with children's alleged interest in knowing key facts about their genetic ancestry, and potentially nonnegligent in terms of not bringing about life under morally problematic conditions.[26]

Suppose I am right that the liberal state need not eradicate assisted reproduction in order to create adequate conditions for moral parenting, but that it must make anonymous gamete donation and commercial surrogacy illegal. The next question to address is whether the state has an obligation to bear (some or all of) the financial costs of accessing the support of fertility clinics, whether or not prospective procreators are also accessing the genetic material or gestational labor of their intimates.

Recall that, in Chapter 1, I argued that the interest in procreative parenting was an interest in loving a child irrespective of the intrinsic properties of the child, and irrespective of the historical-relational properties that arise within the context of the parent-child relationship. As I explained, procreative parents have a normative reason for love because they created their child, and not due to facts about the child or the relationship, rendering the love of procreative parenting the closest we get to unconditional love. Recall also that although this may explain why procreative parenting is not a trivial enterprise such that prospective parents would be under a moral duty to adopt, the case in favor of procreative parenting is not sufficiently strong for there to be a compelling or fundamental interest in procreative parenting. Because adoptive parenting is valuable in its own right, and adoptive parents can be proper moral parents, it is hard to see why the interest in procreative parenting would give rise to *positive* obligations on the part of society to provide the financial resources required for assisted reproduction. It is therefore hard to see why the liberal state should subsidize the costs attached to procreative parenting that go above and beyond the costs of appropriate maternal and pediatric care.[27]

It is also important to remember that assisted reproductive technologies are quite expensive and that this has opportunity costs for those who choose not to parent or those who choose to adopt.[28] After all, resources are limited in a liberal society, and funds spent on subsidized assisted reproductive technologies are funds that are not used for medical procedures that create the conditions for all citizens to lead good lives, such as research and treatment aimed at preventing and curing different types of cancer, heart disease, deadly viruses, and so on. In fact, even those who think that the interest in procreative parenting is a core interest must ask whether the opportunity costs associated with assisted reproductive technologies are worth bearing, given that public resources could be allocated instead to funding more basic obstetric and pediatric research, improving pre- and postnatal care, ensuring that prospective mothers (and trans fathers) receive adequate nutrition, thereby supporting a much greater number of citizens to become procreative parents.[29]

To be sure, there is a reasonable concern that assisted reproductive technologies would in fact be less expensive if the liberal state were more pro-client when regulating the fertility industry.[30] This means that talk of subsidy might be misleading, since the state has largely decided that the costs of assisted reproductive technologies should be high by establishing intellectual property laws that benefit providers as opposed to recipients of assisted reproduction. If that is right, when the state subsidizes assisted reproductive technologies, it merely covers some of the gap between the actual costs and what would be fair for clients; it does not in fact *subsidize* the industry. Now, if that is indeed the case, the liberal state should work toward fairly regulating assisted reproductive technologies so as to make the costs fair to consumers rather than shifting the burden onto the citizenry.

Before we can discuss the question of family formation in the context of adoption, let me summarize the argument so far. The obligation on the part of the liberal state not to facilitate negligent co-procreation by citizens, together with the opportunity costs involved in subsidizing reproductive assistance, count against the claim that there is a positive right to procreation, both in terms of having access to the genetic materials and gestational labor of others, and in terms of having access to financial support from the state. The practical upshot of this discussion is that there is no positive obligation on the part of the liberal state to assist citizens with the biological, technological, and financial resources required for procreative parenting, only an obligation to regulate fertility clinics and the use of genetic material and gestational labor such that the resulting children are the result of responsible (rather than negligent) co-procreation. Such a stance on the ethics of assisted reproduction is supported by the arguments advanced in the first two chapters, which pushed against the idea that procreative parenting counts as a fundamental interest or serves as the only legitimate route to moral parenthood.

3.3. The State and Adoption

In the previous section, we looked at the role that the liberal state must play in family formation via reproduction. As we have seen, such a role is quite minimal since citizens lack a positive right to engage in procreative parenting, and the children who don't yet exist don't have a right to exist, although they have an interest in coming to existence under appropriate care conditions should procreators choose to bring them about.

But what should we think about adoption? Does the state have a duty to facilitate adoption? In this section I answer this question in the affirmative. But instead of appealing to a positive right of citizens to become parents via adoption, I focus on the fundamental interest of existing parentless children to be adopted. As we will see, such an interest is grounded in children's right to be loved, which, in turn, gives rise to a duty on the part of the liberal state to create the conditions for children to find themselves in loving parent-child relationships.

Before I defend this right of children to be loved, let me briefly emphasize that I don't deny that prospective parents also have an interest in adoption. However, as with the interest in procreation discussed in the previous section, we should be careful in defending a positive *right* to adoption on the part of prospective parents. This is because a right to adoption would also require that some procreative parents give their biological children away, something that they are under no general moral obligation to do, unless they fail to count as moral parents. In light of this, we are better off saying that prospective parents have a right to access well-regulated institutions of family creation. As we have just seen, this would mean that fertility clinics should exist as part of a well-regulated social institution, one aimed at preventing negligent co-procreation. And, as we are about to see, when it comes to adoption, this means that screening procedures should not be unduly burdensome, and that all prospective adoptive parents who show themselves to be able and willing to morally commit to the parental role, should be given an equal opportunity to adopt.[31]

So what explains the right of children to be loved such that some of them will have a compelling interest in being adopted? The question of whether children have a right to be loved has recently been addressed in the philosophical literature on children's rights.[32] Two general kinds of skeptical response have arisen in that debate.[33] According to the first, the interest that a child has in being loved is not sufficient to ground a *right* to be loved.[34] The thought here is that children can have their basic interests secured without being loved, so there is no corresponding moral right to be loved. According to the second, children cannot have a right to be loved, because there can be no corresponding duty *to love* on the part of parents. The concern here is that one can have a duty to do something only if it is under one's voluntary control, and there is good reason to think that love largely consists of nonvoluntary psychological dispositions. In what follows, I argue that while it may well be true that no person has a duty to love, the child's right to be loved can still ground a stringent duty on the part of the liberal state to create the conditions for children to be loved. One of those conditions is the establishment of social arrangements that render adoption feasible and desirable to those willing to become moral parents via adoption.

What do I mean by "love" in the context of children having a right to be loved? Philosophers mean different things when they talk about love, and it is plausible to think that love means different things to different people. Notwithstanding the fact that love is a complex type of emotion, it is plausible to think that love has a core feature. As already hinted at in previous chapters, those who love are strongly disposed to care a great deal about their beloved (to, as it were, treat their interests as if they are their own). As Harry Frankfurt puts it,

> Loving someone or something essentially *means* or *consists in*, among other things, taking its interests as reasons for acting to serve these interests. Love is itself, for the lover, a source of reasons. It creates the reasons by which his acts of loving concern and devotion are inspired.[35]

In the case of parents, it is plausible to think that parental love is primarily about a disposition to make all sorts of sacrifices and take on costs in order to benefit one's child. Such a disposition for sacrifice and cost-bearing is already apparent in the day-to-day life of families where so much attention is devoted to securing children's core interests (for example, nutrition and moral education). This disposition, however, becomes particularly salient under difficult circumstances, as when parents need to radically rearrange their life so as to care for a child with special needs, or even take on additional work so as to provide their child with adequate socioeconomic opportunities. Most importantly for our purposes, such a disposition for sacrifice and cost-bearing plays a central role in creating the conditions for children to lead *meaningful* lives.[36]

Now, it may be tempting to dismiss the suggestion that children can and should lead meaningful lives. After all, children lack the requisite level of autonomy necessary to actively engage with many of the activities that give meaning to our existence—that is, projects and relationships that are not only objectively worthwhile, but also subjectively attractive to those who engage with them.[37] In fact, if we think of popular examples of meaningful activities in the philosophical literature on meaning and well-being, such as completing a PhD in philosophy, we might wonder whether meaning is something that is at all available and accessible to children.[38]

Despite the fact that certain projects and relationships are only accessible to adults, there are nonetheless all sorts of activities and relationships that are objectively valuable and that a child will find subjectively attractive. Think of a loving relationship with a sibling, or a child's love of reading. These are things that will make a child's life go better than it would otherwise. But the difficulty for children is that they are often not yet in a position to identify which projects are worthwhile, and they cannot adequately seek many of these worthwhile projects without assistance. Consider how a child may be just as attracted to (say) playing video games, as she would be to engage in imaginative playing with her sibling.[39] Or consider how she might be just as happy to watch low-quality TV as reading age-appropriate literature. Consider also how even low-cost projects such as play dates may require positive intervention on the part of parents. But it is partly for these reasons that loving parent-child relationships play such an important role in children's ability to lead meaningful lives. And as we are about to see, it is partly for these reasons that even well-run children's homes or caring (yet temporary) foster families still fall short of reliably securing children's ability to lead good lives.

To see why parental love is so important for meaning, consider first how the (loving) parent-child relationship itself endows a child's life with meaning. There is no denying that both parties derive meaning from a relationship marked by the deepest and most robust form of human love.[40] But parent-child relationships also play an instrumental role in creating the conditions for children to lead good lives. Consider how those who find themselves in loving relationships with children can ensure that they engage with relationships and projects of worth, by both assisting them to *identify* what is worthwhile and by assisting them to *access* that which is worthwhile. The loving parent is in a position to pay special attention to the child's dispositions and talents, and to facilitate her engagements with things that will confer meaning on her life.[41] The loving parent can help her child see why the relationship with a younger sibling is such an important one, and can create the conditions for them to spend quality time together. Because of children's limited capacity for autonomy, adults who are in loving relationships with children find themselves in a special position to devote the necessary resources, time, and attention to ensure that there is more to their lives than the satisfaction of their basic interests.

We are now in a position to see why a child's right to be loved grounds a duty on the part of the liberal state to facilitate adoptive parenting by prospective parents. In children's homes or temporary foster care arrangements, children do not enjoy reliable access to the intimate relationships that confer meaning on their lives, or that facilitate their access to meaningful projects and other valuable relationships.[42] While such arrangements can secure the conditions for children to enjoy many of their basic interests, it cannot *robustly* secure the conditions for them to engage with projects and relationships that are objectively valuable.[43] After all, when children are loved, they are not significantly vulnerable to losing the relationship over time and in alternative scenarios. While a child social worker or foster carer can always exit the relationship for all sorts of trivial reasons, a parent who loves a child will stick with her if she becomes gravely sick, acquires a disability, or needs to relocate in order to enjoy adequate educational opportunities. The idea here is that when the glue that keeps the parent and the child together is the robust and deep concern of parental love, the child is significantly less vulnerable to losing that relationship.

The same is not true for arrangements where adults are motivated by money or career aspirations.[44]

Assuming that a child's right to be loved is intelligible because we can make sense of the idea that love reliably motivates adults to ensure that children lead meaningful lives, does it then follow that caregivers have a stringent moral duty to feel the emotion of love? There is good reason to be skeptical here. As Mhairi Cowden explains, "Loving cannot be a duty because the structure of rights necessitates that there be a real and achievable corresponding duty.... The emotional component of love may be an unachievable duty."[45] Indeed, if one accepts that stringent moral obligations must be feasible in a strong sense, while also accepting that emotions are not *sufficiently* accessible to us (even though they can *at times* be cultivated or voluntarily brought about), then one must oppose the idea that there can be a stringent moral duty to feel the emotion of love.[46]

But, as I have already indicated, we can conceive of the right of children to be loved as giving rise to a stringent *primary* duty on the part of *the liberal state* and not on the part of parents. The duty in question is not so much to facilitate the development of an emotion, but for the state to do what it legitimately and feasibly can to create the conditions for children to enjoy parental love in the course of their lives.[47] And making adoption more desirable and attractive to prospective parents is one obvious way for the state to discharge this stringent duty it owes children who currently find themselves in state institutional or foster care arrangements. It is also a legitimate way for the state to facilitate the creation of families for those eager to morally commit to the parental role.[48]

3.4. Implications

What, then, are the implications of arguing that a child's right to be loved creates stringent moral obligations on the part of the liberal state? There are four interventions that the liberal state must embark upon in order to make adoption more desirable and feasible to prospective parents, thereby creating the conditions for parentless children to be loved.[49]

The first intervention requires the state to make parental leave schemes available to adoptive parents on the same conditions as enjoyed by procreative parents. Although it is true that parental leave is partly justified by the role of facilitating exclusive breastfeeding (or chestfeeding) for those who choose to do so, and in creating the conditions for birth parents to recover from childbirth, parental leave schemes should be primarily justified by the importance of giving parents and children time and space to bond with one another and become a family. After all, not all mothers can or wish to breastfeed, and not all of them need much time to recover from birth. Moreover, such a focus on bonding when it comes to justifying parental leave sits more easily with feminist calls for procreative fathers to enjoy leave on an equal footing with procreative mothers. But, more generally, given that not all procreative parents gestate, give birth, or breastfeed their children, their interest in accessing parental leave must refer primarily to a compelling interest in bonding with their newborns as early in the relationship as possible.

I take it that irrespective of the age of a child at the time of adoption, the same leave provisions should apply to adoptive mothers and fathers. Both children and parents have a compelling interest in enjoying the conditions for becoming a family after adoption, and the extension of parental leave to adoptive families would go a long way toward creating the conditions for such families to develop strong ties from the very beginning of their life together. The extension of parental leave to adoptive families would also help counter any remaining societal stigma around adoption by allowing the state to communicate that procreation and adoption are equally legitimate ways of starting a family.

Of course, the lack of parental leave for adoptive families in some jurisdictions is not the main reason why prospective parents chose procreation over adoption (if a choice is indeed on the table). As Straehle explains:

> [F]or some, adoption in the current legal and international context is not feasible or too lengthy a process. Others may fear that an adopted child may have special needs that they as future parents won't be able to satisfy, or they may fear that they lack the intuition

and understanding necessary to care for an adopted child, believing instead that a shared genetic heritage may make it easier to face the challenges childrearing may bring.[50]

It is certainly true that there are high levels of anxiety and ambivalence around adoption in liberal societies. This deserves to be acknowledged by the liberal state. But unlike Straehle, who uses these concerns to argue in support of the permissibility of commercial surrogacy, I believe that they must inform a number of pro-adoption interventions on the part of the liberal state, such as legal and mental health support, as well as resistance to mandatory "open adoption"—adoption that preserves some form of contact between child and her biological parents. In what follows, I explain why such interventions are important for adopted children and their parents.

First, the legal support required to navigate the adoption process should be free and adequate for all prospective adoptive parents. Given children's interest in adoption, it is wrong for adoption to only be accessible for wealthy families.[51] Indeed, once parents have morally committed to a child and have worked toward creating opportunities for her to enjoy the goods of childhood, they are under no moral obligation to provide their child with additional socioeconomic opportunities. In fact, as we will see in the second part of this book, the goods of childhood that *parents* are responsible for fostering do not even require substantial financial resources on their part. This means that the liberal state acts wrongly when it puts in place arrangements that make adoptive parenting prohibitive for anyone but the wealthy.

Second, adoptive families should be offered additional free counseling and mental health support for the entire childhood of their adopted child. This is not because adoption itself has a negative effect on children's well-being, but because adopted children might have experienced abuse and neglect prior to adoption and they may require additional mental health support as a result. Although empirical evidence suggests that adoptive children typically make a remarkable recovery after adoption, free psychological support will only make such a recovery more likely.[52] Free counseling and mental health support would also make prospective adoptive parents less anxious prior to adoption, since they would know that should their child experience mental ill health, they would not be left in a difficult financial position as a result.[53]

Finally, the most important step to render adoptive parenting more desirable and feasible for prospective parents requires that the state make adoptive parents legal parents on exactly the same footing as procreative parents. This means that the maintenance of a relationship between the adopted child and her biological parents should always be at the discretion of the adoptive parents. Although there has been a push in many countries for biological parents and adoptees to stay in touch via compulsory "open adoption" arrangements, it is problematic for adoptive parents to lack control over whether the biological parents remain in the child's life.[54] And it is problematic simply because a legal parent is precisely the person who the liberal state sees as having a responsibility to decide which other adults should be in a child's life in light of what is in the child's best interests.[55]

This is not to deny that there is a moral obligation on the part of adoptive parents to be open about a child's genetic and biological history. This entails engaging in age-appropriate conversations about the events that led to a child's existence, as well as the relevant genetic facts that apply to her. But this obligation falls on all parents, not only adoptive ones. Indeed, children should not be deceived about important aspects of their lives merely because it makes parents uncomfortable to have age-appropriate conversations about sex, health, and loss with their children.[56]

But this right to know one's life and genetic history is different from a right to have relationships with other adults irrespective of whether it serves one's best interests. And given that empirical evidence suggests that relationships with one's biological parents are not always in adopted children's best interests, the decision about whether any given relationship is in a particular child's best interest is a decision that should be made by her legal parents, not the state.[57] In the same way as the liberal state does not force procreative parents to foster a relationship between their child and other biological relatives (even when such relationships would clearly be good for the child), it should not force adoptive parents to foster a relationship between their child and her procreators.

To be sure, it may well be that legal (and moral) parents lack a right to exclude other adults from a child's life.[58] It may well be that in liberal societies we give legal parents too much discretion when it comes to who their child should have relationships with. But if that is right, a lack of discretion should apply to all parents, not only adoptive ones. This means that we, as a society, should aim for "open parenting" and that the liberal state should decide who else should be in an ongoing relationship with a particular child. This could mean, for instance, that a parent who is no longer in a relationship with her own parents due to their controlling behavior would still be required to ensure that her child is in a relationship with them. This would be likely to happen because the liberal state would inevitably promote certain relationship types (for example, grandparent-grandchild relationships), even though the important question here is whether any *particular* relationship is in the interest of a *particular* child.

Given that legal (and moral) parents are typically in a much better position to know if their child would benefit from a particular relationship, such a move to open parenting is unlikely to benefit most children. At the very least, the proponents of open adoption must explain why only adoptive parents should not be trusted to make such important decisions on behalf of their children. Or else they must resist the account of moral parenthood defended in Chapter 2, where both adoptive and procreative parents count as proper moral parents, and defend instead an account of moral parenthood whereby adoptive parents remain relegated to the role of mere social or legal parents.

3.5. Objections

In this section I address two direct objections to the arguments presented so far, one that puts pressure on the claim that the liberal state need not be pro-procreation, another that puts pressure on the claim that the liberal state must in fact be pro-adoption. But before I do so, let me respond to a concern that affects all forms of parenting, procreative and adoptive. The concern in question is that it is not the job of the liberal state to facilitate any form of parenting whatsoever, and that it should use its limited resources to assist those in need in the developing world, especially given that a destitute person in (say) the Democratic Republic of Congo is much worse off than a child in a well-run children's home in an affluent liberal state.[59]

To begin with, one clarification worth making is that all the policies and laws I advocate in this chapter are justified by reference to *children's* interest in being parented by individuals capable of securing their interests and creating the conditions for their lives to go well, and not by reference to the interests of prospective parents in becoming parents. The policies and laws in this chapter therefore count as pro-children rather than pro-parenting. Although I do believe that the family can be justified partly due to a valuable adult interest that it serves, I have not argued that the interest in parenting is so fundamental as to give prospective parents a right that their fellow citizens put substantial resources toward making it possible for them to become parents.[60] Although parenting can be an exceptionally valuable project to those who find it subjectively attractive, the same is true of other projects—such as traveling around the world, volunteering for Oxfam, or becoming a novelist. And just as no one has a moral right to be given a round-the-world plane ticket, a position with Oxfam, or a book contract, no one has a positive moral right to become a parent.

But the important point in response to the antiparenting skeptic is that although she is right to point out that poor people in the developing world are typically worse off than children living in state care in affluent liberal states, this fact does not change the special relationship between the state and its child citizens.[61] And it is precisely this relationship between the state and its child citizens that creates an obligation on the part of governments to implement arrangements to protect children's right to be loved, irrespective of how much more good an affluent state could do in poor parts of the world. In other words, it is the special paternalistic relationship between the liberal state and its parentless child citizens that creates an obligation on the part of the former to create the conditions for the latter to be adopted by morally committed parents. That being said, everything I say in this chapter is compatible with the very plausible claim that once the state has secured the conditions for children to flourish, it should move toward improving the lives of destitute people in the developing world rather than simply investing all of its resources in enabling perfect childhoods for its child citizens.

Let me now turn to the objection that I do not take the interest in procreation sufficiently seriously. More specifically, the worry here is that my account permits procreative inequalities between the rich infertile and the poor infertile, as well as inequality between homosexual and heterosexual couples.

My response to this objection is to grant that if we deny that citizens have a positive right to procreate, all sorts of inequalities will arise simply because some citizens will be able to procreate without assistance and others won't. But note that whenever we consider an interest that is not fundamental in a liberal society, such inequalities will inevitably arise. Consider the interest in undergoing cosmetic surgery. Although we may accept that citizens in a liberal society should be able to undergo cosmetic procedures if they so wish (and if they are well informed about the costs and benefits), this does not show that they have a right to have such procedures subsidized by the liberal state, or a right that a surgeon take them on irrespective of their health profile. This in effect creates inequalities between the rich and the poor, and between the healthy and those with health conditions such as diabetes or thyroid disease. Although it is unfortunate for those who miss out on something that they care about, this does not mean an injustice has taken place since the inequality in question is about access to a good (that is, cosmetic surgery) that no one has a positive moral right to.

Moreover, even if it is true that the interest in parenting is more compelling than the interests in traveling around the world, volunteering, or becoming an artist, then such an interest can be promoted with adoption. One of the goals of this chapter is precisely to show that children's right to be loved creates an obligation for the state to make adoption more desirable and feasible, hopefully paving the way for more homosexual couples and low-income families to become adoptive parents.

Let me now move to a concern that has been taken particularly seriously by the critics of international adoption and by those who advocate strong forms of open adoption. The concern in question is that adoption violates a child's fundamental interest in retaining a connection with the cultural practices and materials of her biological ancestors.[62] The worry here is that pro-adoption policies and laws will inevitably sever the connection between the child and the culture of her biological ancestors, thereby taking something extremely important away from adopted children.

I resist the claim that children have an interest in retaining a connection with the cultural practices and materials of a given cultural community *merely* due to a biological connection with their biological ancestors. As I see it, the cultural interest in question is an interest of children to have access to the cultural practices and materials that are necessary for a loving parent-child relationship to flourish. That is, whenever we talk about children's interest in culture and identity, we should be attending to the cultural materials and practices that create the background conditions for parents and children to pursue meaningful activities together. Consider how important it is for a parent and child to speak the same language, or how meaningful it is that they can read the same novels, sing the same songs as children, or celebrate important cultural events together.

However, such an interest can be satisfied irrespective of whether the cultural practices and materials of a child's moral parents are the same as the cultural materials of her biological ancestors. This means that when a child is adopted from cultural environment A and taken to cultural environment B, she acquires a strong interest in having access to the cultural practices and material of B, for that is where her intimate relationships will take place. The thought here is that her cultural proficiency should be on the norms, practices, and materials that will provide her with the background conditions for valuable intimate relationships to arise. Indeed, if we think of culture as giving individuals shared "goals, values, and picture of the world," then it makes sense for children to share goals, values, and pictures of the world with those they will actually explore the world with.[63]

This is not to deny that the liberal state should give parents from marginalized cultural groups all the support they need to parent well, and that, when all else is equal, a prospective adoptive parent who shares the culture of a child's biological ancestry should be given priority in adoption. After all, a shared heritage could help the child seek additional information about her biological ancestry should this become important for her when she grows up. What I do deny in this chapter is that the maintenance of such cultural links is in fact more important for children than their ability to participate in a loving parent-child relationship with an adopted parent who does not share the culture of her biological ancestors.

To be sure, a critic might still worry about the racial dimension of adoption in cases where adoption is not only cross-cultural, but also interracial. She might be concerned that the encouragement of adoption by the state will speed up the extinction of minority languages and practices, which, in turn, will speed up the process of cultural groups themselves dying out. Many critics of adoption, moreover, see interracial adoption as particularly problematic, due to the adoptive parents' alleged inability to understand their child's situation. What should we make of these concerns?

I certainly agree that interracial adoption can be particularly challenging for parents and children, especially in places with fraught racial relations, such as Australia. However, I do not see interracial adoption as being uniquely challenging or challenging in a morally problematic way. After all, parents often lack first-person experience of a myriad of issues that their children may confront in childhood: prejudice on the basis of disability or trans identity, eating disorders, learning difficulties, to name just a few. And yet, we typically believe that parents can play an important role in supporting their child not because they themselves have had similar experiences in childhood, or because we are confident that they already have all the answers, but rather because we expect them to take on the costs and make the sacrifices required for ensuring that their child receive whatever support they need.

With regard to cultural survival, my response is to say that we should be careful not to treat children instrumentally, so that cultural groups get a better shot at persisting over time. And we should be particularly careful not to do so in liberal societies founded upon the values of freedom and equality. Given children's equal moral status and their moral right to be loved, it is more important for them to enjoy loving parent-child relationships than to remain part of a minority cultural group. Moreover, if it is indeed the job of the liberal state to help protect minority cultural groups from dying out, then there are other legitimate avenues for achieving that. For instance, the state can subsidize and encourage cultural practices in public spaces, as well as make sure that minority languages are taught at school. What it must not do is fail to put children's interests front and center when it comes to the establishment of parent-child relationships, and so fail to create the necessary conditions for children to lead good lives qua children.

3.6. Conclusion

In this chapter I have addressed the question of what the liberal state owes its citizens when it comes to the question of family creation. I argue that the liberal state has no obligation to ensure that citizens have access to the reproductive materials, practices, and resources required for procreative parenting, and that its obligations regarding procreation are broadly negative and minimal. In particular, I argue that the liberal state must focus on the familiar rights to bodily autonomy and healthcare for those who choose to engage in procreation.

In addition to lending support to the view that the liberal state should be primarily concerned with bodily autonomy and the provision of adequate healthcare services for procreative parents and their babies, I also defend the claim that, when it comes to family formation, the state should be primarily concerned with arrangements that serve children's interests. In the case of procreation, this requires the state to closely regulate fertility clinics so as to discourage negligent procreative parenting by citizens. In the case of adoption, this requires taking seriously the fact that parentless children have a right to be loved, which grounds a duty on the part of the state to make adoption more desirable and feasible for prospective parents. After all, although foster care arrangements may be able to provide children with one or more moral parents on a temporary basis, only adoption enables the state to discharge its duty of creating adequate conditions for children to be loved in a robust way.

Along the way, I have highlighted the importance of pro-parenting intervention so that all moral parents have the ability to create the conditions for their children to flourish. I have also responded to concerns about inequality in access to procreation, the alleged need for open adoption, as well as concerns about a child's loss of cultural connection with her biological ancestors. In particular, I have resisted the suggestion that group inequalities in the ability to be a procreative parent give rise to an injustice, and that adoptive children have a fundamental interest in staying in contact with their biological parents and their culture. I have done so not because I reject the claim that procreation, biological ancestry, and cultural connections are valuable, but because I reject the claim that these goods must always take priority over other goods, or must be pursued at all costs. I hope that I have developed an account of justice in family creation that considers all fundamental interests, while accepting that not everyone will get what they want—which is something we can live with, so long as children are cared for by moral parents who love them deeply and robustly and are disposed to make the sacrifices necessary to ensure that their childhoods go well.

PART II
CHILDHOOD GOODS

PART II
CHILDHOOD GODS

Introduction

We are now ready to discuss some of the core goods that make for a good childhood. In particular, we are now in a position to move on to the question of what childhood goods parents have a special obligation to foster in the lives of their children.

Before we do that, it pays to revisit the focus of Part I—"Procreation, Adoption, and Parenting." In Part I, I developed a theory of why procreation is permissible, and a theory of why adoptive and procreative parents have equal moral standing vis-à-vis their children. I also explained that the moral parent is the person who adequately promotes and protects the interests of her child up to a moderately high level, and creates the conditions for her life to go well. Finally, I discussed how the state should go about creating opportunities for adults to become parents and supporting them in the course of the parent-child relationship.

In Part II, I will explore three core goods of childhood that parents are primarily responsible for fostering: carefreeness, achievement, and friendship. As we will see, the story behind what is valuable about these goods differs in childhood and adulthood, and we cannot simply apply our favorite philosophical accounts of the nature and value of carefreeness, achievement, and friendship to children without first recognizing that what it means to lead a good life in childhood is significantly different from what it means to do so in adulthood, and even in adolescence. Moreover, although moral parenthood does not depend on any of these goods being perfectly secured, these goods give rise to many obligations that parents must discharge to a sufficient level if they are to count as genuinely creating the conditions for their children's lives to go well.

Now, this is not to say that these goods exhaust a good childhood. Nor do I mean to deny that children have many interests that must be advanced by both parents and the state. It goes without saying that children's core interests in life—bodily integrity, freedom from unnecessary and cruel pain (among others)—are also highly important.[1] But my focus on the interest that children have in accessing the goods of carefreeness, achievement, and friendship is justified due to three important considerations. First, these goods make a significant difference as to whether or not children are able to flourish in childhood. Second, these goods must be understood in somewhat different ways when thinking about the role they play in the lives of children, as opposed to the role they play in the lives of adults. Finally, those interests are best protected and promoted in the context of a parent-child relationship.

It is also important to note is that I will not be focusing on the well-being of children qua future adults. Instead, the goods I am interested in either enable a good adulthood or have merely trivial negative impacts on it. The reason for this is that we should not render childhood subservient to a good adulthood given how important it is for children to lead good lives qua children and to experience certain human goods in distinct ways. For instance, a child who is forced to spend her free time programming rather than playing with her friends misses a core aspect of a good life even if that causes her to excel in computer science later on in life. Similarly, a child who is not exposed to any degree of hardship in childhood is placed in a position of psychological vulnerability in adulthood even if such a lack of hardship enables an idyllic form of childhood. In both cases, there is a trade-off between a good childhood and a good adulthood that parents are morally required to avoid.[2]

Does that mean that I see children and adults as different kinds of creatures, and so endorse the caterpillar picture of childhood, where a child is like a caterpillar, and an adult is like a butterfly? Or do I see children as analogous to saplings, and so as creatures who are in some ways less capable as the creatures they will eventually become later on in their lives?[3] I confess that I find both these analogies, which have been raised in the philosophical literature on children, unhelpful. On the one hand, I do think the differences in terms of cognitive abilities between children and adults are a matter of degree, and not kind. This means that children are unlike caterpillars in that they don't become completely different beings when they grow up. On the other hand, I resist the assumption that childhood is in some ways defective, and that growing up always entails becoming better at being a member of the human species. Rather, I see the process of growing up as one where we strengthen some of our abilities, and weaken others. Children are, all things considered, neither better off nor worse off when they mature into adults.

In Part II, we will explore some of the consequences of this way of thinking about childhood, but one upshot worth flagging here is that if there were a magic pill that allowed us to skip or remain in a given life stage, it would not be irrational to skip childhood or to stay as a child for many decades until death.[4] It would just be deeply regrettable, because the person who would never get to be a child, or never get to be an adult, would miss out on the distinctive goods of childhood (for example, carefreeness) and adulthood (for example, self-determination). Their lives would be in some important ways impoverished.

It is also important to recognize that the person who never gets to be a child or an adult misses out on experiencing certain goods in profoundly different ways throughout their lives. Indeed, as we will see in Chapter 4, carefreeness is a special good of childhood and not adulthood. Moreover, as we will discuss in Chapters 5 and 6, achievement and friendship play somewhat different roles in childhood and adulthood, and so to achieve as a child, or to have a friend as a child, is to experience these goods in ways that are no longer possible in adulthood.

In what follows, I will operate with a narrow understanding of childhood, which sees childhood as starting some time after infancy, with the development of basic social skills and self-awareness, and ending some time around puberty, when adolescence begins and the adolescent acquires the ability and interest in exercising a much greater degree of autonomy in her life.[5] This means that I am primarily interested in young people who have begun to develop their practical reasoning skills, but have not developed them to such a degree that they can enjoy many of the rights and responsibilities of adulthood. I am unsure about which ages should be used as proxies for each life stage, but on a very conservative notion of childhood, it would start roughly at age 3 and finish roughly at age 12. On a less conservative (and more plausible) notion, it would start at age 2 and end at age 14.

Why focus on this narrower group, rather than on anyone who is not yet an adult? My answer is that children are the first age group that creates an obligation on parents to support them with leading a good life, requiring actions that go well beyond merely protecting basic interests and providing a secure loving relationship. Indeed, with babies and toddlers, it suffices to meet their biological needs, and to provide them with attention and affection. After all, children in this age group have too little understanding of the world around them to be deemed sufficiently capable of many of the projects that make a life meaningful. As for adolescents, I believe the obligations of parents toward this age group decrease significantly, since adolescents are in a much better position to identify worthwhile projects and pursue them independently. This means that parents should play a more supervisory role in the lives of adolescents, ensuring that they are paying enough attention to the risks and harms involved with certain projects and relationships, and that they have an adequate grasp of the long-term consequences of their actions.[6]

In short, childhood is the stage where human beings are most dependent on their parents for leading *meaningful* lives, and this creates special obligations on parents to create the conditions for children to pursue activities that are both subjectively attractive and worthwhile. Moreover, such dependence brings with it a heightened vulnerability to domination since parents can easily coerce and manipulate their children into adopting certain values and pursuing certain projects and relationships on the basis that such values, projects, and relationships best conform to the lives parents envisage for their children, as opposed to what the children themselves find attractive. This, in turn, creates stringent negative obligations on parents not to abuse their power, and to make sure that the paternalism they exercise in the lives of their children either serves the protection of children's interests or facilitates engagement with projects and relationships that the children themselves find enjoyable. As I hope to show in the following three chapters, parents can enable good childhoods by creating the conditions for children to be carefree, to achieve in positive ways, and to enjoy close friendships with other children.

4
Carefreeness

4.1. Introduction

What do children need in order to lead good lives? One familiar answer is that, among other things, children need the opportunity to play.[1] That is, children need the opportunity to engage in playful activities, which can include sports, make-believe, games, role-play, and unstructured exploration of their environment. This familiar answer finds expression in the Convention on the Rights of the Child, which stipulates that "every child has the right to rest and leisure, to engage in play and recreational activities appropriate to [their age] and to participate freely in cultural life and the arts" (Art. 31). In contrast, the Universal Declaration of Human Rights, which applies to persons of all ages, only mentions the right "to rest and leisure, including reasonable limitation of working hours and periodic holidays with pay" (Art. 24). So, it seems, play is understood by political leaders as a special good of childhood and not a special good of adulthood.

Philosophers too have found this familiar view quite compelling. Virtually everyone interested in philosophical questions relating to childhood believes that the activity of play is an important part of a childhood well lived. The disagreement among philosophers working on childhood is over whether play is instrumentally or intrinsically valuable to a good life, and whether playing, broadly conceived, should be seen as a special good of childhood, or rather as a good that contributes to the well-being of any person irrespective of age.[2]

One influential position in this debate has been put forward by Anca Gheaus, who claims that play is both intrinsically and instrumentally valuable, and that not only children, but also adults, "should have the freedom to cultivate and enjoy capacities to learn and play a lot more than they are typically able to in highly competitive and efficiency-driven societies."[3] Gheaus does not go so far as to claim that the interest of adults in play rises to the level of a human right, but she supports policy proposals that would see society arranged to permit adults meaningful opportunities for play if that is something they are attracted to.[4]

In this chapter, I want to take the debate in a somewhat different direction. My aim here is twofold. First, I want to investigate the relationship between play and another good typically associated with childhood: the good of carefreeness. Moreover, because it is plausible to hold that play does not exhaust a good childhood, I also want to investigate the relationship between carefreeness and other valuable childhood goods. After all, it seems plausible to claim that other goods that are not directly aimed at protecting and promoting the bodily interests of the child, such as loving relationships and education, are also valuable childhood goods, even if not special childhood goods. I want to suggest that carefreeness counts as a precondition for any of these childhood goods constituting a good childhood, while not counting as a precondition for adults to enjoy a good adulthood. By looking closely at the relationship between carefreeness, play, and other childhood goods, I hope to mount a compelling case for the conclusion that carefreeness is a necessary component of a good childhood, but not a necessary component of a good adulthood.

The discussion is structured as follows. In Section 4.2, I briefly motivate a hybrid view of well-being, one that takes both objective goods and subjective endorsement of these goods as jointly necessary for a life to go well. In Section 4.3, I defend an account of carefreeness that I believe best captures the significance of carefreeness and the role it plays in the pursuit of a good adulthood. In Section 4.4, I move on to the relationship between carefreeness and the lives of children. I show that the psychological disposition of carefreeness is a precondition for valuable goods to constitute a good childhood. In Section 4.5, I discuss some of the implication of this discussion for the parent-child relationship. One upshot of my discussion is that a child who is allowed to play and who has loving parents, but who lacks the psychological disposition of carefreeness, leads an impoverished life, even if she might lead a good life in adulthood.

4.2. On Well-Being

The philosophical literature on well-being is primarily interested in answering the following question: What does it mean for human lives to go well? This literature can be roughly divided into three main camps. Some theorists focus on facts about a person's circumstances that make her life go well.[5] Others focus instead on facts about a person's mental states.[6] And, finally, some theorists defend hybrid accounts of well-being, which combine subjective and objective elements.[7]

One compelling version of a hybrid theory holds that an agent leads a good life insofar as facts about her circumstances combine with her mental states in an appropriate way. Such a hybrid theory requires that fulfilling both an objective and a subjective condition are jointly necessary for well-being.[8] Indeed, in the first part of this book, I took for granted that such *joint-necessity* hybrid theories are promising ways of thinking about well-being. In particular, I endorsed Susan Wolf's own hybrid account for the purposes of theorizing about the role of parental love in children's lives. In this section, I briefly survey what I take to be the most compelling arguments in support of such hybrid accounts. Although I lack the space to discuss the merits of alternative accounts, I hope to convince the reader that joint-necessity hybrid accounts of well-being are quite promising, and that we have good reasons to theorize about children's well-being under the assumption that they are in fact correct.

What can be said in favor of joint-necessity hybrid accounts? In recent decades, several philosophers have endorsed the position that subjective and objective elements are jointly necessary for a life well lived. Joseph Raz, for instance, makes it clear that the objective value of a person's life goals is not all that matters when assessing how well her life goes. The question of whether such goals are endorsed by the agent also matters. As he puts it, "[Such goals] contribute to a person's well-being because they are his goals, they are what matters to him."[9] In a similar vein, Shelly Kagan defends the view that well-being requires that one's enjoyment be properly connected to objective goods.[10] And, as we have already seen in previous chapters, Susan Wolf argues that a good life is a meaningful life, and that meaning arises when we engage in projects and relationships that are both subjectively attractive and worthwhile.[11]

To illustrate: if it is equally morally good for a 10-year-old child that she learns a second language or owns a dog, but her parents can only afford one of these projects, it seems quite plausible that the subjective importance *she* attaches to each project should guide their decision-making process. Indeed, an account of well-being that recommends to the parents that they simply flip a coin seem to miss a core element of what it means for a life to go well. Equally, an account of well-being that recommends to the parents that they take the child's preferences into account, but that her preferences merely add to her overall well-being, does not seem to take seriously the necessity of endorsement for a project or relationship to partly constitute a good childhood. A relationship with a dog will partly constitute a good life only if the child delights in the companionship of a dog, but not if she is uncomfortable around animals. Similarly, the ability to speak another language and engage in depth with another culture will partly constitute a good life only if the child has a sociable disposition and is curious about other cultures, but not if she is an introvert who shows no interest in cultural diversity or knowledge. (Note that because children are appropriate targets of paternalistic intervention, some valuable goods will need to be secured by parents and the liberal state irrespective of whether the child is in fact subjectively attracted to them. Education is the obvious example in this context. This does not change the fact that were the child to become subjectively attracted to such goods, they would also contribute, in a constitutive manner, to her leading a good childhood).

Finally, support for joint-necessity hybrid accounts of well-being can be found in the work of proponents of the capabilities approach, which aims at providing an account of well-being for the purposes of securing human development and achieving social justice.[12] For these theorists, subjective attraction to valuable doings and beings is constitutive of well-being. Indeed, theorists working on the question of which capabilities matter morally have focused their attention on the capabilities that allow persons to achieve valuable functionings, rather than any capability, such as the capability to count the blades of grass in one's backyard. Moreover, such valuable functionings are taken to be a function of what persons have reasons to value.[13] But unlike standard objective list theories, which focus solely on the ingredients of a good life, the capabilities approach supports the claim that a life goes well insofar as the valuable functionings that are achieved are in fact endorsed by the agent. As Serena Olsaretti explains, "On this view, it is necessary both that certain objects that are present in one's life be valuable (where their being valuable is not a function of the person's attitude), and that one deem them in some way valuable for oneself."[14]

To return to the example of the parents deciding how to benefit their child, we can claim that a child achieves the valuable functioning of affiliation with another species if she is given a dog after expressing a desire to care for one, rather than being forced to own a dog because her parents are themselves animal lovers. In contrast, a child does not achieve any valuable functioning when she persuades her parents to buy her a number of violent video games. In the first case, the functioning of being part of a cross-species friendship contributes to a good life not only due to the child's endorsement, but also due to the fact that there are objective reasons to value a friendship with a nonhuman animal. In the second case, the functioning of playing violent video games does not contribute to a good life despite the child's endorsement, since there are no objective reasons in support of virtual violence. Endorsement of a set of childhood beings and doings are necessary but not sufficient for the pursuit of a good life, since the functionings at stake must also be the sorts of things one has reason to value.

As we have just seen, there are compelling arguments in support of the view that a good life requires both engagement with valuable goods, and some form of endorsement of such goods on the part of the agent. Moreover, such joint-necessity hybrid accounts can make sense of both adults' and children's well-being, since both age groups can and do engage with valuable relationships and projects in the respective life stage they find themselves in, and both age groups can and do endorse such relationships and projects to a lesser or greater extent. Or so I will argue in Sections 4.3 and 4.4. For now, I explore the implications of endorsing joint-necessity hybrid views of well-being for our understanding of the relationship between carefreeness and the pursuit of a good life in adulthood.

4.3. Carefreeness and Adulthood

Before we can be clear on how and why carefreeness matters for children, we must first clarify the relationship between carefreeness and a good life in adulthood. Because carefreeness plays different roles in adulthood and childhood, knowing more about carefreeness in adulthood will put us in a better position to understand the role that carefreeness plays in the lives of children.

Let me start the discussion by defining the state of being "carefree." On a standard definition: to be carefree is to be free "from care or anxiety." That is, a maximally carefree person is one who has nothing worrisome in her mind. She never frets about the state of the economy, the possibility of a new world war, the likelihood of her marriage breaking down, and so on. A person who is not at all carefree, on the other hand, is someone "experiencing worry or nervousness, typically about the future or something with an uncertain outcome; in a troubled or uneasy state of mind as a result of such worry."[15]

There are two ways of understanding carefreeness. One can think of it as an occurrent state of mind, or one can think of it as a psychological disposition. The two are obviously related, since a person disposed to worry often finds herself in a worrisome state of mind, for instance. In this chapter, I will take "being carefree" to mean having a mental life whereby an agent is disposed to experience the world without worry, even though there will be some moments where she will experience an array of negative emotions associated with stress and anxiety.

What is required for someone to count as being carefree? I take it that carefree persons are sufficiently devoid of stress and anxiety partly due to their psychological makeup and partly due to their personal and sociopolitical circumstances. Some persons are much more prone to worry and stress than others, even when they have had similar upbringings and even when their life conditions are not significantly different. At the same time, however, personal and sociopolitical conditions play a key role in one's ability to lead a carefree life. Being able to reliably enjoy personal projects or securely access the goods of intimate relationships is obviously important for finding oneself devoid of serious concerns. A person who loves cycling, but lives in a city where cycling is extremely dangerous, cannot enjoy an important personal project without some degree of stress. Similarly, a person whose best friend is a war journalist cannot but feel constantly concerned about her friend. And, of course, being able to provide for one's basic needs makes a significant difference to one's ability to be carefree. A wealthy person living in an affluent state is in a much better position to lead a carefree life than a poor person living in a developing state, all else being equal.

Now, it could well be that there are coping strategies that can be developed by any person in any circumstance, making her capable of leading a carefree life irrespective of her personal circumstances. I take it, though, that we are justified in assuming that such coping strategies are not always available, and that some agents might not find them desirable. The important philosophical question that arises for us is whether such a lack of carefreeness affects their ability to lead good lives.

Before we can answer this question, it pays to revisit a core commitment of joint-necessity hybrid accounts of well-being: objectively valuable projects and relationship must be in some sense endorsed by the agent for them to contribute to a good life. Indeed, theorists defending hybrid accounts of well-being refer to enjoyment, pro-attitudes, subjective attraction, attachment of subjective importance, and a sense of ownership over valuable projects and relationships, all of which can be best captured by the language of endorsement.[16] In fact, endorsement seems to be the most helpful notion in this literature since it encompasses both cognitive and affective responses.[17] A schoolteacher will endorse her profession if she believes that she is a great educator or if she feels a great deal of joy and satisfaction around children (or both). Similarly, a crime journalist will fail to endorse his profession if he believes that he is an impostor or if he experiences a great deal of melancholy every time he covers a crime (or both).

Notice that although endorsement can take place by both cognitive and affective means, the two can come apart in many instances. A schoolteacher might strongly believe that she is a great educator and yet find children unpleasant. A crime journalist might believe that he is typically incapable of finding information that goes beyond what has already been made public by the police, and yet feel excitement every time he works on a new story. This raises the question of whether there is in fact endorsement on the part of such agents, given that their beliefs and emotions pull them in different directions. I take it that in cases involving adults, either beliefs or emotions can do the trick, although endorsement will certainly be stronger in cases where both obtain.[18] After all, compelling self-regarding reasons in favor of participating in a valuable project or relationship can secure endorsement of a project or relationship even when all affective responses to it are negative. This is why the schoolteacher above endorses teaching as a vocation, despite not "enjoying" the job. By the same token, one or more sufficiently strong positive affective responses to a valuable project or relationship can secure endorsement even when the agent struggles to find self-regarding reasons in their favor and lacks sufficiently strong reasons against it. This is why the journalist above endorses crime journalism as a profession despite struggling to find compelling self-regarding reasons that justify his lifelong devotion to journalism.

So how does carefreeness enter into the picture? If carefreeness is a disposition not to feel stressed or worried, then carefreeness is not necessary for a good adulthood. After all, many adults endorse a life of worry and responsibility so as to realize valuable goods that they care deeply about. The humanitarian delivering aid in war-torn South Sudan, the writer tapping into his own neuroses for writing brilliant books, the brain surgeon operating on the worst types of brain cancer will all be leading a good life if it is true that they have access to self-regarding reasons that lead them to endorse such projects despite the immense stress and anxiety that they cause. Indeed, the humanitarian worker knows that her vast cultural knowledge can render aid projects more effective. The writer knows that she has important stories to tell. The doctor knows that her perfectionism gives her patients a good shot at surviving. And, of course, there is no denying that humanitarianism, literature, and medicine are the sorts of objectively valuable projects that hybrid theorists believe can constitute a good life.

But if being carefree is not necessary for a good adulthood, then why do we think that adults also lose something important if they find themselves constantly worrying and feeling the weight of an array of life responsibilities? As is clear from the examples above, some people do choose or benefit from such a life, and it is not at all obvious that they deserve our pity. The neurotic writer might respond that if she were differently disposed, her novels wouldn't be as deep and confronting. She might go so far as to claim that were she to become carefree, she would be unable to write with any level of depth. The surgeon might raise a similar response, claiming that the stakes in her job are simply too high for her to approach life in a carefree manner.

What explains this, I think, is that an adult's more complex evaluative capacity (that is, capacity for self-reflection; capacity to acquire relevant moral knowledge; adequate sense of time; ability to recognize foreseeable costs, risks, and opportunities attached to certain actions; and so on and so forth) allows her to be subjectively attracted to worthwhile projects even when positive affective responses to these projects are lacking. After all, human adults are the sorts of creatures that often give a great deal of weight to whether or not their goals are being achieved or fulfilled over time, and this can render them quite tolerant of an array of negative affective responses that may accompany the pursuit of such goals. This means that adults can be satisfied with their lives even if they do not feel happy with the projects they are currently engaged with.[19] Indeed, the humanitarian worker in Sudan who finds her job stressful can step back and evaluate humanitarian assistance as a desirable project to engage in despite the stress involved. She might hope that the experience will set her up for a career in politics, land her a dream job at the United Nations, or simply make her a better, more compassionate, person.

But what about persons who would like to be sufficiently carefree, but who cannot afford to be so? Doesn't that show that being carefree is in fact necessary for a good adulthood? I don't think so. For a good to be necessary to the positive evaluation of a stage of life, it has to be the case that without that good, positive evaluation is not possible. And, as we have just seen, we can in fact positively evaluate the lives of many adults who lack the disposition of being carefree. In fact, we can say that many adults lead wonderful lives despite not being carefree, and they do so because they choose a life that is inimical to carefreeness, or they believe that their difficult circumstances will enable the enjoyment of valuable goods that would otherwise not be available.

At this stage of the discussion, it is important to make two observations. Carefreeness can, in some circumstances, make endorsement of valuable projects and relationships more likely simply by preventing core negative affective responses in relation to such projects and relationships from arising. This does not lead us to the conclusion that carefreeness is necessary for endorsement on the part of adults, and therefore necessary for a good adult life. Second, my understanding of carefreeness departs significantly from other philosophical accounts on the topic. Anca Gheaus, for instance, claims that although carefreeness is more readily accessible to children, it is still available to, and valuable for, adults. For Gheaus, carefreeness is the good of experiencing "trust and love wholeheartedly and unstructured time during which children engage in fantasy play, experimentation, and undirected exploration of the world and of their minds."[20] She also believes that the good of being carefree makes for a good adulthood, despite its being obviously true that children typically find it easier to be carefree than adults do, and typically benefit more than adults from enjoying this good.

Gheaus and I disagree about how to best conceive of the good of carefreeness. She understands carefreeness as the enjoyment of unstructured time, as well as engagement in fantasy play, experimentation, and undirected exploration of the world and of one's mind. I, on the other hand, see it as a disposition that affects all the other pursuits in a person's life, including her structured time. As I understand it, a carefree adult is an adult who is disposed to approach life in a carefree manner even when undertaking paid work, fulfilling caring responsibilities, or engaging in any activity that requires a great degree of focus and responsibility. (Similarly, a carefree child is a child who does not frequently experience stress and anxiety, whether or not she is having unstructured fun, playing with friends, doing household chores, or looking after a young sibling for a short period of time. I will return to the case of children in the next section.)

There might be one point of broad agreement between us, however. Although Gheaus is not explicit about this, at times she seems sympathetic to a joint-necessity hybrid theory of well-being, since she makes it clear that adults should not be forced to play.[21] She might therefore believe that endorsement matters for a good life, which would mean that carefreeness is valuable for a person only if she endorses it.[22]

Despite this potential point of agreement, Gheaus's understanding of carefreeness as an objectively valuable set of activities will have as a result that these activities can contribute to the life of an adult in a way similar to things like loving relationships, and the pursuit of knowledge and aesthetic enterprises, so long as persons are not forced by the state to lead a carefree life. That is, carefreeness will count as one of the many ingredients of an objective list aimed at describing what is in fact required for a person's life to go well. By contrast, my understanding of carefreeness as a disposition does not allow for carefreeness to be on a par with other objectively valuable activities and projects. Rather, carefreeness as a disposition merely makes it easier for endorsement on the part of adults to take place by preventing crippling negative affective responses to valuable projects and relationships. Carefreeness thereby plays at best an instrumental role in a joint-necessity hybrid account of adult well-being. But because endorsement of valuable projects and relationships can still take place via cognitive means alone, its instrumental role is in fact replaceable by subjective reasons for endorsement.

Before I conclude this section, let me note one explicit advantage of adopting my understanding of carefreeness as a disposition rather than following Gheaus in her understanding of carefreeness. The definition of carefreeness as a disposition allows us to refer to adults as carefree even when they do not enjoy unstructured time, or engage in fantasy play, experimentation, and undirected exploration of the world and their minds. A cheerful adult woman who structures her whole day so as to maintain her garden under difficult weather conditions, to help look after a sibling with a severe disability, and to fundraise at the local shops can be leading a carefree life if it is true that none of these pursuits creates crippling anxiety and stress in her life. Indeed, many adults have highly structured lives with a great deal of responsibility, and their overall approach to the worthwhile projects and relationships they engage with seems far more relevant to how we evaluate their lives than their engagement with a very specific set of activities, even if those activities are valuable.

To summarize the discussion so far, I have argued that we should understand carefreeness as a disposition that affects all the projects and relationships in a person's life, rather than a set of activities that persons engage in. I have also argued that there are good reasons to believe that a good adult life requires that agents endorse the valuable projects they engage in either by acting on self-regarding reasons in their support or by displaying positive affective responses in their favor. This leads to the conclusion that carefreeness is not in fact necessary for a good adulthood. In the next section, I show that in the case of children, positive affective responses to valuable projects and relationships are in fact necessary for endorsement, and argue that this makes carefreeness necessary for a good childhood.

4.4. Carefreeness and a Good Childhood

We are now in a position to argue for the claim that being carefree is necessary for a child to lead a good life. The idea is this: a childhood full of stress and anxiety is necessarily impoverished even if it is full of other goods. A child who receives an excellent education, has parents who love her, and is given ample opportunity to play still fails to experience a good childhood if her mental life is so constituted that she is never or rarely able not to feel concerned, worried, or stressed. Harry Brighouse and Adam Swift get close to my own view of carefreeness in the following passage:

> Childhood is a period during which it is possible to enjoy being carefree, and not to have to bear responsibility for decisions about others or, to a considerable extent, one's own interaction with the world.... A child who knows that her participation in the labour market is essential for her family's survival misses out on one of the special goods of childhood; so does the child who is the main carer for his severely epileptic parent.[23]

To be sure, Brighouse and Swift don't go so far as to claim that children who work or care for their parents don't enjoy a good childhood. What we are told in their discussion of carefreeness is that children who bear significant responsibility during childhood miss something of great value. The trouble, of course, is that this claim is compatible with the further claim that these children could have made up for such a loss by accessing other special goods of childhood, or by appealing to self-regarding reasons that would secure a level of endorsement of their responsibilities.[24] In what follows, I show that the children above don't enjoy a good childhood precisely because their personal circumstances render them unable to be carefree. I also show that precisely because these children are not carefree, they can neither authoritatively endorse their caring responsibilities nor the other valuable goods in their lives.

The argument to follow has three premises, which I defend below.

P1. A good childhood requires endorsement of the valuable goods that are present in one's childhood.
P2. Endorsement requires positive affect in the case of children.
P3. A sufficient level of positive affect requires carefreeness.
C: A good childhood requires carefreeness.

4.4.1. The Case for P1

This is a philosophical premise, and one that follows directly from my commitment to a joint-necessity hybrid account of well-being. As I alluded to with the case of the parents deciding whether to give their child a dog or language lessons, it seems quite important for a theory of well-being to be able to prescribe valuable projects and relationships for children to engage with, as well as require endorsement on their part.

For one, children find themselves in a position where they can adequately respond to a full array of valuable activities and relationships. One such valuable activity is play, which is no doubt the least controversial good of childhood. But children can also participate in real friendships, experience beauty qua beauty, achieve in sports or the arts, and so on and so forth. And as we will see in more detail in the next chapters, there is good reason to think that such projects and relationships contribute to a good childhood in a way that merely playing violent video games does not.

Apart from being able to pursue valuable relationships and projects, children are able to endorse such relationships and projects to a greater or lesser extent. Some are attracted to music and want to learn an instrument; others would rather do something else with their time. Some are very sociable and love playing with other children; others are happy to play by themselves. Despite the objective value of these activities being the same for each child, there is a great deal of variation in how much subjective attraction is at play. A theory of well-being that is oblivious to these variations fails to capture an important part of what it means for a childhood to go well.

In addition to being incomplete, any theory of well-being that rejects P1 faces some serious difficulties. Recall that according to joint-necessity hybrid accounts of well-being, P1 is true because endorsement of valuable goods is necessary for well-being. Those who reject hybrid accounts will therefore have to follow one of two paths. Either they will need to subscribe to subjectivist accounts and, by implication, reject the necessity of worthwhile goods in the lives of children, or they will need to push for objectivist accounts, where endorsement becomes irrelevant. In the former case, such a critic will have to accept that violent video games partly constitute a good childhood in case the child endorses such games. In the latter case, she will have to commit herself to the claim that a friendship with a dog partly constitutes a good childhood even when a child does not feel comfortable around animals. Both of these results seem implausible.

Now, none of this is to deny that because children are legitimate targets of paternalistic intervention by parents and the state, they will sometimes lack choice about which projects to engage in. But even when children have had no say over some of the valuable goods in their childhoods, there remains a question about whether or not they have come to endorse them, which, in turn, will affect whether or not such goods have contributed, in a constitutive manner, to their leading a good life.

4.4.2. The Case for P2

The premise that endorsement requires positive affect in the case of children is also a philosophical premise, but it relies on empirical claims about how children respond to the valuable projects and relationships they engage in. The idea here is that, unlike adults, children's cognitive abilities are not sufficiently developed so as to produce, via cognitive means, authoritative endorsement of worthwhile projects and relationships. This means that when it comes to children, there can only be authoritative endorsement via positive affect.

Now, it is well known that children have different thought patterns and priorities from adults, but the question is why exactly this is the case. Psychologists specializing in childhood point to numerous factors. The most obvious one is that children have more limited life experience than adults, and so have less expertise to draw on in the course of their childhoods. But the difference between adults and children goes much further than the degree of expertise they have access to. There is also a significant difference in cognitive abilities between children and adults, due to the former having relatively immature capacity for self-reflection and self-perception, a high degree of optimism (which leads to an inability to realistically assess risks and costs), and also an overestimation of their positive values.[25]

Indeed, such cognitive differences between adults and children have led Tamar Shapiro to go so far as to refer to childhood as a predicament. In her discussion on the status of children, Shapiro draws attention to how a child lacks a "principled perspective which would count as the law of her will."[26] That is, a child doesn't yet have a practical identity with a realistic insight into her values (and their overall ranking), so as to be able to authoritatively adjudicate between conflicting motivational claims. Of course, children can appreciate reasons for and against different actions, but they cannot adequately evaluate these reasons in light of established values and moral beliefs, for they don't yet possess values that are sufficiently established, nor do they possess a fully developed capacity to acquire relevant moral knowledge and to engage in complex moral reasoning. This is why we take children to be appropriate targets of paternalistic intervention, and do not believe they are wronged by being denied the opportunity to make high-stakes decisions about their own lives.

This difference between the authority of the judgments of children and adults about their own good is a crucial step in my argument. When discussing endorsement of valuable projects and relationships on the part of adults, I merely pointed out that when positive affective responses are lacking, adults can still identify self-regarding reasons in their favor. That is, the humanitarian worker in Sudan who is anxious about the activities associated with her profession can still appeal to the value of becoming a better person as her reason for persevering with that type of work. But, of course, for that reason to be hers in any meaningful sense, we must presuppose an agent who has sufficient moral knowledge that is relevant to the case at hand, an adequate sense of what kind of person she is, what she would like to achieve in her life, a good sense of time, and what it means to commit to a project for a certain period of time. We also need to presuppose an agent who has a good enough grasp of the risks, costs, and opportunities involved with different life choices. This means that when she identifies whatever self-regarding reason in support of being a humanitarian worker, she has gone through a complex deliberative process that allows us to say that the reason in question is indeed her own. As Shapiro puts it, an adult "is one who is in a position to speak in her own voice, the voice of one who stands in determinate, authoritative relation to the various motivational forces within her."[27]

For comparison, imagine a nine-year-old child who has volunteered to look after a grandparent with dementia for two hours every evening. Let us imagine that the work does not jeopardize any of her core interests. Now suppose that she finds it stressful and difficult, but believes that family members should always stick with each other. What shall we make of this reason? Should we take it as authoritative in the way we would take the reason of an adult doing the same work?

If we take the cognitive limitations of children seriously, then we cannot possibly trust that this reason is the outcome of an adequate deliberative process. This child might believe that the ability to please her family is the only source of meaning in her life, but in reality she is just going through a phase where she finds it hard to value the other worthwhile projects and relationships she engages with. Or she might non-culpably hold the clearly false belief that morality requires children to make sacrifices for others whenever they have the opportunity to do so. She might also underestimate the opportunity costs associated with her caring obligations, by not realizing that two hours each day will take away precious time playing with an older sibling who will soon move out of home.

At this stage, it is important to be careful not to let our attitudes favoring caring relationships obscure the fact that this child's reasons lack authority. The point is not that caring obligations are not objectively good and that good reasons cannot be provided in their favor, but simply to note that a child lacks the ability to adequately evaluate whether such caring obligations should play such a prominent role in her life given her lack of enjoyment. Moreover, the point is not that children cannot cite good reasons for undertaking this kind of work, but simply to note that such reasons are not authoritative because of children's underdeveloped deliberative capacities. In fact, if we were to take children's deliberative capacity as authoritative due to the fact that they can sometimes produce good reasons in favor of worthwhile projects, we would also need to take bad reasons in favor of worthless projects as authoritative as well. They are, after all, produced by the same psychological process or mechanism. This would in effect spell out the end of justified comprehensive paternalism toward children.[28]

Does this mean that endorsement is not possible in the case of children? Not at all. Recall that endorsement can take place via positive affect, and that children can come to endorse a project or relationship on the basis that it produces joyfulness, satisfaction, pleasure, amusement, delight. These positive affective responses might not be enough to render a child immune from paternalistic intervention (for it seems that paternalism tracks a lack of authority over one's reasons, rather than a lack of endorsement of one's projects and relationships), but it is certainly enough for assessing how well her childhood goes. This is why the child who loves her school is in a significantly better position than the child who despises every second of her education, even if their academic achievements are on par.[29] This is also why the child who delights in her caring obligations, and is able to pursue such obligations in a way that does not jeopardize her current and future interests, engages with a project that no doubt contributes, in a constitutive manner, to her leading a good childhood.

4.4.3. The Case for P3

The premise that a sufficient level of positive affect requires carefreeness is fully empirical. Social psychologists have discovered that positive and negative affect are not independent from each other at any given period of time. According to one expert,

> [E]ach type of affect clearly tends to suppress the other, although the mechanism by which this occurs is not yet clearly understood. [Moreover], because of the suppressive mechanism, the two types of affect are not independent in terms of their frequency of occurrence.[30]

In other words, the more a person feels positive affect, the less she will feel negative affect, and vice versa.

This suppression mechanism could explain, for example, why children who report feeling happy are more likely to perform well academically, for their happiness allows them to develop positive affective responses to schooling and education.[31] It could also explain why children who report feeling happy show more imagination and creativity during play, for their happiness allows them to develop positive affective responses to play.[32] That is, carefreeness creates space for children to authoritatively endorse the valuable projects and relationships in their lives. Stress and anxiety have exactly the opposite effect.[33]

Notice though that the mere fact that highly stressed and anxious children will at times display positive affective responses to valuable projects and relationships will not suffice for endorsement. The valuable projects and relationships that contribute to a meaningful life typically extend across a nontrivial period of time, or are in fact ongoing. For positive affective responses to count as endorsement, they have to be present for most of the time in which they are pursued. A child who only occasionally feels joy in the playground or the classroom does not in fact endorse play or education, since what is actually needed is for her to feel this way for most of the time during which she pursues these valuable projects.[34]

This completes my case for the conclusion that carefreeness is a necessary good of a childhood well lived, because children need to have enough mental space for developing positive affective responses that secure endorsement of worthwhile projects and relationships. Unlike adults, who can endorse worthwhile goods merely on the basis of how well they fit with their life goals, children's endorsements are authoritatively mediated via their affective responses. Children will therefore fail to endorse play, loving relationships, and education, for instance, when they constantly find themselves worried or stressed. Although we can concede that many children in stressful circumstances still have access to valuable goods, we shouldn't be naive in thinking that these by themselves constitute a good childhood. If we want children to lead good childhoods, they must be carefree.

4.5. Implications

I now want to finish the discussion by saying a few words on who is responsible for ensuring that children lead carefree lives, as well as asking what exactly this entails in terms of concrete actions on the part of parents.

First, it is important to acknowledge that the liberal state can play a role in creating the conditions for children to lead carefree lives, by ensuring that parents themselves are not suffering from things like housing or food insecurity, which can lead to a great deal of stress and anxiety for families. The state can also promote carefreeness and play by designing the curriculum and structuring school hours to provide children with plenty of opportunities to engage in carefree play in the day and ensure that they are not constantly concerned about homework, tests, and assignments. Obviously, the concrete educational policies that strike the best balance between academic growth and carefreeness are matters for psychologists, education experts, and social scientists. Similarly, the concrete welfare policies that support low-income families with children and that create enough of an incentive for labor-market participation are matters for experts other than philosophers. But I hope that this chapter has helped to explain why children should not find themselves constantly worrying about schooling and other aspects of their life irrespective of the effects this will have on their adulthood.

But still, this is a book about the goods that parents are primarily responsible for, and so I want to end the discussion by highlighting the ways that parents can foster the special good of carefreeness in the course of the paternalistic relationship they enjoy with their child. One obvious way that parents can help children lead carefree lives is by not instrumentalizing their childhood. Indeed, the more parents make clear that children's educational accomplishments (and other forms of achievements) matter for their success in adulthood, the more children are being invited to develop negative affective responses to the valuable things that give meaning to their childhood, such as schooling, sport, and artistic projects. This is not to say that children should be completely shielded from the realities of adult life, but just to note that too much transparency can be counterproductive. Children will do better at school if they are given the space to develop pro-attitudes to education. Children will be better musicians if they are given the space to develop pro-attitudes to music. And so on and so forth. And being carefree is necessary for such pro-attitudes to arise in the first place.

It is important to stress the fact that carefreeness also relies on children having a sense of security about their lives. This is true when it comes to knowing that the loving relationship with a parent is enjoyed robustly, as well as knowing that access to the basics of life such as housing and nutrition is guaranteed irrespective of what else happens down the track. (Obviously some families don't have secure access to adequate housing and food, but, as we have alluded to in Chapter 3, this is typically because the state has failed that family, rather than the family having failed the child.)

Finally, parents should ensure that children have secure access to the other projects and relationships that matter in their lives. One uncontroversial good is the good of play. In the next two chapters, I discuss two other goods of childhood: achievement and friendship. I explain why they matter, and why, again, parents have a special obligation to ensure that children have reliable access to them in the course of their childhood.

4.6. Conclusion

In this chapter I argue that carefreeness is necessary for a good childhood because carefreeness is necessary for children to endorse the valuable projects and relationships in their lives. This means that carefreeness should be taken just as seriously as play when it comes to thinking about what it means for children to lead good lives qua children. I also argue that this creates important obligations for parents, such as the obligation not to instrumentalize their children's childhood and to provide them with a strong sense of security. In the next chapters, we will look at other goods that parents are primarily responsible for fostering. We will start with the good of achievement, and finish with a discussion on the good of friendship.

5
Achievement

5.1. Introduction

In the previous chapter I argued that carefreeness is necessary for a good childhood, and that carefreeness counts as a special good of childhood. That conclusion might have come as a surprise to some readers, since carefreeness is sometimes understood as encompassing certain kinds of activities that don't exhaust a good childhood.

In this chapter, the surprise might come from the other direction. I will argue that achievement in childhood, as currently expressed in the social imaginary of liberal societies, does not always contribute to a good childhood. In fact, I will argue that childhood achievement often gets in the way of a good childhood precisely because it makes children much less carefree than they would otherwise be. The upshot of the discussion will be that when we see children excelling at musical instruments, drama, sports, and academic disciplines, we might actually be looking at a so-called "childhood bad." As I hope to show, whether or not these kinds of achievements contribute to a good childhood will depend entirely on what is in fact driving a child to excel in a particular domain.

Now, the argument in this chapter might seem entirely misguided to those who recall achieving wonderful things in childhood and feeling as if such projects did contribute to their experiencing a good childhood despite not even remembering the motives behind their own quest for achievement. Those who remember winning a spelling contest, a sports tournament, or who learned a new language in a very short period of time might be somewhat confused by the claim that achievement can be detrimental to a good childhood. After all, they might not remember exactly what was going on in their minds, but they may clearly recall the satisfaction of having succeeded in a difficult enterprise.

In response to this common experience, I will explain how a concept in the vicinity can help draw a distinction between good and bad forms of achievement. Indeed, I will show that what we might call "intrinsic achievement" can in fact partly constitute a good childhood, but that some strict conditions must obtain. And, as we will also see later in the discussion, such conditions create stringent obligations on parents, both positive and negative in content.

The discussion is structured as follows. In Section 5.2, I briefly discuss the connection between achievement and joint-necessity hybrid accounts of well-being. In Section 5.3, I discuss achievement in adulthood and show that motives do not seem to matter for the question of whether a specific project rises to the level of achievement. In Section 5.4, I show that the opposite is true in childhood, and that, in fact, motives are key for assessing the value of a child's achievement. In Section 5.5, I discuss the most important practical implications of the discussion. I conclude this chapter by showing that only enjoyment-driven or curiosity-driven achievements constitute a good childhood. Instrumental forms of achievement get in the way of children enjoying good childhoods.

5.2. Achievement and Well-Being

What is the precise connection between achievement and well-being? Before we can get clearer on the role that achievement plays in a good life, we need to be clear on what achievement is. According to Gwen Bradford, achievement must meet (at least) two conditions: the credit condition and the difficulty condition.[1]

The first condition requires that a given process or product is "properly attributable or credited to the agent."[2] This means that achievement cannot be the result of sheer luck. If I accidently leave my soda-making equipment outside, and the next day I notice that my mixing stick had frozen upright in the liquid, thus inventing a Popsicle, this does not really count as an achievement, no matter how delicious this invention is.[3] Similarly, if I sit a university entrance exam without having studied at all, and decide to select answers randomly, then getting a place at a university as a result of sheer luck is not an achievement.

After all, even a toddler who has not yet learned to read could choose answers at random, get lucky, and then be accepted into a university degree. In other words, outcomes that are a matter of luck alone are not achievements.

But being able to appropriately attribute a process or product to an agent is not the only condition for achievement. Difficulty seems to matter a great deal as well. When I successfully go through the automatic checkout machine at the supermarket, I don't achieve anything, since it is fairly easy for someone like me, who does not suffer from a severe form of intellectual impairment, to follow their prompts, as well as fairly easy to abide by the principle that I ought to pay for each product that I take home. By contrast, if I design a complex machine that helps solve an important social problem, such as a voting machine that prevents large-scale fraud, then I have in fact achieved something remarkable.

Although virtually all philosophical accounts of achievement give some prominent role to difficulty, there is a puzzle about effortless achievements on the part of highly competent agents.[4] For instance, is it really an achievement for an award-winning chef to cook a perfect turducken? It is certainly an achievement for any amateur cook, but perhaps not for someone who can do so painlessly.

One response to this sort of case is to bite the bullet and say that when something is very easy for an agent, despite being difficult for most other people, it does not count as an achievement for that agent.[5] Bradford argues for this response when considering the case of a violin virtuoso effortlessly playing the Paganini Caprices.[6] According to Bradford, the virtuoso does not achieve anything, because playing the Paganini Caprices is too easy for him. Achievement then relies on an understanding of difficulty that is relative to the level of effort required on the part of the agent.

I take it, though, that this response is highly counterintuitive. How could it be that the award-winning chef does not achieve anything given the low level of effort required of her when cooking a perfect turducken? Most importantly, how could it be that my slightly burned turducken counts as more of an achievement merely due to the sweat and tears involved? Something seems to be amiss in an account of achievement that leads to this sort of result.

There are three plausible ways of including such cases while simultaneously preserving the idea that difficulty matters for achievement. The first response is to deny that there is such a thing as effortless achievement, by noting that even the best violin virtuoso knows that things can go terribly wrong if he gets distracted, and so needs to apply his utmost attention and focus to the outcome he is trying to achieve. This means that even when things look effortless, there is still a level of cognitive effort that is not at all trivial.[7]

Another response is to have an objective understanding of difficulty. Turducken might not be difficult for an award-winning chef, but it is difficult for most people, and that is the sense of difficulty we are interested in.[8] Perhaps part of what is valuable about achievement is that it involves a process or product that many or most individuals are not easily capable of bringing about.

A more promising response, however, is to say that the difficulty can lie in acquiring the skills, even if the exercise of the skills is no longer difficult. This response insists that we must look at difficulty at earlier points in time, and then describe the acquisition of a skill in the past as the real achievement rather than the exercise of that skill. The thought here is that it is in fact quite difficult to master all the skills required to get to the point where one can easily cook a perfect turducken, such as perfectly deboning birds, perfectly cooking and inserting the stuffing, learning to calculate the roasting time, and so on. In that case, the achievement in question is to become the sort of chef who can easily make a perfect turducken. In the same way, the real achievement of a violin virtuoso playing the Paganini Caprices is to have become so excellent at playing the violin that she can perfectly and effortlessly play pieces beyond the skill of most musicians.

At any rate, irrespective of how we decide to solve this puzzle, one thing is clear: difficulty does seem to be at the heart of achievement. And a process or product that can be brought about effortlessly, with the use of skills that were also acquired effortlessly, will not count as achievement.

Now, before we can look at achievements both in adulthood and in childhood, we must attend to a final crucial question: How does achievement contribute to well-being? Or, more specifically, how does being credited with difficult processes or products contribute to one's leading a good life?

Most influential philosophical accounts of the value of achievement are perfectionist accounts, whereby achievement's significance lies in the exercise of distinctive human capacities, such as our rational and physical capacities.[9] For perfectionists, well-being just is the exercise of characteristically human capacities, and achievement involves the exercise of such capacities at a high level due to the difficulty involved. Indeed, for perfectionists, achievements contribute to well-being, because they undoubtedly contribute to human flourishing.[10]

Despite perfectionists having an easy time explaining why achievement helps us fare well, I believe that joint-necessity hybrid theories of well-being are better suited to explaining how achievement may partly constitute a good life. These theories, recall, require that agents endorse a project or relationship that is objectively good for it to contribute to a life well lived.[11] This is because the cases of achievement that most contribute to a good life are precisely those where the agent is subjectively attracted to a difficult project, and the project itself is worthwhile. Moreover, while perfectionist accounts can be silent on whether or not the agent endorses the project, joint-necessity hybrid theories will require a level of endorsement on the part of the agent for the achievement in question to partly constitute a good life.

Indeed, the important point here is that while perfectionist accounts of well-being may include in their list of goods achievements which have neutral or even negative value, joint-necessity hybrid theories will pick a class of achievements as contributing to a good life precisely because the agent is subjectively attracted to a difficult yet worthwhile enterprise.[12] Writing a brilliant novel, helping bring about important social change, finding the cure or vaccine for a deadly illness are the sorts of achievements that seem to most contribute to a good life. This may be due to the connection between worth and fulfillment. After all, it seems plausible to claim that the more worthwhile a project is, the more fulfillment an agent will derive from it.

Bradford, who herself advocates a perfectionist account of achievement, seems to agree that joint-necessity hybrid theories capture the most valuable forms of achievement.[13] As she puts it,

Achievement is also particularly well-suited to accounts that include both objective and subjective components because one might think that achievement alone is not sufficient, as is illustrated by John Stuart Mill in his *Autobiography* or Tolstoy in *A Confession*, who both experience despair in spite of achievement. So perhaps, it is just not achievement [which matters] but active engagement with worthwhile projects.[14]

There is much more to be said about achievement and its connection to well-being, but this brief discussion will suffice for our purposes. At its core, achievements are difficult processes or products that are brought about by agents primarily due to their abilities. Moreover, achievements certainly contribute to a good life when they are subjectively attractive and worthwhile. But, to return to the question of this chapter, how should we think of achievement in childhood? Now that we have a plausible definition of achievement in mind, and a sense of what is valuable about achievement, we can turn to the question of whether we should think of achievement differently at different life stages. In the next two sections, I will argue that there is good reason to think that different forms of achievements will contribute to a good childhood and a good adulthood. And, as we will see, this creates stringent obligations on the part of parents to ensure that children are achieving in ways that make their childhood go well, rather than badly.

5.3. Achievement in Adulthood

Before we are better positioned to compare achievements in childhood with achievements in adulthood, we must first look at the relationship between motives and achievement. This is because one obvious difference between childhood and adulthood achievement is that adults are typically motivated to achieve for reasons that children lack access to. That is, children may, for instance, not understand why someone wants to get a job with greater responsibilities than they presently bear, or why it matters to an artist that a famous critic reviews her work irrespective of whether they admire it. Moreover, as discussed in the previous chapter, even when such reasons are intelligible to a child, a judgment that such reasons could apply to her would not be authoritative because she lacks a "principled perspective which would count as the law of her will."[15] Indeed, even if a child can make sense of the idea that responsibility can be rewarding or that critical feedback by someone one respects can be valuable, it is still not the case that a child can authoritatively judge that it is in fact good for her to acquire more responsibility in her life, or that it is good for her to have her artistic work scrutinized by a highly regarded art critic.

In light of the reasons that typically move adults to achieve, but that may not suffice to render a child's quest for achievement authoritative, how should we think of the role of motives in achievement when thinking at a more general level?

In the philosophical literature on achievement, motives do not seem to play an important role when it comes to describing whether something counts as an achievement. That is, philosophers writing on achievement don't specify motive conditions for a process or product to count as an achievement. The result here is that we should understand achievements as difficult processes or products that are brought about by agents primarily due to their abilities and irrespective of their motives.

How should we evaluate this lack of a motive condition? When we look deeper into this omission, it seems warranted. After all, the brilliant novel will count as an achievement irrespective of why the author decided to write it. That is, it does not seem to matter whether she did it to become globally famous, make a lot of money, influence politics, avoid lockdown boredom, or impress the person she is in love with. Whatever the motive, the brilliant novel counts as an achievement.

The same is true of the scientist who discovers the cure for a dreadful disease. It does not matter whether she does it to secure tenure, win a handsome prize, get back at a senior colleague who denied her an opportunity early on due to her working-class background, and so on and so forth. Again, whatever the motive, the cure counts as an achievement.

Of course, the question of what counts as an achievement is different from that of how achievement contributes to well-being. But here, too, motive does not play a central role. After all, for joint-necessity hybrid accounts, it does not matter why the author or the scientist endorses the project, so long as that project is subjectively attractive and objectively valuable. Indeed, if an agent is subjectively attracted to a worthwhile project, then it contributes to a meaningful life, and by extension, to a good life, irrespective of what is actually driving the agent.

To be sure, it is possible for there to be evil achievements, which means that agents can be motivated to do difficult things in order to bring about a morally problematic outcome.[16] The teenager who teaches himself to code in order to engage in online banking fraud achieves something impressive and bad. The art-lover who manages to steal the Mona Lisa from the Louvre achieves something exceptional. But again, such cases are easy for joint-necessity hybrid accounts, for they fail to meet the objective condition. Stealing is simply not a worthwhile activity. This means that the fraudster and the robber achieve something remarkable, but such achievements do not even partly constitute a good life.

So what explains this disconnect between achievement and motives such that agents need not be moved by a "good" reason in order for the achievement to constitute a good life? I think such disconnect is merely the byproduct of a psychologically plausible account of how achievement contributes to a good life. Human beings are often motivated to achieve wonderful things out of petty motives. In fact, many great achievers throughout history have been deeply flawed individuals. Some of them might have achieved not in spite of their psychological weaknesses, but precisely due to them. Ernest Hemingway, for instance, has been accused of being a hypercompetitive boaster motivated by sheer vanity.[17] Some have suggested that Picasso's sexually voracious behavior was an integral part of his creative process.[18] These are very common human stories. Moreover, the motives in question don't seem to change the verdict that Hemingway's novels and Picasso's paintings count as great human achievements, and that such achievements were precisely the things that both artists had going for them in terms of well-being.

Now, I do not mean to suggest that motives do not matter when we make an overall assessment of the person who successfully engaged with a difficult product or process. We can in fact judge human beings for having or lacking a good will, and the amount of praise we afford someone is likely to depend on how we assess their motives. The point of this section is simply to highlight that valuable achievements do not seem to require a motive condition, and that all sorts of motives are still compatible with achievement partly constituting a good life. Or, at least, this seems to be the case for adults. In the next section, I show that things are much more complicated for children, and that certain kinds of motives are in fact crucial for an achievement to partly constitute a good childhood.

5.4. Achievement in Childhood

So how exactly should we think of achievement in childhood? On the face of it, it may look as if childhood is a particularly good stage of life to achieve remarkable things. After all, childhood is a stage of life where children enjoy certain skills, cognitive abilities, and capacities to a different extent from adults, and this lends itself to engaging in an array of difficult processes and products. For instance, in childhood it is easy to get lost in one's own world and so easy to stay focused when undertaking certain kinds of projects. In childhood, it is easy to learn certain things very fast, and to be open to new possibilities due to a lack of experience with things being a certain way for a long time. This lends itself to creativity and imagination.

But childhood is also a stage of life where human beings typically have a distinctive relationship to their bodies. That is, they are less "careful" when interacting with the physical environment around them, and less fearful of being injured. This means that they are more inclined to test their physical abilities and limits.

One relevant question is whether these differences between adults and children render the latter more disposed to certain forms of achievements than the former. Anca Gheaus, when engaging with the perfectionist account of achievement put forward by Gwen Bradford, answers this question in the affirmative. As she says: "In virtue of their creativity and drive to explore the world, children in general are more capable of genuine achievement than adults in general."[19] Gheaus goes on to suggest that if we follow Bradford in believing that the value of an agent's achievements depends on agents' full exercise of their characteristic human capacities, then achievement will come easier to children than to adults because children are particularly good at being "all one can be."[20]

Now, Gheaus may well be right that children are better than adults at exercising their human capacities. Or, at least, Gheaus may be right that children are better at exercising their characteristic child-capacities than adults are at exercising their characteristic adult-capacities. This would entail that Gheaus is correct to claim that children are particularly good at achieving. However, the important question for our purposes is whether achievements contribute to children leading a good life. And, as I hope to show in the remainder of this section, the answer to this question is much more nuanced than child-rearing practices in liberal societies would have us believe. More specifically, my answer to this question is that achievements can contribute to a good childhood, but many forms of achievements that children are strongly encouraged to undertake actually make their childhood go worse than it would have gone without the achievement in question.

Why so skeptical of achievement? Unfortunately, in liberal societies many children are encouraged to achieve for purely instrumental reasons. That is, many children are told that if they practice a musical instrument or a sport for many hours a day, they may become a famous musician or sports star when they grow up. Or they are taken to audition for acting roles in advertisements and movies and are told that this will make them and their family rich. Other children are encouraged to excel academically in order to make their parents or family members proud. And so on and so forth. As we will see, such forms of achievement not only do not partly constitute a good childhood, but are also likely to make it harder for children to enjoy the other goods in their lives.

Consider first the case of musical instruments and sports. There is a world of difference between becoming excellent at the piano or soccer because one really enjoys practicing the relevant skills, and doing so merely because one wants to be famous. In the first sort of case, the child derives joy from expressing herself musically, or has a lot of fun playing with others in the field, and this counts as them endorsing that activity. And note that it counts as endorsement despite the difficulty involved, since enjoyment can obtain despite effort also in the case of children. In the second case, the child derives no joy from it, but persists merely because she believes that fame is a good thing. Now, of course, whether or not fame is valuable is irrelevant for our purposes here, since what is at issue is children's ability to assess whether fame is worthwhile *for them*. That is to say, even if we agree that fame can be overall positive, a child is not capable of deciding *with authority* whether fame is something that will make her life go well.

Indeed, recall that in the previous chapter, we established that children can only endorse objectively valuable activities and projects via positive affect, because they lack the cognitive capacities to authoritatively evaluate the worth of the projects they undertake merely on the basis of reasons. As we saw, this is because they lack a practical identity with a realistic insight into their values (and their overall ranking) to be able to authoritatively adjudicate between conflicting motivational claims. They also lack the ability to adequately evaluate risks and costs, as well as to identify all the core demands of morality, which makes it hard for them to assess the worth of a pursuit against a background of conflicting demands on their time and attention. This means that children are very different from adults, who can in fact authoritatively decide that becoming excellent at the piano is what will make their life meaningful, even if they actually dislike the process of becoming good at it.

Another way of drawing a distinction between an achievement that partly constitutes a good childhood and one that does not is to recognize that a child always knows if she feels joy when playing the piano or when playing soccer.[21] What she does not yet know is if she is the kind of person who can build a good life partly on the basis of being excellent at playing the piano or soccer. And until she knows that (something that will become clearer in late adolescence or in adulthood), she had better not waste her precious (and short!) childhood years doing things that she does not in fact enjoy. She had also better not find herself in a position where doing such things will make her feel so miserable that she cannot enjoy the other goods in her life.[22]

Consider now the case of child actors. Again, some children love to act and to role-play and they may do so extremely well. These are some of the children who end up acting in movies, TV series, and advertisements. Now, some of these children will love to role-play so much that they will jump at any opportunity to do so with others.

If acting will also make the family better off financially, this is a positive byproduct, but such children might be equally happy to join a local amateur theater group. These children no doubt enjoy acting, and acting projects will count as achievements that make their childhood go well. Such cases are in stark contrast, however, with the case of a photogenic child who is pressured by her parents to take on acting roles because she is good at it, and because the family could do with the money. In this case, the child is not moved by the sheer joy of acting, but on the basis of a reason (that is, financial benefits) that she is incapable of authoritatively acting on. The result here is that acting projects undertaken by a pressured child will not count as an achievement that makes her childhood go well.

Finally, consider the case of children who excel academically. Some of them do so because they love a subject and are intensely curious about that domain of knowledge. I myself recall falling in love with history at a very early age and simply devouring any history entry in any encyclopedia I could lay my hands on. As a result, I consistently achieved very good grades in history. But that was always a byproduct of being curious about what people did in the past, how they lived their lives, and what kind of societies they created. I never achieved in history for the sake of being an achiever. I achieved in history as a byproduct of my passion for the discipline.

Now compare that with another achievement of my childhood. At age nine, I was told by my parents that if I made no mistakes whatsoever in any of my math tests for that school year, I would receive a typewriter as a present. This offer had the positive intention of encouraging me to focus on my math assignments (apparently, I was good at math, but very bad at focusing. The typewriter was used as a carrot, so I would remember the importance of paying attention). But, of course, the offer had an unintentional side-effect: it made me worry about my performance at school. Indeed, I wanted the typewriter so much that I studied very hard for a whole year, practicing the different problem sets so much that it became second nature. This, in turn, led to a significant level of stress. Now, there is no doubt that getting perfect scores in math for a year counted as an achievement. But, as I am suggesting in this chapter, this form of achievement does not contribute to a good childhood.

As is now clear, achievements in childhood require positive affect so that they come to partly constitute a good childhood. When children achieve in a joyless fashion merely for the sorts of reasons that will appeal to an adult, those achievements do not play a role in their leading a good childhood. This is why it is so important that children engage with noninstrumental forms of achievement: difficult processes that they find fun, or that they are curious or passionate about. Otherwise, what they are doing is wasting their efforts on something that is not enjoyable and does not contribute to a good childhood, when they could instead be making an effort in a domain that brings about joy, satisfaction, pleasure, amusement, and delight.

Waste is not the only issue here, however. The more negative affect involved in learning an instrument, playing a sport, acting, or excelling in an academic endeavor, the less carefree a child will be. And the less carefree she is, the less space she has to enjoy the other goods in her life. Indeed, recall how in the previous chapter, we learned that positive affect and negative affect are not independent from each other at any given period of time, and that the more a child feels positive affect, the less she will feel negative affect, and vice versa.[23] A child who is made miserable by the violin-practice regime put in place to make her into a famous musician in adulthood is a child who is constrained in her ability to feel positive affect toward the other valuable projects and relationships in her life. This means that the stress spills over into other activities and makes them less enjoyable, making them, in turn, less likely to partly constitute a good childhood. The result here is that a parent cannot accept the lack of enjoyment attached to violin practice, but then justify it on the basis that the child has plenty of other enjoyable things in her life. For it could well be that those long hours practicing the violin cause so much stress that she barely enjoys all the other good things in her life. In other words, it could well be that the violin lessons make a carefree childhood impossible, taking away something that is in fact necessary for her to lead a good life in childhood.

The same would be true for other forms of instrumental achievements. Upon realizing that the math challenge was not something I enjoyed pursuing, my parents could not justifiably point to all the other good things in my life and claim that there were enough of them to make up for the fact that math practicing was now causing me great stress. For it may well be that in that academic year, I was not a carefree child, and this placed me in a position where I could not enjoy all the other valuable things in my life. That is, it could well be that in that academic year the valuable things in my life did not constitute a good life because I was psychologically incapable of endorsing them via positive affect.

This is not to suggest that parents should not act paternalistically in the domain of education. It would have been entirely legitimate for my parents to see to it that I acquired a sufficient level of math skills so I could acquire a good education and function later on in my life. But no child needs to get perfect scores in math in order to acquire a good education; what parents owe their children is precisely that they acquire the academic skills that will enable them to choose from an array of professional opportunities later on in their lives. Parents do not owe their children the level of academic excellence that clearly goes well beyond functioning, and can come at the cost of a carefree childhood.

So far, we have seen that achievements can partly constitute a good childhood, but that this depends on the motives driving such achievements. Children who excel in a difficult endeavor primarily due to joy, curiosity, and passion are in a completely different position from children who excel for pure instrumental reasons, and who do so in a joyless fashion. The latter group is simply not achieving in a way that makes their childhood go well. The upshot for us is that achievement in childhood partly constitutes a good childhood when it meets the credit condition, the difficulty condition, the objective-value condition (as discussed in Section 5.2 above), and what we might call the positive-affect condition.

But what of children who find an activity to be intrinsically motivating but also stressful? They might not be pushed by anyone else to pursue that activity, but they still don't enjoy it. How should we think of such cases?[24]

I think such cases would be quite rare in childhood, given that children are typically attracted to projects that produce positive affect. However, you can certainly imagine a child who finds an activity both intrinsically motivating and unpleasant. Perhaps she cannot help but feel that she should be surfing every day, just because it is something obvious to do where she lives. Yet, when she is surfing, she feels constant dread and angst. Why think in such cases that the achievement in question is bad?

Again, given that children can only endorse the valuable projects in their lives via positive affect, surfing does not partly constitute a good childhood in this case. It is true that if she becomes a great surfer in childhood, she has achieved something remarkable. But the point here is precisely that not all achievements on the part of children partly constitute a good childhood. In this case, either the achievement does not contribute positively to a good childhood or it actually gets in the way of a good childhood. It all depends on whether the stress involved is significant enough to make it hard for this child to endorse the other valuable things in her life.

Let me now move to another objection which must be addressed head on. The objection takes the following form: it may be true that when children do not enjoy the achievements they are encouraged to undertake, such achievements do not partly constitute a good childhood. But this fact does not settle the question of whether such achievements are desirable, all things considered. After all, many such achievements are not about enabling a good childhood, but rather are about enabling a good adulthood. They are about equipping children with certain skills at a stage of their lives when it is easier to acquire those skills, an investment potentially enabling them to employ those skills to achieve remarkable things later on in their lives. In other words, the objector may agree with me that such achievements do not partly constitute a good childhood, while insisting that they are valuable merely on the basis that they pave the way for a good adulthood.

This is a very important objection, and I am sure this way of thinking is behind the decision of many parents to pressure their children to stick with an instrument, drama classes, or a sport long after it is clear that the child is not enjoying it. When pressed to explain why they want their child to achieve in a certain domain despite the child's lack of endorsement, the parents might say that they want their children to lead good lives, and that being very good at something is one sure way of leading a good life as an adult.

Now, this objection rests on one empirical assumption that will be false in some cases. The assumption is that one cannot excel in adulthood unless one has picked up the skills in childhood. In fact, many adults excel in many domains despite acquiring the relevant skills only in adolescence or adulthood. Denis Rodman famously started to play basketball seriously only after high school.[25] Acclaimed novelist Edwidge Danticat only learned English at age 12.[26] Three-time Grammy award winner Bill Withers only learned to play the guitar in adulthood.[27]

Still, for every case of a late bloomer, there are hundreds of other achievers who started developing the skills in a certain domain very early in their lives. There is no denying that learning an instrument, language, sport, or academic discipline in childhood will increase the likelihood of achievement in adulthood. The philosophical question is whether a worse childhood, due to the child not enjoying the achievement in question, can be justified on the basis that it will pave the way for achievement in adulthood.

As I see it, such a trade-off cannot be justified, since both childhood and adulthood are equally valuable life stages that play an important role in human beings leading good lives. Although children and adults pursue the good differently, with the first doing so as part of intimate loving relationships, and the second as part of an autonomously chosen life plan, both groups are capable of engaging with projects and relationships that are both subjectively attractive and worthy of that attraction. Moreover, each life stage has goods that are distinct to that life stage. Children get to play for a great part of their childhood. Adults get to make autonomous decisions about different aspects of their lives. This means that a rich all-round human life is in our best interest, and a better adulthood simply cannot justify the imposition of a bad childhood on a child.

It is also important to recognize that joyless achievement in childhood merely increases the likelihood of achievement in adulthood; it does not guarantee it. Moreover, a joyless childhood may well have the effect that the future adult will lack other skills that are often essential for achievement. Indeed, being good at something is often only part of the equation. Being resilient, attentive to one's own emotional needs, able to make certain kinds of sacrifices, as well as having the social skills required to get others to support one in achieving can also be very important. Although in some domains, such as chess, one may be able to achieve without any support from others, in many other fields, one will get nowhere alone, no matter how talented. The point here is that joyless achievement may well backfire, and you might end up with an adult who lacks the other skills required to translate effort into something remarkable.

In fact, the route to achievement in adulthood may be through precisely not making achievement overly salient in childhood. A child who is given a great deal of space to experiment in domains she is curious or passionate about, without parental pressure to follow through, may well become the sort of mature well-rounded individual who is truly capable of excelling in whatever pursuit she puts her mind to. So even for those who genuinely believe that childhood has less value than adulthood, there is a genuine empirical question about whether joyless achievement can do a better job of paving the way for achievement in adulthood than a childhood of carefreeness and experimentation. For it could well be that when it comes to most of the greatest achievers of our times, their childhood was one where they enjoyed many goods in life, and only developed high-level skills in things that they were genuinely curious, interested, or passionate about.

5.5. Implications

Let me now turn to the question of what this discussion means for parents and society at large. At the societal level, the obligation remains the same as that outlined in the previous chapter: it is paramount that the liberal state play a role in creating the conditions for children to lead carefree lives, by ensuring that parents are themselves not parenting under significant stress. It is also paramount that school does not become a place dreaded by children and that the stress of school does not spill over into other aspects of a child's life.[28]

But, of course, when it comes to achievement, the main obligations will fall on parents. For one thing, there is a stringent negative obligation not to impose a difficult project on a child merely for reasons that appeal to the parents, no matter how well intentioned those parents may be. Indeed, achievements have to be child-led, and it is only positive affect on the part of the child that serves as a signal that the project in question will contribute to a good childhood. Recall that a child is not the sort of creature who can authoritatively act on reasons in favor of a project, no matter the strength of those reasons. This is why even the parent who pressures her child to develop a set of skills which can one day lead to major social benefits acts wrongly if it is clear that the child does not enjoy developing such skills. If it is obvious to parents that their child is not curious, interested, or passionate about a given achievement, then they must refrain from imposing it on the child, no matter how noble their intentions.[29]

But parents also have positive obligations when it comes to achievement. And the obligation in question is to bear moderate costs to support the child in pursuing an achievement that she endorses, but cannot pursue by herself. The cost condition is essential here. Parents are not required to take on high costs in terms of time and resources in order to support achievement in childhood. It does not matter how much I loved history in childhood; I had no claim that my parents take me on international trips to Europe or the Middle East, or that they buy me more books than they could easily afford. The obligation they had was simply to give me time and a reasonable amount of resources for me to independently pursue my love for the subject.

Of course, parents are allowed to bear high costs if they so like, and there is a sense in which parent and child can achieve remarkable things together when parents support their child to achieve in a domain the child is passionate or curious about. This can add even more meaning to both their lives and be something that makes their relationship even more valuable. Think of the parent who supports a child's love for music by spending most of the discretionary time and resources supporting the child to develop her skills. In such a case, one might plausibly claim that when the child becomes a great musician, the child and parent have achieved that together. Although there is no obligation here, it is certainly a wonderful thing when a child is passionate about a difficult project, and her parent goes well above and beyond what is required to support the child in that endeavor. This is precisely the sort of action that readily flows from parental love and from parents seeing the good of their child as their own. And, as we have learned in the first part of this book, this disposition to take on costs and make sacrifices in order to support a child in acquiring meaning in her life is precisely what makes parental love distinctively valuable.

5.6. Conclusion

In this chapter, I defend an understanding of achievement that allows for childhood achievement to constitute a good childhood. However, I argue that in order for achievement to count as a good of childhood, it must also meet an objective-value condition and a positive-affect condition (in addition to the credit condition and the difficulty condition specified by Bradford).[30] This is because children can only authoritatively endorse worthwhile projects and relationships via positive affect. The upshot of the discussion is that achievement partly constitutes a good childhood when it is worthwhile and when the child feels satisfaction, pleasure, amusement, or delight. And of course, intrinsic achievements—projects driven by enjoyment and curiosity—are precisely the ones likely to produce positive affect. Difficult projects driven for pure instrumental reasons are unlikely to do so.

Apart from highlighting the fact that positive affect is necessary for a project to partly constitute a good childhood, I noted that there are opportunity costs involved in pursuing a joyless achievement when a child could potentially be pursuing a joyful one. I also highlighted how a lack of positive affect is likely to render a child much less carefree, making it more difficult for her to enjoy all the other valuable projects and relationships in her life. I concluded the discussion by explaining how parents should go about supporting their children in achieving in ways that do make their childhood go well.

6
Friendship

6.1. Introduction

In the last two chapters, I discussed two goods of childhood in detail. In particular, I argued that carefreeness is necessary for children to lead good lives, and that achievement can be a constituent of a good childhood if some strict conditions are met. The discussion so far has raised a number of implications for parents, from negative obligations not to impose stressful activities on children and not to pressure them to pursue excellence in a given domain, to positive ones such as to take steps to ensure that children feel a strong sense of security in their lives.

In this chapter, I discuss one final good of childhood that parents are primarily responsible for fostering: the good of friendship. Although philosophers have spilled a lot of ink theorizing about the nature and value of friendship in adulthood, very little philosophical attention has been paid to friendship in childhood. And yet childhood friendships often shape children in profound ways, and the friendship bonds children enjoy can be extremely meaningful to them. Childhood psychologist Judy Dunn puts the point well: "friends *matter* to children. We are missing a major piece of what excites, pleases, and upsets children, what is central to their lives even before school, if we don't attend to what happens between children and their friends."[1] Moreover, as philosophers Harry Brighouse and Adam Swift have emphasized in their work, children are particularly spontaneous, self-disclosing, and trustworthy, which are qualities that bear directly on the dynamics of particular friendships.[2] I will argue that such facts about childhood friendship have direct implications for philosophical views on the nature of friendship. In fact, taking childhood friendship seriously will lead us to embrace one particular way of understanding the nature of friendship: the drawing view advocated by Dean Cocking and Jeanette Kennett.[3]

But thinking carefully about friendship in childhood does not only have important theoretical implications for the philosophy of friendship. It also has important practical implications for family life. For one, there are relevant differences in how children and adults go about pursuing their friendships that matter for evaluating the merits of particular friendships. But, most importantly, understanding the nature and value of childhood friendship is important for identifying exactly what role parents ought to play in children's relationship with their friends. I hope to show in the course of this discussion that parental interventions aimed at ending (or even weakening) such friendships are often misguided and disrespectful to children qua creatures with independent and equal moral standing. Conversely, parental interventions that help create the conditions for children to pursue the friendships they care deeply about are among the most important things parents can do to help their children flourish.

The discussion is structured as follows. In Section 6.2, I discuss the nature of friendship and show how childhood friendship tells against the "mirror" and "secrets" views of the nature of friendship, and in favor of the "drawing view," advocated by Dean Cocking and Jeanette Kennett. In Section 6.3, I discuss the role that morality plays in regulating friendships in adulthood, which supports the view that some adult friendships should not be initiated, and if initiated, should eventually be abandoned. In Section 6.4, I show that the governing conditions for childhood friendships are somewhat different from the governing conditions for adulthood friendship, and that very few childhood friendships are problematic in the way that adulthood friendships can be. This means that there is very little room for paternalistic intervention in the lives of children when it comes to their pursuit of particular friendships. One upshot of this discussion is that if we put unstructured play aside, friendship is the domain where children ought to enjoy the greatest degree of freedom in their lives, partly because paternalism in the sphere of childhood friendship fails to take children's current interests seriously, and partly because such freedom is crucial for the development of an authentic self who can make autonomous decisions later on in life.

6.2. Friendship and Well-Being

What is the nature of friendship and how does it contribute to a good life? A common-sense view of friendship is that close friends enjoy each other's company, care for each other deeply, and engage in shared activities that make each other's life go better than it would otherwise. Philosophers too are attracted by this simple picture. Laurence Thomas argues that when it comes to close friends, "*the raison d'etre* for their interaction is the delight that they take in being with one another."[4] This common-sense view is also nicely captured by Nancy Sherman, who adds that "we experience a friend's happiness or sorrow as our own. Accomplishments and failures, which are not explicitly our own, are nonetheless, through an extension of self, sources of pride and shame."[5]

But although this picture gets things partly right, more needs to be said about close (or companion) friendship if we are to distinguish it from other valuable relationships, such as those between relatives, siblings, and even certain kinds of professional collaborations. And, as already alluded to in the introduction, another important desideratum for a successful theory of the nature of friendship is to make sense of friendship across all life stages: from childhood to adolescence, from adulthood to old age.

Now, it may be that friendship in one particular life stage best approximates what the ideal friendship looks like. Nothing in this chapter precludes that conclusion. But given that many people will point to their childhood friends as the best friends they have ever had in their lives, and given that, in childhood, friends are disposed to act in ways that are particularly effective at strengthening the loving bond they enjoy with one another (think of sleepovers, the overt displays of affection that would be unthinkable for many adults, especially men, or the sheer amount of time that children are willing to offer each other), we had better not endorse a theory of the nature of friendship that has the result that children cannot be companion friends.[6]

And yet, this is precisely the result we get from two of the main contenders in the literature: the mirror view and the secrets views.[7] As we are about to see, both these contenders are ill suited to making sense of friendship in childhood, because they theorize about agents who already have a sufficiently established practical identity, a good understanding of what morality requires, as well as a full grasp of the distinctiveness of the relationship they enjoy with their close friends. Luckily for us, the drawing account advocated by Cocking and Kennett does not run into similar trouble. Although the authors themselves have not extended the account to cover childhood friendship, I will show that it does in fact capture an important element of close friendships across all life stages: "that we are distinctively disposed to engage in each other's activities and to be responsive to the way the other thinks and feels about things."[8]

But before I explain why the drawing view should guide us in thinking about friendship across all life stages, it pays to understand exactly why the other two main contenders fail to do justice to children's friendship. Consider the mirror view first. The idea here is that the choosing of a close friend, and the ongoing pursuit of that friendship, involves the recognition of each other's good character. More importantly, by forming a friendship bond, close friends mutually acknowledge that they share not only love and concern for one another, but also that they are similar in virtue. The mirror view takes its name from the central role that friendship allegedly plays in the acquisition of self-knowledge: by reflecting each other's positive characteristics, close friends provide each other with an important insight into who they really are. This view goes back to Aristotle, who is skeptical that people who are markedly dissimilar could be genuine friends. As he puts it,

> How could they be friends when they neither approved of the same things nor delighted in and were pained by the same things. For not even with regard to each other will their tastes agree, and without this (as we saw) they cannot be friends.[9]

The first thing to note about this view is that if companion friends provide us with a mirror so as to acquire a valuable form of self-knowledge, such a mirror image will be mostly ineffective in the case of children. Children lack sufficient knowledge of their constantly evolving values and traits to learn anything especially deep about themselves from their close friends. Children also lack sufficient knowledge about the world and about human psychology to adequately evaluate their motives and the motives of others in the course of an intimate relationship.[10]

Another reason to be skeptical of the mirror view is that children (perhaps even more so than adults) are often attracted to children who are very different from themselves. Who can forget the friendship between the extrovert and daring hypochondriac girl obsessed with death and the quite sensible (and somewhat fragile) boy in the film *My Girl*? What makes that film so touching is precisely the fact that although an adult struggling with a myriad of deadly allergies would have had very little patience for a healthy hypochondriac, the little boy is incredibly forgiving, understanding, and supportive of his best friend.

But the main reason why the mirror view does not work for children can already be found in Cocking and Kennett's discussion of the nature of friendship. When focusing on adult friends, they call attention to the fact that even adults shape one another in profound ways by directing one another to different pursuits and by interpreting one another in ways that are profoundly illuminating. They accuse the mirror view of incorrectly implying that "we come to friendship as fully formed and self-sufficient individuals."[11] And, of course, such an assumption is even more problematic in the case of children who are being "formed" by their intimate relationships to a much greater extent than the adults around them, and are particularly vulnerable precisely due to their lack of self-sufficiency.[12]

Consider now the secrets view, which understands friendship as a relationship marked by a deep bond of mutual trust. According to the secrets view, what distinguishes friendship from other relationships is that we are disposed to show aspects of ourselves to our close friends that we are not disposed to share with anyone else. Moreover, we tell our close friends our deepest secrets, both because we wholeheartedly trust them and because we want to signal to them how important they are in our lives. Laurence Thomas, the most prominent defender of this view, goes so far as to argue that friendship between people whose lives are open books is virtually impossible since "there can be no friendship if we cannot convey [intimate trust]."[13]

Although it is true that some children do share secrets with their close friends, such secrets are often unrelated to self-disclosure.[14] That is to say, they might tell a friend what they really think of their teacher, or break the news that Santa isn't real, but they don't typically have the sort of private life that comes with (say) an understanding of one's sexuality and sexual desires, past and current moral failures, and strong preferences in politics and social relations which may be embarrassing or controversial. That is to say, unlike adults' secrets, children's secrets are unlikely to convey anything that will give other children a deep insight into their character. And again, even if it did, children lack enough knowledge about the world and about human psychology to make too much out of a secret that has been shared with them.

But the problem with the secrets view runs deeper in the case of children. On the one hand, children are typically trusting of others and prone to overshare with anyone willing to listen. Apart perhaps from those entering adolescence, they don't see friendships as obviously distinct from other relationships when it comes to self-disclosure.[15] For instance, they are more likely to signal the distinction between a friendship and a classmate relationship by (say) not showing a great level of affection toward a fellow pupil than by intentionally keeping aspects of their life hidden in the classroom. Moreover, the whole idea of self-disclosure is somewhat absurd in the case of children. Because they are still in a process of psychological development, they have not yet formed a stable self that can be appropriately disclosed to others as a meaningful act of friendship.

Cocking and Kennett take issue with the secrets view even when it comes to adults. As they explain,

> [I]t is the value we assign to the hopes and concerns we share with each other (whether we wish them to be kept private or not) and the fact that we choose to talk to each other about what matters to us that contributes to the growth of intimacy between us. Thus, as my friend, you do indeed gain what [Laurence] Thomas calls "a commanding perspective" on my life but access to my secrets need play very little part in this.[16]

How, then, do children develop intimacy with their close friends, given that they are not typically in the business of engaging in deep conversation about what matters to them? This is a particularly interesting question. Children mainly share their concerns, fears, and hopes with their close friends via fantasy (or imaginative) play. Studies from 1930s to the 1980s show that the themes that children appeal to in fantasy play have not changed significantly over 50 years, and in fact seem to tap into the most important elements of children's lives—from jealousy of siblings, power relations with parents, abandonment, separation, loss, and birth in the 1930s to lost-and-found, danger and rescue, death and rebirth in the 1980s.

Other qualitative studies also support the claim that children use fantasy play as a way of fostering intimacy with their close friends. Judy Dunn shares the example of a four-year-old girl in her studies, who suggests to a close friend that they play that their "Mommies have gone away and left us, and we are afraid."[17] Vivian Paley shares the story of a four-year-old boy who is upset about the birth of his baby brother, refuses to discuss it with his teacher, but insists on playing the role of a baby over several weeks when playing with his two close friends. The theme of the play changes over time until he takes on the role of "mother" and finally moves on to be the "hunter" who provides for the family.[18]

In light of the particular dynamics of childhood friendship, it is clear that philosophical accounts of the nature of friendship which reject the sharing of secrets as a necessary constituent of friendship will be much more accommodating of children's friendship. After all, a young child might share her deep concerns with her close friend in the context of fantasy play, which will often take place in front of teachers, parents, and other children. Her close friends will then help her address her fears and concerns, as well as pursue her interests by supporting her to continually communicate them via play. And, even in the case of older children who may be better at expressing themselves and less dependent on fantasy play for addressing their fears and concerns, the sharing of secrets might not be a prominent aspect of the friendship. An eight-year-old child might tell her entire classroom about how an older sibling has not been very interested in playing with her recently, but it is her close friend who might take special note of that disclosure and try to create additional opportunities for them to play together.

If the mirror and the secrets views are not successful in accommodating childhood friendship, what, then, is the alternative? I believe that the drawing view of the nature of friendship gets to the heart of friendship across all life stages. The key idea here is that "as a close friend of another, one is characteristically and distinctively receptive to being directed and interpreted and so in these ways drawn by the other."[19] The result here is that companion friends don't see themselves in each other as the mirror view suggests, or necessarily reveal themselves via the disclosure of well-kept secrets, but rather see themselves *through* each other. Companion friends are, in a sense, each other's creators.[20] Or, as Cocking and Kennett put it, "the self in friendship is, in part, a thing that is constituted by and particular to that friendship."[21]

So how do close friends help to create each other? Cocking and Kennett point to how companion friends direct one another to particular projects that can come to play an important role in their lives. For instance, I might have been someone who never cared for politics, but after many conversations with my close friend about how our political leaders have failed to address growing inequality in our country, I may end up caring for politics as much as she does, and suddenly find myself joining the local branch of a political party which my friend is actively involved with. As Cocking and Kennett explain: "To say, then, that one is directed by one's close friends is to point to the distinctive ways in which one's choices are shaped by the other and one's interests and activities become oriented toward those of the friend."[22] Indeed, 10 years after joining my friend's party, I might win an election and go on to hold values and develop attitudes about social and political issues that I would not have held had I not met her. I will also go on to live a life that is different from the life I would have led had I not fallen in love with politics as a result of loving my friend.

This distinctive kind of responsiveness to our close friends' values and interests is also present in childhood. I might have been a very sporty child until I became close friends with a child who had a physical disability that prevented her from playing most sports. Suddenly I found myself playing Monopoly every weekend, which then led to a broader interest in board games, which we chose to pursue together as part of our close friendship. As a result, we both developed important skills, traits, and values that we would not have developed otherwise, such as attention to detail or a love of long and slow conversations.

Cocking and Kennett also highlight the ways in which we are distinctively receptive to how our close friends see us. Indeed, I might have always seen myself as a person who cares deeply about freedom of speech, and yet, after confiding in my close friend about my views on certain kinds of speech, I might have realized that my overall position on the topic was much less rigorous and coherent that I might have thought. But it is not that my friend's response to my disclosure pointed to new facts or moral considerations I was not aware of. Rather, it was the fact that *she* was particularly unimpressed by some of my arguments which led me to believe that I should do a better job of thinking through those difficult issues.

Similar dynamics are at play in childhood friendships. Empirical evidence suggests that a childhood friendship "is often the first relationship in which children begin to care about and try to understand someone else, and to respond to the feelings, needs and troubles of another."[23] Studies also suggest that children show heightened sensitivity to moral and social issues when a friend, as opposed to a sibling, is involved. Comments that indicate awareness of moral norms around reciprocity and care are much more common after a conflict with a friend has been resolved, as opposed to conflict with a sibling.[24] This means that children will have a heightened level of receptiveness to what their close friends have to say about their behavior. For instance, when playing Monopoly with my friend and other children, she might remark that I am always ganging up against her. Again, it is not that I was completely unaware of my competitiveness. But it was through my friend that I first got a glimpse that my competitiveness could be making the game much less enjoyable for others.

Note, though, that such a comment from a childhood friend would not have made me learn anything too deep about myself as a child, such as learning that I am overly competitive and that such competitiveness will be detrimental to my ability to make friends and lead a good life. Rather, such a remark by a childhood friend might have led me to begin to understand how certain kinds of behavior can negatively affect the people I care deeply about. My childhood friend's remark did not then give me a deep insight into my traits and values. Rather, it gave me a reason to try to keep my competitive side in check—a reason which might have been absent in childhood had I never met (and cared deeply for) this friend.

It is time to take stock. I have argued that taking childhood friendship seriously leads us to embrace the drawing view of the nature of friendship. Childhood friends play a pivotal role in our becoming the people we are today, and an account of the nature of friendship has to adequately account for that. Unlike the mirror and secrets views, the drawing account identifies a constitutive feature of close friendships across all life stages: that close friends direct and interpret one another in ways that contribute to each other's identity and to the choices they make in the course of their lives.

This is not to deny that parents, teachers, siblings, and others also have profound effects on the people children grow into. The point is simply that close childhood friendship distinctively and characteristically leads to children espousing certain values, having certain preferences, and seeing the world in a certain way.[25] Indeed, had my parents tried to talk to me in early adulthood about the importance of politics, I might have just rolled my eyes. Had my sister complained that I was too competitive when we were both young, I might have just shrugged my shoulders. Earlier in this chapter, I argued that we had better not endorse an account of the nature of friendship that had as a result that children could not meet the bar for companion friendship. The drawing account shows that children not only meet the bar, but well exceed it, for we are all the people we are today partly due to the friends we had in childhood. Some of those very same friendships continue to shape us in profound ways today.

6.3. Friendship in Adulthood

Now that we know a bit more about the nature of friendship, it is worth thinking about how friendships contribute to a good childhood in particular, and a good life more generally. But before we turn our attention to children, it is worth looking at the question of justification when it comes to adult friendships. As we will discuss in the next two sections, there are important differences between childhood and adulthood friendships that matter when it comes to evaluating whether particular friendships are good for the child who participates in them.

Questions of justification for particular intimate relationships are, of course, bound up with the question of whether there are normative reasons for love. In Chapter 1, I endorsed the position that there are normative reasons for love, and that love is a result of lovable facts about the person combined with facts about the relationship.[26] That view will have as a result that we have normative reasons for loving our close friends because of their positive qualities (which can include both moral and nonmoral traits and dispositions), and because of how such qualities have been partly shaped by our history of interaction.[27] Were I to meet a new person who is even more concerned about inequality than my best friend, and who is even more involved in politics than she is, I would *not* be justified in "upgrading" my friendship. For the history we share shapes the people we are today and gives us normative reasons for continuously loving each other.

But I also noted in Chapter 1 that, unlike parental love, adult friendship love is both less deep and less robust. One implication of this is that I am less likely to take on costs and make sacrifices on behalf of my close friends than I am on behalf of my children. But another implication is that friendship has stricter governing conditions. There can be strong reasons not to invest in a particular friendship that do not apply in the case of parent-child relationships.

One of these reasons has been well articulated by Jessica Isserow, when explaining why we should not be friends with bad people. Although Isserow follows Thomas in acknowledging that there is a sense in which friendships develop unexpectedly and spontaneously, she emphasizes the fact that we do make a choice about whether or not to pursue such friendships.[28] And that choice has significant moral import. For when we choose to pursue a friendship, we inescapably evaluate that person favorably.[29] And, unfortunately, sometimes such positive evaluation is unjustified, because of the fact that "there are particular moral flaws that no wholly decent person should tolerate."[30] Isserow's important insight is that even when it comes to our relationships with our close friends, we must remain properly responsive to certain values and moral considerations. And this means that we must either refrain from initiating or we must in fact terminate a friendship with people who behave in ways that are deeply morally problematic. Doing otherwise would lead to an objectionable form of moral complacency, one that no doubt prevents such friendship from adding any degree of meaning to our life.[31]

But apart from the danger associated with moral complacency, friendships pose another threat to a life well lived. The danger comes from when a friendship crowds out space in our lives, leaving no room for other things that matter to us. This dynamic is, of course, more apparent in some pathological romantic relationships. Sometimes lovers become so obsessed with one another that they go down a path of falsely believing that romantic love suffices for a good life. But close friends can make a similar mistake, and the costs can be equally high: to pursue an intimate relationship, at the expense of everything else that is valuable, is to lead a particularly impoverished life. For although all meaningful projects and relationships contribute to a good life, they are valuable for different reasons, and so contribute to a good life in distinct ways. Indeed, it seems quite plausible to hold that a meaningful life requires more than just one valuable project or relationship.

To be sure, terminating the relationship is not always necessary in such cases, since close friends can come to realize that they are both missing out on other goods and can thereby make a concerted effort to get the balance right. But when a friend makes her friendship conditional on exclusivity, then the other friend must end the relationship even if the friend is motivated by insecurity rather than malice. Indeed, Thomas makes the following relevant plea for caution when examining the role that particular friendships can play in our lives: "It is one thing to be intrigued, fascinated, and even captivated by a person . . . it is another thing to lose entirely one's sense of reason and perspective on things."[32] An important question for the next section is whether it makes sense to talk about children losing themselves within a companion friendship. This matters for deciding whether it is appropriate for parents to act paternalistically toward their children in the domain of friendship.

6.4. Friendship in Childhood

In the previous two sections, we discussed how the drawing view of the nature of friendship can help us make sense of friendships across all life stages. For all close friends direct one another toward certain projects and interests, and all close friends interpret each other in ways that bring about change in how they perceive themselves in relation to their intimates, or at least in how they act toward those around them. The idea is that all close friendships lead to a process of co-creation. I am my close friend's co-creator, and she is mine. We would simply be different people had we not pursued our intimate relationship over the years.

It is important to emphasize, however, that although the drawing view sees close friends as having this profound effect on the self, the account does not depend on such effect being fully positive. My close friends might have played a major role in my becoming more attuned to social injustice than I might have been otherwise, but they might have also strengthened some of my shortcomings.[33] Perhaps I am more judgmental of others than I would have been otherwise. But so long as the friendship is on the whole sufficiently valuable, and I am subjectively attracted to it, it adds meaning to my life.

And, of course, although this account provides us with a much less moralized picture of the nature of close friendship than some of the alternatives, it is still compatible with the claim that some friendships are not justified on moral and prudential grounds. I have already discussed two examples of such problematic adult friendships. One is the case of a close friend who has a bad character. The other is the case of a close friend whose dependence on you crowds out space for other meaningful projects and relationships. Although the major moral challenge that comes with close friendships is the challenge of reconciling the partiality we display toward our close friends with the impartial demands of morality, sometimes moral and prudential reasons will count against the friendship itself, not the act of benefiting a friend at the expense of other needy members of the moral community.[34]

What about childhood friendship? Do children have moral and prudential reasons against pursuing a particular friendship? In this section, I want to take seriously the insight from the drawing view: that children will direct each other toward certain values and projects and will interpret each other in ways that have a profound effect on the self. I also want to argue that, unlike adult friendship, the governing conditions of childhood friendship are significantly less strict. And this is a direct byproduct of what kind of creature a child is, as well as the fact that—save in some extreme cases of cruelty—it makes no sense to say that children can be bad people. And, as we will see, this will have important implications for whether parents are permitted to act paternalistically toward their children when they believe that a particular friendship is not in their child's current or future interests.

Consider first the issue of moral complacency. Does it make sense to say that children are being morally complacent when they stay close friends with a child who engages in "challenging" behavior? I believe not. There are two reasons for this. First, children do not yet have a sufficiently developed capacity to acquire moral knowledge and engage in complex moral reasoning. A child who tolerates another child's constant lies, for instance, is in no way displaying a problematic form of moral complacency. After all, she is unable to adequately assess how problematic lying is in general, whether there are excusing conditions that apply to her friend, what would be the consequences of a world where people lied all the time, and so on. She is also not yet sufficiently attuned to the values of honesty and integrity in the way that adults are (or should be). In other words, moral complacency itself requires epistemic and moral resources that children lack.

But another problem that comes with suggesting that children should not stay friends with children who engage in challenging behavior is that evaluating the behavior of children as morally problematic is itself a morally suspect endeavor. For in the same way as children lack the moral and epistemic resources to avoid being morally complacent, they lack the moral and epistemic resources to adequately understand the moral implications of their actions. Indeed, a child who constantly lies to a close friend does not disrespect her friend. And the close friend who thereby tolerates those lies does not disrespect herself. For even the ability to adequately respect oneself and others requires abilities and knowledge that children lack. But so long as these children are on track to acquire the capacities for acquiring moral knowledge, and engaging in complex moral reasoning, these friendships may well make each of them more competent moral agents later on in life. For not only do friendships in general play a crucial role in developing a concern for the needs of others, but particular friendships may play an important role in the development of certain moral attitudes.[35] The lying friend might be particularly attuned to the value of generosity given that her friend had displayed a great deal of that in course of their friendship. The forgiving friend might become particularly attuned to the value of honesty. Although she never ended the friendship on the basis of the lies, the lies did bother her, and she became an adult who took honesty and integrity particularly seriously.

Now, of course, I am not denying that the lying child might instead make her friend grow desensitized to the badness of lying. There is certainly an element of luck when it comes to how different relationships will affect the moral sensibilities of different children. The important point to emphasize here is that the drawing view is not committed to claim that the process of co-creation we find in friendships in general, and in childhood friendship in particular, will necessarily lead to friends becoming more similar in character over time. As Cocking and Kennett make clear: the interpretation that takes places in friendship "may very well serve to confirm and sharpen those features in respect of which we are different."[36]

Moreover, I suspect that when children are given the love and support they need to develop morally, the capacities for acquiring moral knowledge and for engaging in complex moral reasoning which they are in the process of developing will be sufficiently robust so as not to be significantly undermined by the many problematic exemplars they will inevitably encounter in their lives.[37]

At this stage, it is also important to emphasize that I am also not denying that there are moral limits even when it comes to childhood friendships. A child who is already displaying clear signs of extreme cruelty is one who is hard to be friends with. But such cases are rare. Most children engage in challenging behavior that is not so much cruel but troubling, such as lying, saying inappropriate or disrespectful things, and stealing. But in these cases, it is simply too early to tell if such behaviors are indicative of the person the child will be, or of the life stage she finds herself in. And it is exceptionally problematic for the moral community to give up on this child before she actually acquires the moral and epistemic resources to act morally. Children, of course, seem to know this intuitively, and so are willing to tolerate a great deal of challenging behavior from their close friends.

Let me now turn to the second case discussed in the previous section. The concern there was about friendships that become so obsessive as to leave very little room for other things that matter. Should children be pressured to end such friendships? If such a friendship gets in the way of a carefree childhood, then, like the scenario involving a cruel friend discussed above, it is problematic for the child to continue to invest in that friendship, for there can be no positive affect toward the friendship itself, nor toward other valuable projects and relationships when a particular friendship causes crippling stress and anxiety.[38] But often such friendships in childhood are a result of the delight that each child takes in each other's company. Such obsessive friendships in childhood are also a temporary result of the kind of creatures children are. Because children are unable to step back from their projects and relationships and critically evaluate whether they have achieved a balance between all the things they care about, they might inadvertently temporarily ignore other things that matter.

Given how much positive affect matters for a good childhood, however, it is not clear that preventing a child from engaging in such obsessive relationship is a good idea. Rather, it seems that parents ought instead to support their children to become better at attending to the compelling reasons in favor of different projects and relationships, and so to speed up the process by which a previously "obsessed" child becomes sufficiently capable of adequately attending to all the other things that matter in her life.[39]

Hence, because children are forming their values and developing their practical identity in the course of their childhood, as well as responding to the world via affect, it is not surprising that they can go through a stage in their lives where all they care about is a certain friend, and are therefore particularly open to following that friend's lead in terms of activities and projects, especially if the friendship itself brings about a great deal of joy and delight to the child. For parents to actively attempt to end such friendships is for them to act in a way that clearly fails to grasp the nature of childhood and the nature of friendship, as well as the important role that friendships can play in children's lives.

6.5. Implications

Let us now move to the question of who is responsible for ensuring that children enjoy friendships in their lives, and what exactly this entails in terms of concrete actions.

To begin with, it is clear that schools can play an important role in fostering friendships by giving children enough space for getting to know each other and for socializing. Mary Healy, one of the only philosophers to tackle the question of childhood friendship head on, is quite correct to suggest that

> most teachers can identify children who have difficulties forming relationships and problems in reaching out in friendship to others, so they can identify opportunities for children to form friendships through shared or paired activities, giving children the opportunity to get to know others.[40]

But, of course, the main obligation that arises from recognizing the value of childhood friendships falls on parents. As I hinted in the previous section, a particularly important obligation is not to act paternalistically in the domain of friendship, save in the extreme cases of cruelty, anxiety, and distress discussed above. Let me now expand on this point.

When we think about parents engaging in effective paternalism in the lives of their children, we are thinking of competent agents who genuinely know best what is in their children's current or future interests. When a parent forces her child to go to school, eat a healthy diet, minimize screen time, she is no doubt acting in ways that are justified. In fact, given that children cannot protect and promote all of their interests, parents are morally required to act paternalistically toward children in many domains of their lives. But note that in all these cases, there is a clear answer to the question: what are children's interests? It is just obvious that a child will be harmed by a lack of education, by childhood obesity, or by overexposure to screens.[41] In other words, the parent is undoubtedly protecting and promoting her child's interests in education and health.

In the case of childhood friendship (and putting aside the cases of cruelty, anxiety, and stress discussed above), the answer to the question of whether a particular friendship is good or bad *for a child* will depend on whether the child enjoys the relationship. Any evaluation on the part of the parent that a child's friend is not good for her on account of traits or behavior of the friend that the parent themself does not approve of will entail a mistake. For to judge another child's traits negatively *on behalf of* one's child is to assume that children have a formed practical identity and moral outlook such that there is a genuine clash between the values and moral outlooks of the two children. But, as I have discussed above, this fails to capture the fact that children are developing into agents over time, and it is not at all clear how any particular friendship will affect the child's identity and moral sensibility. The upshot here is that the very judgment on the part of a parent that a particular friendship benefits or hinders their child due to her friend's character is to put the cart before the horse. For in the case of a child, particular friendships will in fact partly determine what values and moral sensibilities will be established in the first place, and which character will emerge at the end.

Now, of course, parents might not be acting *on behalf of* their child. They might want to interfere with a friendship because they want to control the very development of their child's character. A parent might then feel that a wild and disruptive childhood friend will lead to an unruly adolescent son, or that an overly girly friend in childhood will lead to a gender-conforming adult daughter, and so on and so forth. But this type of control on the part of the parent is extremely disrespectful to children, who can come to care deeply about their close friends, and to participate in childhood friendships that are quite meaningful. It is also extremely disrespectful to children when parents feel entitled to manipulate them for the parents' own ends. Parents don't own their children and don't have a right to decide what kind of adults their children will become. This follows directly from the commitment that children are creatures with equal and independent moral status, and not objects to be tampered with at parents' discretion. Parents can certainly indirectly *influence* the child's values and disposition in the course of an intimate loving relationship they enjoy.[42] But they cannot actively deprive their children of the exposure to the other values and worldviews which are so crucial for the development of an authentic self.[43]

Apart from the wrong of disrespect, there is also a great deal of value in children being *directed* by and *interpreting* others by themselves.[44] A child might know more about the situation involving a friend and be more sympathetic toward that friend's behavior. The unruly friend may be part of a household where both parents work long hours to put food on the table. It may become clear that the friend is acting out because he does not get enough attention. Similarly, it is also possible that a child might see something valuable in a friend that the parent is completely oblivious to. The overly feminine child might actually be the sharpest and bravest child at school, and the girly aspect of her behavior quite superficial. Indeed, children can be highly perceptive, and can come to learn important life lessons in the course of their childhood friendships. For parents to deprive them of such an opportunity to learn important lessons via direct experience is for them to treat their children with contempt and disrespect. Although it is tempting to dismiss the value of exploration in childhood, because children don't yet have a fully developed capacity for autonomy, we should be sensitive to how children can gain a deeper understanding of the world around them if they are given some freedom to experiment and explore by themselves, as opposed to having a whole life script developed and laid out in advance for them.[45]

This is not to deny that parents can offer advice and use friendship experiences to teach their children important moral lessons. If we return to the case of the lying friend above, it is certainly permissible, if not required, for a parent to express a condemnation of lying within the context of that particular friendship. The same is true of parents who call attention to the aggressive or rude behavior of a friend, and emphasize that such actions can be really hurtful to the more sensitive children in the classroom. But it is important to realize that parental intervention comes in degrees, and some interventions will count as manipulation or coercion, whereas others won't. The thought here is that there is a world of difference between a parent who explains that lying or bullying is bad, while also acknowledging that some children need time to learn to do the right thing, and the parent who actually forbids her child from ever interacting with that friend again.[46]

Indeed, if the parent cares about the moral development of her child, it seems that advice is the most likely avenue to produce the desired effect. After all, if the parent ends the friendship, the child might feel so much resentment toward the parent that valuable moral lessons are likely to be lost in that process. Moreover, parents can always emphasize that sometimes we make bad choices because we are dealing with a life challenge that others might not be aware of (thereby signaling the values of sympathy and understanding). They can also emphasize that part of what it means to be a good friend is to help our friends make good choices in life and to be there for our friends if they are going through a tough time (thereby signaling the values of generosity and kindness). In other words, challenging behavior on the part of a child's friend she cares deeply about can create opportunities for parents to help their children become more competent moral agents than they would have been otherwise.

Let me conclude the discussion by also noting that the good of childhood friendship also gives rise to positive obligations on the part of parents. Given that children cannot pursue many friendships by themselves, parents should take on moderate costs to support children in their pursuit of such friendships.[47] This could mean, for instance, organizing play dates or attending events with other parents one is not particularly fond of. It could mean driving the child to see a friend, or making sure the child has enough time during the week to spend with everyone she cares about.[48]

But it could also mean even more costly actions. For instance, it might mean traveling to another part of the country to accompany one's child in visiting a friend who has moved out of town. It might even mean not moving to a different part of the city when the reasons for the move are not sufficiently compelling (for example, better shops, slightly easier commute), if that would significantly impact the ability of one's child to spend enough time with her close friends. The thought here is that parents have an obligation to take on moderate costs in terms of time, opportunities, and financial resources in order to support their children in pursuing the friendships they care deeply about.

To intentionally leave children to their own devices when it would clearly make it impossible for them to enjoy the friendships that matter to them is to do a poor job in creating the conditions for children to flourish in the course of their childhood.[49]

6.6. Conclusion

In this chapter, I explore one of the core goods of childhood: companion (or close) friendship. I argue that philosophers working on friendship must take childhood friendships seriously if they are to adequately identify the constitutive feature of close friendships. More specifically, I lend support to the drawing view of the nature of friendship, which understands companion friendship as a type of relationship where parties are distinctively and characteristically prone to direct and to interpret one another in ways that contribute to each other's identity and to the choices they make in the course of their lives.

Apart from supporting the drawing view, I have also discussed in detail the governing conditions of childhood friendship, and the relationship between a close friendship and a good childhood. This discussion has several implications for parents. It tells us why paternalism in the domain of childhood friendship is typically deeply problematic, and why it often entails unjustifiable forms of coercion and manipulation. I have also argued that, given the prominent role of childhood friendship in a good childhood, parents are required to take on moderate costs in support of friendships that their children care deeply about.

Notes

Part I, Introduction

1. Throughout the discussion, I will make normative assumptions that are compatible with the most promising versions of virtue ethics, consequentialism, and deontology.
2. Luara Ferracioli, "Citizenship for Children: By Soil, by Blood, or by Paternalism?," *Philosophical Studies* 175 (11) (2018): 2859–77: Luara Ferracioli, *Liberal Self-Determination in a World of Migration* (New York: Oxford University Press, 2022).

Chapter 1

1. A previous version of this chapter was published as Luara Ferracioli, "Procreative-Parenting, Love's Reasons and the Demands of Morality," *Philosophical Quarterly* 68 (270) (2018): 77–97. Note that some minor changes have been made to the text.
2. For the ethics of mitochondria donation, see Tina Rulli, "What Is the Value of Three-Parent IVF?," *Hastings Center Report* 46 (2016): 38–47.
3. More controversially, my definition leaves out cases where the intention to parent arises after procreation has already occurred. This will be true of surrogate mothers who want to keep the child after birth or persons who have their genetic material used by someone else without their consent. The reason why I leave such cases aside is because I am here interested in meeting the two challenges that arise for procreation carried out *for the purpose* of parenting. Cases where the intention to parent arises after procreation need not meet the first challenge, only the second. In Chapter 2, I develop an account of moral parenthood that tells us when a gestational or genetic connection gives procreators a moral right to parent.
4. Daniel Friedrich, "A Duty to Adopt?," *Journal of Applied Philosophy* 30 (1) (2013): 25–39; Travis N. Rieder, "Procreation, Adoption and the Contours

of Obligation," *Journal of Applied Philosophy* 32 (3) (2015): 293–309; Tina Rulli, "Preferring a Genetically-Related Child," *Journal of Moral Philosophy* 13 (6) (2016): 669–98. Thomas Young, "Overconsumption and Procreation: Are They Morally Equivalent?," *Journal of Applied Philosophy* 18 (2) (2001): 183–92.

5. Young, "Overconsumption and Procreation," 183.
6. Rulli, "Genetically-Related Child," 693. My emphasis.
7. If it is indeed true that procreation necessarily violates the vital interests of existing or future people, then the procreative challenge simply cannot be met. However, given that there are moderately feasible reforms that can decrease consumption and waste, it seems worth trying to meet it. Of course, it may well be that only limited procreative parenting (e.g., one biological child) can be justified because only limited procreative parenting does not violate the vital interests of others. Everything I say here is compatible with this position, although in other work I argue that the environmental case for limited procreation is weak. See Luara Ferracioli, "On the Human Right to Found a Family," in Jesse Tomalty and Kerri Woods (eds.), *The Routledge Handbook of the Philosophy of Human Rights*, forthcoming.
8. This view is meant to be a compromise between two extreme positions in ethics. The first has it that personal projects and relationships cannot be given any priority by the agent, and that one's life can be rightly overruled by morality. This view questions the moral permissibility of (say) academic philosophy when other professions are more congenial to a life of service. The second position has it that personal projects and relationships can be given priority over the demands of morality, regardless of content. This view makes it permissible for a pot smoker to spend all of her resources smoking weed when she could instead donate to charity. For a defense of one such compromise view, see Samuel Scheffler, *The Rejection of Consequentialism* (Oxford: Clarendon Press, 1982). For a similar framework, see Rulli, "Genetically-Related Child," 677–78.
9. One might deny the possibility of such a world by insisting that competent biological parents are necessarily better suited to meet their child's needs. According to David Velleman, human beings have a need to associate with their biological relatives because of how biological ties help us understand our own traits, inclinations, and aptitudes. Although Velleman may be right that children benefit from associating with people who share similar traits or dispositions, it is not obvious that a biological connection needs to be in place. After all, if I am an extrovert adoptive parent of a shy child, I can make sure that my adopted child spends time with my introvert friends so she can see different models of navigating the world as a shy

person. See David Velleman, "Persons in Prospect," *Philosophy and Public Affairs* 36 (3) (2008): 245–66.
10. Liam Shields, "How Bad Can a Good Enough Parent Be?," *Canadian Journal of Philosophy* 46 (2) (2016): 163–82.
11. Ibid.
12. I assume that a correct theory of well-being is a hybrid one, where subjective attraction and objective attractiveness come together to endow our lives with meaning; see Susan Wolf, *Meaning in Life and Why It Matters* (Princeton: Princeton University Press, 2010). Note that the arguments in this chapter are compatible with any theory of well-being that is not merely subjective. In Part II of the book, I will discuss hybrid theories in more detail, and will in fact rely on them for developing an account of the value of carefreeness and other goods of childhood.
13. David Benatar, *Better Never to Have Been: The Harm of Coming into Existence* (New York: Oxford University Press, 2006).
14. Stuart Rachels, "The Immorality of Having Children," *Ethical Theory and Moral Practice* 17 (3) (2014): 567–82.
15. For a justification of the family based on the fiduciary role of parents, see Harry Brighouse and Adam Swift's work in "Parents' Rights and the Value of the Family," *Ethics* 117 (1) (2006): 80–108; and *Family Values: The Ethics of Parent-Child Relationships* (Princeton: Princeton University Press, 2014). For a justification based on intimacy and affection, see Colin Macleod, "Liberal Equality and the Affective Family," in David Archard and Colin Macleod (eds.), *The Moral and Political Status of Children* (Oxford: Oxford University Press, 2002), 212–30.
16. Luara Ferracioli, "Why the Family?," *Law, Ethics and Philosophy* 3 (2015): 214. Note that Christine Overall is also skeptical that parental love is unconditional: *Why Have Children? The Ethical Debate* (Cambridge: MIT Press, 2012), 212–17.
17. Luara Ferracioli, "The State's Duty to Ensure Children Are Loved," *Journal of Ethics and Social Philosophy* 8 (2) (2014): 1–19.
18. For the notion of a modally demanding value, see Philip Pettit, *The Robust Demands of the Good: Ethics with Attachment, Virtue, and Respect* (Oxford: Oxford University Press, 2015).
19. Neil Delaney, "Romantic Love and Loving Commitment: Articulating a Modern Ideal," *American Philosophical Quarterly* 33 (4) (1996): 339–56; Simon Keller, "How Do I Love Thee? Let Me Count the Properties," *American Philosophical Quarterly* 37 (2) (2000): 163–73.
20. Ferracioli, "State's Duty," 13–15.
21. Ferracioli, "Why the Family?," 216.

22. See Brighouse and Swift, *Family Values*, 51.
23. As I will discuss in Chapter 2, such social or legal parents do not count as moral parents.
24. Not everyone will agree with me. Philip Pettit, for instance, suggests in passing that parental love is on a par with romantic love when it comes to their degree of robustness (*Robust Demands*, 34). I think Pettit is wrong about this, and that parental love presents us with the deepest and most robust form of caring we find in human relationships. To see why, consider the difference in attitudes toward the end of romantic and parental love, be it due to abandonment or death. First, consider the case of an abandoned lover or child. While we find the former regrettable, we don't typically feel the same sort of incomprehension as when we hear of a parent who has walked away from an already established morally benign parent-child relationship. Consider also our attitudes to love and mourning. Again, we respond with sheer relief to the news that a mourning lover has moved on after some time, but we tend to expect parents to never quite recover from the death of a child, even though we hope they manage to lead as meaningful a life as possible under such tragic circumstances.
25. For a defense of the claim that love has reasons and so can be justified, see Niko Kolodny, "Love as Valuing a Relationship," *Philosophical Review* 112 (2) (2003): 135–89. For a critique, see Harry Frankfurt, *The Reasons of Love* (Princeton: Princeton University Press, 2006).
26. For a discussion of the quality view, see Bennett Helm, "Love," in Edward N. Zalta (ed.), *The Stanford Encyclopedia of Philosophy* (Fall 2009 ed.). For a defense of the relationship view, see Kolodny, "Love as Valuing." For hybrid accounts, see Delaney, "Romantic Love"; Keller, "How Do I Love Thee?" Note that there is also a common ideal that we should love a person in her particularity, not because of her qualities: see Gregory Vlastos, "The Individual as an Object of Love in Plato," in his *Platonic Studies* (Princeton: Princeton University Press, 1972), 3–34; Pettit, *Robust Demands*, 31–32. I worry that such a view, although celebrated in works of art and literature, collapses into a no-reasons view. As Kolodny puts it: "The beloved's bare identity, however, cannot serve as a reason for loving her. To say 'She is Jane' is simply to identify a particular with itself. It is to say nothing about that particular that might explain why a specific response to it is called for" ("Love as Valuing," 142).
27. For an illuminating discussing of these accounts, see Sara Protasi, "Loving People for Who They Are (Even When They Don't Love You Back)," *European Journal of Philosophy* 24 (1) (2016): 214–34.

28. One might respond to this case by arguing that Ada's love in case 4 is in fact justified, but that society fails to give her the recognition she deserves. This is interesting, but I am not sure it works. Unlike procreation, where there is already a *normative* reason for love, due to the biological connection between parent and child, there is no *normative* reason for love prior to the establishment of a relationship between child and adoptive parent. There are certainly expectations, which might *explain* love but not *justify* it. Society responds the way it does precisely because it finds Ada's behavior inappropriate, even if it can sympathize with her.
29. Rulli, "Genetically-Related Child," 691–92.
30. See Tina Rulli, "The Unique Value of Adoption," in Françoise Baylis and Carolyn McLeod (eds.), *Family Making: Contemporary Ethical Challenges* (Oxford: Oxford University Press, 2014), 110–28.
31. Rulli, "Genetically-Related Child," 691–92.
32. My dual-interest account requires that the interests of the parent and child are jointly secured rather than traded off for one another (unless the stakes are extremely high). For a dual-interest view that is consequentialist in nature, see Shields, "How Bad."
33. I focus on many of the core interests of children in Part II of this book.
34. S. Matthew Liao has defended the interest in procreative parenting via an appeal to human rights. The challenge for such a view is that unlike goods such as access to adequate nutrition, many persons can and do lead quite flourishing lives without engaging in procreative parenting. See S. Matthew Liao, *The Right to Be Loved* (New York: Oxford University Press, 2015).
35. Overall, *Why Have Children?*, 215.
36. Ibid., 214.
37. Anca Gheaus, "The Right to Parent One's Biological Baby," *Journal of Political Philosophy* 20 (4) (2012): 432–55.
38. Ibid., 436. In recent work, Gheaus focuses only on the putative relationship and leaves the issue of costs aside. See her "Biological Parenthood: Gestational, Not Genetic," *Australasian Journal of Philosophy* 96 (2) (2018): 225–40.
39. For additional criticisms, see Liao, *Right to Be Loved*, 151–78; Brighouse and Swift, *Family Values*, 108–9.
40. For another discussion that equates procreating with already being in a *relationship* with a child, see Sam Shpall, "Parental Love and Procreation," *Philosophical Quarterly* 73 (1): 206–26.
41. For a discussion of unrequited love, see Protasi, "Loving People."

42. Margaret Olivia Little, "Abortion, Intimacy and the Duty to Gestate," *Ethical Theory and Moral Practice* 2 (3) (1999): 311. For the claim that pregnancy can, at times, rise to the level of a meaningful *project*, see Amy Mullin, *Reconceiving Pregnancy and Childcare: Ethics, Experience, and Reproductive Labor* (Cambridge: Cambridge University Press, 2005); Rulli, "Genetically-Related Child."

43. Sam Shpall argues that in some cases procreative parenting is not likely to make an agent a more loving parent. I agree. And that is why agents deciding whether or not to engage in procreative parenting should be attentive to whether or not they are the kind of agent who is likely to be moved by the weighty pro tanto reason for love that arises as a result of procreation. If they are not in fact likely to be moved by it, they should consider adopting a child instead of pursuing procreative parenting. For a discussion, see Shpall, "Parental Love and Procreation."

Chapter 2

1. These so-called parental duties are different from the alleged duty to parent (or the duty to enter into a parent-child relationship with a particular child). Note that an account of moral parenthood can accept that the more autonomy a child has, the less paternalism is justified on the part of the parent. Moreover, an account of moral parenthood can allow for moral parents to remain in that role even when their child reaches adulthood. After all, should the adult child become incapacitated, the moral parent would be permitted to step in and make decisions on behalf of the adult child.

2. See J. L. Hill, "What Does It Mean to Be a 'Parent'? The Claims of Biology as a Basis for Parental Rights," *New York University Law Review* 66 (3) (1991): 353–420. For an account that picks out doctors in fertility clinics and matchmakers, see, for instance, James Lindemann Nelson, "Parental Obligations and the Ethics of Surrogacy: A Causal Perspective," *Public Affairs Quarterly* 5 (1) (1991): 49–61. For an account that does not pick out gestating and intentional parents, see, for instance, Rivka Weinberg, *The Risk of a Lifetime: How, When, and Why Procreation May Be Permissible* (New York: Oxford University Press, 2015). The under- and overinclusiveness of causal accounts has given rise to the charge of extensional inadequacy by its opponents. See Teresa Baron, "A Lost Cause? Fundamental Problems for Causal Theories of Parenthood," *Bioethics* 34

(7) (2020): 664–70; Giuliana Fuscaldo, "Genetic Ties: Are They Morally Binding?," *Bioethics* 20 (2) (2006): 64–76.

3. See David Archard, "What's Blood Got to Do with It?," *Res Publica* 1 (1) (1995): 91–106; Elizabeth Brake, "Willing Parents: A Voluntarist Account of Parental Role Obligations," in David Archard and David Benatar (eds.), *Procreation and Parenthood: The Ethics of Bearing and Rearing Children* (Oxford: Oxford University Press, 2010), 151–77.

4. This question is about who has the responsibility of acting as a parent, which is different from the question of who (if anyone) has the parental obligation to ensure that the child has a parent. For this distinction, see David Archard, "The Obligations and Responsibilities of Parenthood," in Archard and Benatar, *Procreation and Parenthood*, 103–14. See also Jeffrey Blustein, "Procreation and Parental Responsibility," *Journal of Social Philosophy* 28 (2) (1997): 79–86; Nelson, "Parental Obligations"; Lindsey Porter, "Why and How to Prefer a Causal Account of Parenthood," *Journal of Social Philosophy* 45 (2) (2014): 182–202; Weinberg, *Risk of a Lifetime*.

5. Anca Gheaus argues that the morally relevant causal aspect of creation is gestation, and that it is the gestating parent (and supporting partner if there is one) who has a right to parent a particular child: "The Right to Parent One's Biological Baby," *Journal of Political Philosophy* 20 (4) (2012): 432–55; "Biological Parenthood: Gestational, not Genetic," *Australasian Journal of Philosophy* 96 (2) (2018): 225–40. Note, though, that Gheaus might disagree that her account counts as a causal account due to its focus on the *relationship* between fetus and gestating parent. As for the voluntarist view, a particularly sophisticated position has been put forward by Elizabeth Brake (in "Willing Parents"), who argues that the costs of parenting are too high and context-sensitive for the parental role to be plausibly considered the content of a compensatory-based obligation to the child. For her, such demanding obligation can only arise as a result of consent. See also Onora O'Neill, "Begetting, Bearing, and Rearing," in Onora O'Neill and William Ruddick (eds.), *Having Children: Philosophical and Legal Reflections on Parenthood* (New York: Oxford University Press, 1979), 25–38.

6. Tim Bayne and Avery Kolers, "Toward a Pluralist Account of Parenthood," *Bioethics* 17 (3) (2003): 221–42 at 241.

7. See Brake, "Willing Parents."

8. See Archard, "What's Blood"; Samantha Brennan and Robert Noggle, "The Moral Status of Children: Children's Rights, Parents' Rights, and Family Justice," *Social Theory and Practice* 23 (1) (1997): 1–26; Peter

Vallentyne, "The Rights and Duties of Childrearing," *William and Mary Bill of Rights Journal* 11 (3) (2003): 991–1009.

9. See Barbara Hall, "The Origin of Parental Rights," *Public Affairs Quarterly* 13 (1) (1999): 73–82; Jan Narveson, *Respecting Persons in Theory and Practice* (Lanham, MD: Rowman and Littlefield, 2002).

10. See Harry Brighouse and Adam Swift, *Family Values: The Ethics of Parent-Child Relationships* (Princeton: Princeton University Press, 2014); Matthew Clayton, *Justice and Legitimacy in Upbringing* (Oxford: Oxford University Press, 2006); Colin Macleod, "Conceptions of Parental Autonomy," *Politics and Society* 25 (1) (1997): 117–40.

11. Anca Gheaus, "Biological Parenthood," argues that an account of moral parenthood should be in line with a dual-interest or a child-centered account of the family.

12. For the fiduciary account, see Brighouse and Swift, *Family Values*. For the intimacy account, see MacLeod, "Conceptions of Parental Autonomy." For the focus on cost-taking and sacrifices, see Luara Ferracioli, "Why the Family?," *Law, Ethics and Philosophy* 3 (2015): 205–19.

13. See Chapter 1. See also Ferracioli, "Why the Family?" Here I focus on the relevant disposition for parenting well, but that does not mean that physical and psychological conditions are irrelevant for one's ability to act on one's disposition. Quite the contrary: one's psychological and physical conditions are important for one's ability to act on one's disposition, and so I will be assuming that the well-disposed parent suffers from no physical or psychological incapacity to parent sufficiently well.

14. It is not clear if Brake's voluntarism account (in "Willing Parents") meets or fails this desideratum. She says that "those taking on the obligation [must] be able to carry them out" (152), and that to undertake the obligation involves "awareness of the role and its obligations and that what one is doing amounts to entering it, and further, that one wishes, or intends, or at least believes oneself to be thereby taking on the role" (170). The obvious questions are: What is meant by ability here? And what threshold does Brake have in mind? There is a sense in which Mary *is* able to take on the role. The question is whether she is able to robustly perform the role in a way that creates the conditions for the child to lead a good life. But note that even if Brake's account meets this desideratum, it still fails to meet the relationship desideratum, which I discuss at the end of this section.

15. Causal accounts can only accommodate adoption by going pluralist and accepting that parental duties can be transferred, and that the *acceptance* of the parental role (i.e., consent) can also ground moral parenthood.

16. As Robert Sparrow nicely puts it, "the social relation of parenting, marked by the provision of love and care, is more important to the well-being of both parents and children than any genetic relation (between them)": "Cloning, Parenthood, and Genetic Relatedness," *Bioethics* 20 (6) (2006): 308–18 at 312.
17. See Chapter 1 for a discussion. See also Gheaus, "Right to Parent"; Christine Overall, *Why Have Children? The Ethical Debate* (Cambridge, MA: MIT Press, 2012).
18. Joseph Millum has argued that the right to parent is generated by the performance of parental work, and that parental work includes any work aimed at the flourishing of the child. For Millum, moral parenthood ends when the child no longer requires parental work. As I see it, the relationship desideratum also raises a problem for Millum, since the question of who is entitled to *parent* a child can still be relevant in adulthood when an adult child is either temporary or permanently incapacitated. In such cases, we want to point to an essential feature of the parent-child relationship that explains why parents should be able to make decisions about their (adult) child's well-being as opposed to being placed in the same position as any other bystander. And, of course, parents of adult children are no longer in the business of doing parental work, but they are still morally committed to the child. For Millum's account, see *The Moral Foundations of Parenthood* (New York: Oxford University Press, 2018)
19. Note that if the property changes over time, we no longer have a monist account in place. As we will see, a moral commitment account gives the same answer to the questions of who has a right to acquire parental rights and who has a right to hold on to these rights. A philosopher who wants to treat such questions as separate is in danger of abandoning monism by appealing to additional considerations, or of giving the same answer in ways that lead to odd results. Indeed, treating these questions as separate has theoretical costs, since both the acquisition and the maintenance of parental rights are fundamentally about who counts as the moral parent of a child.
20. For notable exceptions, see Sam Shpall, "Moral and Rational Commitment," *Philosophy and Phenomenological Research* 88 (1) (2014): 146–72; Joseph Walsh, "Commitment and Partialism in the Ethics of Care," *Hypatia* 32 (4) (2017): 817–32.
21. Walsh, "Commitment and Partialism."
22. Shpall, "Moral and Rational Commitment."
23. In "Moral and Rational Commitment," Shpall argues that a promise is a paradigm case of moral commitment, but that agents can promise to do

things, and become committed to doing them, without believing them to be morally valuable. Contra Shpall, I think that there is a difference between promises and moral commitments, and that only promises which are perceived as morally valuable (and are in fact morally valuable) rise to the level of a *moral* commitment.

24. Such lack of value recognition does render Mary's loving actions toward Jay less robust across time and alternative circumstances. For the notion of a modally demanding value, see Philip Pettit, *The Robust Demands of the Good: Ethics with Attachment, Virtue, and Respect* (Oxford: Oxford University Press, 2015).

25. There is an issue of how often and to what extent a person must express that she values a project for it to rise to the level of a moral commitment. As with concepts that are both scalar and binary, there is a threshold that applies here and that renders someone morally committed to a project. But there is also some vagueness that makes it hard to be precise about where that threshold lies.

26. How about people who through bad luck are hopeless at adequately expressing the recognition of the moral value in place? In such cases, it is regrettable that they find themselves in such a situation, but is still true that their projects or relationships do not rise to the level of a moral commitment. Note, though, that failure to morally commit due to bad luck is an important consideration when we are in the business of assessing blame. I thank Teresa Baron for encouraging me to address this point.

27. This claim is compatible with the claim that sometimes moral parents must engage in certain kinds of wrongdoing in order to protect the interests of their child. But the kind of wrongdoing that is compatible with moral commitment does not rise to the level of egregious moral wrong, such as the violation of core basic rights—e.g., rights against being assaulted, kidnapped, killed, or prevented from pursuing the projects and relationships one cares deeply about. Note that the claim here is also compatible with the claim that sometimes one must violate basic moral requirements because the moral stakes are extremely high. In such cases, the agent is not violating a basic moral requirement *for the pursuit* of a project, but rather averting something terrible from happening. For instance, if the Red Cross needs to kill a politician in order to avert a large-scale war, members of the organization are not failing in their moral commitment to humanitarianism, but rather discharging a stringent duty that would fall on any similarly situated agent. I thank Christian Barry and Holly Lawford-Smith for encouraging me to say more about the relationship between moral commitment and moral action.

28. What about someone who conceives a child by deception—a woman who tells her male partner that she is infertile when she is not? My account delivers the result that she does not count as a moral parent since she has in fact violated the basic demands of morality in order to enter into a parent-child relationship. Note that this case is somewhat different from cases involving abduction, so I leave open whether such a person could potentially count as a legal parent. I thank Suzanne Uniacke for suggesting this very interesting case to me.

29. It is true that in many cases of adoption, there will be a moral commitment only *after* the adoptive parents take the child home and start parenting her (although there are morally acceptable avenues for adoptive parents to commit even before signing an adoption document; they can, for instance, regularly visit a child in care and so develop the relationship before signing the legal document). One might think that this introduces unfairness between biological parents and adoptive parents, but I think it just recognizes the fact that adoptive parenting and procreative parenting start differently. A theory does not introduce an unfair advantage toward biological parents by recognizing basic biological facts, but by ruling out the possibility that adoptive parents could ever count as proper moral parents.

30. The bar for moral commitment is obviously quite low in pregnancy since a gestating parent who chooses not to engage in actions that are harmful to the fetus does enough to protect her biological interests. Once the child is born, she thereby acquires a number of other nonbiological interests, which require more effort on the part of her moral parent(s). For instance, babies and toddlers require affection and a secure sense of attachment. Preschool children require opportunities to play and some degree of moral education. Older children require an opportunity to enjoy projects and relationships that they themselves find attractive. (I shall return to the goods of childhood in the second part of this book.) If, at times, due to severe depression or some other form of impairment, the moral parent cannot protect and promote the interests of her child, this gives rise to a duty on her part to see to it that someone else can step in and play a kind of surrogate parental role. But note that if the moral parent still has ultimate authority over the child during such an arrangement, she will remain the moral parent throughout. If, however, the moral parent transfers ultimate authority to someone else for a long period of time, then, at some point, this other person becomes a moral parent.

31. Anca Gheaus, who defends a gestational account of moral parenthood, argues that nongestating prospective parents can become moral parents by supporting the gestating parent with the costs of pregnancy. I agree with

Gheaus that supporting a gestating parent is one way of expressing moral commitment, but I hope it is clear why such an act should not be necessary for moral parenthood. An *intentional* genetic parent (with the intention and the relevant dispositions to parent well) who is prevented by the gestating parent from supporting her with the costs of pregnancy, but tries his best to express commitment, will count as a moral parent in my account. See Gheaus, "Right to Parent"; "Biological Parenthood."

32. See Chapter 1 for the claim that procreative parenting is morally permissible, and that prospective parents are not under a moral duty to adopt. But even if I am wrong about the moral permissibility of procreative parenting, I can still be right about the grounds of moral parenthood. These are compatible, yet separate, theories.

33. In childhood, parents must necessarily act paternalistically in order to create the conditions for their child's life to go well. In adulthood, moral parents create such conditions by respecting the autonomy of their adult children, by being disposed to take on a high degree of cost in order to support them should they ask for help, and by being committed to act paternalistically should the adult child become incapacitated. This is why in adulthood, a moral parent remains a moral parent and does not become a friend. It is true, though, that the question of moral parenthood is most relevant in childhood, given that paternalism is an ongoing, salient, and inescapable feature of that stage of the relationship.

34. The moral commitment account might lead to more parental scarcity than voluntarist accounts due to its having higher expectation of parents, but the latter will also be faced with the problem that, in many cases, there is no moral parent for a particular child. I thank Suzie Killmister for raising this important point.

35. It is true that once causal parents fail to discharge their parental duties to a significant extent, they will lose the moral right to parent. However, it is awkward for the proponents of the causal theory that it counts as a *moral parent* someone who was never willing to discharge those duties in the first place.

36. I leave open the possibility that mediocre parents necessarily count as abusive and/or neglectful, and that there is in fact no separate category of parental mediocrity. I thank Rivka Weinberg for raising this possibility.

37. There is nothing incoherent about a position that accepts a legal right and a legal duty to do something on the part of an agent who simultaneously lacks a moral right or moral duty to do that thing. For example, I might have a legal right to vote in my state of original citizenship, but lack the moral right because I haven't resided there for many years. In such a case,

the legal right to vote may be justified by reasons other than the existence of a moral right to vote.
38. Such stringent duty may justify penalties in the form of fines or community service for those who procreate willy-nilly.
39. For a similar point, see Archard, "Obligations and Responsibilities," 112. Now, why not say that procreators should have at least a duty to try to morally commit, given their role in the child's existence? I am very sympathetic to this view, but if ought implies can, we first need to settle the empirical question of whether one's values are subject to one's control such that one can be under a duty to commit morally to a project or relationship.
40. Narrow versions of the voluntarist account, which require that parents sign some sort of legal document, might be able to avoid parental proliferation, but only at the pain of ruling out the possibility of moral parenthood by those who do not qualify as legal parents in a given society, such as homosexual couples.
41. For a defense of the claim that children can benefit from having more than two parents, see Kalle Grill, "How Many Parents Should There Be in a Family?," *Journal of Applied Philosophy* 37 (3) (2020): 465–84. For the Aristotelian concern that children cannot have too many parents if they are to be adequately cared for, see Nancy Sherman, "Aristotle on Friendship and the Shared Life," *Philosophy and Phenomenological Research* 47 (4) (1987): 602–7.
42. It is true that sometimes couples procreate and then separate. However, it is precisely because of the risk that separation will lead to a situation where parties violate each other's parental commitments that prospective parents should not procreate together if their relationship (romantic or otherwise) is under crisis. In cases where parenting starts as a joint commitment and ends with a separation, former partners owe it to each other not to jeopardize the other's relationship with the child. After all, it is not in the interest of the child to have a moral parent who for selfish reasons does not allow the other moral parent to discharge her own parental duties. It is also not in the interest of the child to find herself in a relationship with a stepparent who adequately plays the parental role (and is, as a result, seen as a parent by the child), but has her authority constantly undermined by an ill-disposed biological parent. The result here is that moral parents who jeopardize the relationship of other moral parents will at some point lose their own moral right to parent.
43. The parent-child relationship is then profoundly different from (say) a friendship, and other intimate relationships involving only adults who stand in a position of equality vis-à-vis one another. Indeed, my friendship

with Anna does not conflict with Alex's friendship with Anna, since neither I nor Alex is in the business of exercising authority in Anna's life. If, on the other hand, we were both Anna's parents, then we would need to coordinate how we simultaneously discharge our parental duties so that we would not negatively affect each other's ability to parent well.

44. Given the interest in procreative parenting defended in Chapter 1, procreators have a moral claim to commit if they so wish. It is therefore problematic to prevent procreators by force or deceit from morally committing to the parental role. How about family members who share a genetic tie or history with a child? As I see it, there is an important difference between family members who love the child and spend time with her, and those who play the parental role proper. There is also an important moral difference between the family member who encourages a couple to become parents via procreation, and the parents that actually take on the costs of pregnancy and commit to an existing fetus in the womb. Indeed, the favorite aunt does not become a parent simply because she encouraged procreation or because she loves the child. She becomes a parent at the moment in which she is invited by the existing moral parents to play the parental role proper. Indeed, so long as a parent still has the ultimate say over a child's well-being, she is the one playing the parental role, not other loving members of the family.

45. This case raises the tricky question of whether the couple should remain in contact with the child. I think that the answer here depends on the empirical question of how much psychological damage follows the severing of the bond between a very young child and those she mistakenly takes to be her parents. Small setbacks to the child's interest would not justify putting the biological mother in such a position that it would be very hard for her to resume her parental role. Significant setbacks to the child's interests would. Any dual-interest theorist needs to nominate the party whose interests count for more in case of genuine conflict between the parties. I assume that the interests of *children* should have more weight because they are the more vulnerable party to the relationship. For a discussion, see Liam Shields, "Parental Rights and the Importance of Being Parents," *Critical Review of International Social and Political Philosophy* 22 (2) (2019): 119–33.

Chapter 3

1. Australian Institute of Health and Welfare, "Child Protection Australia 2019–20," Child Welfare Series no. 74, Cat. no. CWS 78 (Canberra: AIHW, 2021).
2. Amy Conley Wright, Betty Luu, and Judith Cashmore, "Adoption in Australia: Past, Present and Considerations for the Future," *Australasian Law Journal* 95 (2021): 67–80.
3. For facts about adoption in Australia, see AdoptChange.org.au.
4. AdoptChange, "Modern Families: Attitudes and Perceptions of Adoption in Australia" (Sydney, 2015), 3, https://engonetac.blob.core.windows.net/assets/uploads/files/Assets/FINAL-AdoptChange-ResearchAugust2015.pdf.
5. For other accounts, see Jurgen De Wispelaere and Daniel Weinstock, "State Regulation and Assisted Reproduction: Balancing the Interests of Parents and Children," in Françoise Baylis and Carolyn McLeod (eds.), *Family-Making: Contemporary Ethical Challenges* (Oxford: Oxford University Press, 2014), 131–50; Carolyn McLeod, "The Medical Nonnecessity of In Vitro Fertilization," *International Journal of Feminist Approaches to Bioethics* 10 (1) (2017): 78–102.
6. For arguments focusing on exploitation, see Laura Purdy, "Surrogate Mothering: Exploitation or Empowerment?," *Bioethics* 3 (1) (1989): 18–34; Stephen Wilkinson, "Exploitation in International Paid Surrogacy Arrangements," *Journal of Applied Philosophy* 33 (2) (2018): 125–45. For the right of children to know their origins, see Inmaculada de Melo-Martín, "The Ethics of Anonymous Gamete Donation: Is There a Right to Know One's Genetic Origins?," *Hastings Center Report* 44 (2) (2014): 28–35; Kimberly Leighton, "Analogies to Adoption in Arguments against Anonymous Gamete Donation," in Baylis and McLeod, *Family-Making*, 239–64.
7. Christine Straehle, "Is There a Right to Surrogacy?," *Journal of Applied Philosophy* 33 (2) (2016): 146–59; Suzanne Uniacke, "*In Vitro* Fertilization and the Right to Reproduce," *Bioethics* 1 (3) (1987): 241–54. See also Sarah Hannan and R. J. Leland, "Childhood Bads, Parenting Goods, and the Right to Procreate," *Critical Review of International Social and Political Philosophy* 21 (3) (2018): 366–84.
8. Uniacke, "*In Vitro* Fertilization," 247.
9. Straehle, "Right to Surrogacy," 151.

10. For the claim that there is a moral duty to make friends, see Stephanie Collins, "Duties to Make Friends," *Ethical Theory and Moral Practice* 16 (5) (2014): 907–21.
11. Here I am just relying on a common-sense view of who counts as a procreator. For a more detailed common-sense definition, see James Lindemann Nelson, "Special Responsibilities of Parents Using Technologically Assisted Reproduction," in Baylis and McLeod, *Family-Making*, 185–97. Note that any such causal definition will run into trouble at the margins, but given that the definition of co-procreator advanced here is not meant to pick out the people who count as a moral parents, but rather the people who must take reasonable steps not to procreate negligently, it becomes less important for the concept of co-procreator to avoid overinclusiveness. After all, the costs attached to a duty not to procreate under problematic moral conditions are much less burdensome than the costs attached to performing the parental role.
12. Note that although there is more uncertainty in public debates about whether the surrogate mother counts as a co-procreator, the reasons in favor of her inclusion are quite compelling, given that she provides all of the nourishment required for the fetus to develop, and that the fetus cannot survive outside the womb for a large proportion of the pregnancy. See Teresa Baron, "Nobody Puts Baby in the Container: The Foetal Container Model at Work in Medicine and Commercial Surrogacy," *Journal of Applied Philosophy* 36 (3) (2019): 491–505.
13. For a discussion of this sort of case, see Nelson, "Special Responsibilities of Parents," 190.
14. For this argument in more detail, see Luara Ferracioli, "On the Value of Intimacy in Procreation," *Journal of Value Inquiry* 48 (1) (2014): 349–69.
15. Ibid.
16. Ibid.
17. And even if the psychologist were to meet the prospective parent over several years, there is reason to be skeptical that adequate assessment would follow. This is because psychologists get to know their clients well precisely because their clients are willing to fully review themselves for the pursuit of self-knowledge. If they were instead seeking therapy to acquire a good that required them to display certain traits, the whole process would produce entirely different results. See Ferracioli, "Value of Intimacy," for a detailed discussion. Also, note how it seems morally wrong for a couple to procreate as soon as they start a relationship without knowing each other well, merely because their common friend tells each one of them that the other

would be a good parent. Given the stakes associated with co-procreation, it is negligent not to make that assessment oneself.
18. As Laurence Thomas puts it, "the amount of time spent together enables friends to observe the behavior of one another over a wide range of the social roles which each occupies, and to do so in a variety of contexts. This, in turn, enables each to have a very informed picture of how each expresses himself in his various roles . . . a complete picture of a person is not to be had if our observations are limited to only one of the social roles which that individual occupies. Nor, a fortiori, is one to be had if we are unfamiliar with the variety of ways in which the person may express himself in that role. This is because it is primarily through role expression that traits of character and personality are revealed or that we can come to have a sense of the contours of those traits": Laurence Thomas, "Friendship," *Synthese* 72 (2) (1987): 217–36 at 229. Note that moral agents might still make a poor assessment of an intimate, but at least they tried and were not acting negligently. Moreover, although it is hard to know where to draw the threshold of knowing well enough that someone will be a moral parent, it is intelligible to claim that moral agents should only go ahead with co-procreation if they are reasonably confident that moral parenthood will follow.
19. For this argument, see Reuven Brandt, "The Transfer and Delegation of Responsibilities for Genetic Offspring in Gamete Provision," *Journal of Applied Philosophy* 34 (5) (2017): 665–78; James Lindemann Nelson, "Parental Obligations and the Ethics of Surrogacy: A Causal Perspective," *Public Affairs Quarterly* 5 (1) (1991): 49–61; Rivka Weinberg, "The Moral Complexity of Sperm Donation," *Bioethics* 22 (3) (2008): 166–78.
20. Nelson, "Special Responsibilities of Parents," 189.
21. This is not to say that sperm donors acquire a moral obligation by virtue of acting negligently. The claim is simply that they do something morally wrong. See Chapter 2 for a discussion of who counts as a moral parent to a child, and why procreation is neither necessary nor sufficient for moral parenthood.
22. And, as Jason Hanna puts it, "there is considerable value in a system under which medical professionals offer their services without first engaging in an extensive review of patient's personal life": "Causal Parenthood and the Ethics of Gamete Donation," *Bioethics* 33 (2019): 267–73 at 271.
23. See David Benatar, *Better Never to Have Been: The Harm of Coming into Existence* (New York: Oxford University Press, 2006).

24. Ferracioli, "Value of Intimacy." Note that the core issue here is not anonymity or financial rewards, but the lack of an intimate relationship between co-procreators. Anonymity and financial rewards serve as good proxies for the liberal state, however, since an anonymous gamete donor is typically not in a relationship with prospective procreators, and family and friends typically do not charge their loved ones when they volunteer to gestate a fetus on their behalf.

25. One might claim that the state need not make anonymous gamete donation and commercial surrogacy illegal, because the state does not have a duty to prevent a citizen from playing a benign causal role in someone else's harmful act. So, for instance, the state should not prevent me from leaving matchsticks around in case they find themselves in the pocket of a pyromaniac. But this misunderstands the argument here. I am not relying on a causal story whereby gamete donors and surrogate mothers inadvertently enable child abuse or neglect by a third party. Rather, I am arguing that co-procreating is only permissible when one is reasonably confident that moral parenthood will follow; otherwise one is acting negligently. The state enters the picture because it owes it to potential children to minimize negligent forms of co-procreation. Here is a parallel case: in some states there are laws preventing children from walking to school by themselves below a certain age. Now, of course, the liberal state should treat child kidnapping as the horrendous crime that it is, and attach serious penalties to anyone who kidnaps a child. But it is entirely legitimate for the state to also prevent parents from acting negligently by allowing very young children to walk to school by themselves. This is not because a parent who allows her four-year-old to walk to school by herself will in some sense play a morally problematic causal role in the kidnapping if it takes place. Rather, it is *negligent* for parents to make that decision, and it is entirely appropriate for the state to take that option off the table. I thank Liz Harman for encouraging me to address this point.

26. I say potentially here because family members and friends would still need to adequately assess the parental competency of prospective parents. This is not to deny that some friends and family members might do a lousy job of making that assessment, but at least in such cases, the liberal state has discharged *its duty* to potential children by creating the sociopolitical conditions for citizens not to co-procreate negligently.

27. At this stage, it might be helpful to compare meaningful vocations, such as academic philosophy, with procreative parenting. Like procreative parenting, the pursuit of a meaningful vocation for its own sake can be quite valuable for many individuals. This explains why philosophers, writers,

and poets don't act wrongly when they chose to pursue a career in philosophy, literature, or poetry, rather than volunteering for Oxfam in poor parts of the world. However, neither the pursuit of a meaningful vocation nor procreative parenting is such a fundamental activity that agents who are attracted to them have a positive right to have the pursuit of that activity subsidized by the liberal state. And note that such activities are not fundamental, despite people often being devastated for not succeeding in becoming pregnant or making a living out of an activity they love. Thanks to Elizabeth Cohen, Stephen Macedo, Tina Rulli, and Hannah Tierney for helpful discussions on this point.

28. For instance, in Australia, the average out-of-pocket costs of a single IVF cycle range from AUD 3,400 to AUD 4,400. See Margaret Ambrose, "'I Started Working Two Jobs': The Real Cost of IVF," *Sydney Morning Herald*, September 24 2021. See also McLeod, "Medical Nonnecessity."

29. For this argument in detail and in the context of embryo editing, see Inmaculada de Melo-Martín, "Reproductive Embryo Editing," *Hastings Center Report* 52 (4): 26–33.

30. Thanks to Dan Halliday for suggesting this possibility to me.

31. Does the preceding discussion imply that every time an adoption agency transfers parental rights to adoptive parents, it acts wrongly by allowing adoptive parents to become legal parents without first assessing their competency via an intimate relationship? The reason why there is a difference when it comes to adoption is that there is already a child who needs care and so the best we can do is to put in place screening procedures that get as close as possible to the sort of knowledge we would acquire through intimate relationships (e.g., visits by social workers, interviews with psychologists, etc.). In other words, screening by adoption and government agencies is the best we can do under the nonideal conditions of having to grant legal parenthood to a child who already exists and who would benefit significantly from parental love. Moreover, note how the costs of false positives for neglect and abuse are very different in the cases of procreation and adoption. In the case of procreation, no one is harmed, since nonexistence is not harmful to the child who does not get to exist. By contrast, the child who is not adopted by a competent prospective parent is in fact harmed. So the stakes are somewhat different in both cases, which justifies treating them differently. See Ferracioli, "Value of Intimacy," 368. For an interesting discussion around assessment of parental competency on the part of biological and adoptive parents, see Jurgen De Wispelaere and Daniel Weinstock, "Licensing Parents to Protect Our Children," *Ethics*

and *Social Welfare* 6 (2) (2012): 195–205; Hugh LaFollette, "Licensing Parents Revisited," *Journal of Applied Philosophy* 27 (4) (2010): 327–42.

32. Mhairi Cowden, "What's Love Got to Do with It? Why a Child Does Not Have a Right to Be Loved," *Critical Review of International Social and Political Philosophy* 15 (3) (2012): 325–45; Mhairi Cowden, "A Need Is Not a Right," *Critical Review of International Social and Political Philosophy* 15 (3) (2012): 359–62; Luara Ferracioli, "The State's Duty to Ensure Children Are Loved," *Journal of Ethics and Social Philosophy* 8 (2) (2014): 1–19; S. Matthew Liao, "The Right of Children to Be Loved," *Journal of Political Philosophy* 14 (4) (2006): 420–40; S. Matthew Liao, "Why Children Need to Be Loved," *Critical Review of International Social and Political Philosophy* 15 (3) (2012): 347–58.

33. There are also other kinds of skeptic, like those who think that rights talk is misguided, or that children cannot be right-holders. Here I assume that rights exist, that they protect interests of sufficient importance to impose correlative duties on others, and that children can be right-holders.

34. Cowden, "What's Love Got to Do."

35. Harry Frankfurt, *The Reasons of Love* (Princeton: Princeton University Press, 2004), 37.

36. Ferracioli, "State's Duty."

37. See Susan Wolf, *Meaning in Life and Why It Matters* (Princeton: Princeton University Press, 2010).

38. Ibid.

39. Note that the recognition that something is objectively valuable need not take place at the time of engagement. While as children we can be quite obsessed with our video games, as adults we can recognize that it was our loving relationships with friends, siblings, and parents that conferred meaning on our childhood.

40. See Chapter 1 for a discussion.

41. Although Adam Swift and Harry Brighouse do not directly address the question of whether children have a right to be loved, some of their discussion on the role of the family in an egalitarian society alludes to the sorts of activities that confer meaning to the child's lives. See their "Parents' Rights and the Value of the Family," *Ethics* 117 (2006): 80–108.

42. For a more detailed discussion, see Ferracioli, "State's Duty."

43. For the notion of a modally demanding value, see Philip Pettit, *The Robust Demands of the Good: Ethics with Attachment, Virtue, and Respect* (Oxford: Oxford University Press, 2015).

44. Could they be motivated by morality? A concern here would be that when someone is "eager to help the sick or the poor, any sick or poor person will do": Frankfurt, *The Reasons of Love*, 43. That being said, those who are motivated by morality could still come to love their adopted child. So even if people are motivated by morality prior to adoption, it is important that they are also disposed to love, for love will ensure that children enjoy the relationship robustly.
45. Cowden, "What's Love Got to Do," 326. This is obviously not to deny that children have a right that parents do a good job of parenting, which gives rise to a duty to parent in an adequate fashion.
46. I think Liao is correct to say that the claim that emotions are never commandable is too strong. For this discussion, see S. Matthew Liao, "The Idea of a Duty to Love," *Journal of Value Inquiry* 40 (1) (2006): 1–22.
47. Here I endorse a strong notion of feasibility of the sort expressed by the principle of "ought implies can."
48. Making contraception more easily accessible, and so decreasing the rate of unwanted pregnancies, is another approach the liberal state should undertake in order to create the conditions for children to enjoy parental love; see Ferracioli, "State's Duty." See also Isabel V. Sawhill, *Drifting into Sex and Parenthood without Marriage* (Washington, DC: Brookings Institution Press, 2014).
49. De Wispelaere and Weinstock also put forward a pro-adoption account, but one that allows for the partial subsidy of assisted reproductive technologies; see De Wispelaere and Weinstock, "State Regulation."
50. Straehle "Right to Surrogacy," 148. Rivka Weinberg makes a similar point: "adoption is not ideal, as it often leaves children feeling abandoned and rejected and can result in parents temperamentally poorly matched with their children." Rivka Weinberg, *The Risk of a Lifetime: How, When, and Why Procreation May Be Permissible* (New York: Oxford University Press, 2015), 44.
51. See also McLeod, "Medical Nonnecessity."
52. See Jesús Palacios and David Brodzinsky, "Review: Adoption Research: Trends, Topics, Outcomes," *International Journal of Behavioural Development* 34 (3) (2010): 270–84.
53. Of course, ideally this form of support would be available for all families, biological and adoptive.
54. Australia has gone so far as to make it a mandatory practice, and contact between adoptee and the birth family is expected to be facilitated by adoptive families until the child turns 18. For open adoption in Australia, see Wright et al., "Adoption in Australia."

55. This is not to deny that the liberal state can override legal parents' decisions on what is in a child's best interests. The point is simply about which agent is typically thought to have the authority to make decisions about which relationships children should have access to.

56. For the concept of adoptee vulnerability, see Mianna Lotz, "Adoptee Vulnerability and Post-adoptive Parental Obligations," in Baylis and McLeod, *Family-Making*, 198–221.

57. For the claim that no system of adoption is inherently superior, see Harold D. Grotevant, Yvette V. Perry, and Ruth G. McRoy, "Openness in Adoption: Outcomes for Adolescents within Their Adoptive Kinship Networks," in David Brodzinsky and Jesús Palacios (eds.), *Psychological Issues in Adoption: Research and Practice* (Westport, CT: Praeger Publishers / Greenwood Publishing Group, 2005), 167–86.

58. For a discussion, see Anca Gheaus, "Arguments for Nonparental Care for Children," *Social Theory and Practice* 37 (3) (2011): 483–509.

59. See Stuart Rachels. "The Immorality of Having Children," *Ethical Theory and Moral Practice* 17 (3) (2014): 567–82.

60. Rivka Weinberg argues that procreative parenting is a particularly enriching life experience, and Ingrid Robeyns believes that procreative parenting is important for our self-understanding as humans. Although these arguments could be appealed to in order to resist the claim that there is moral duty to adopt, I am not convinced that they are strong enough to justify a positive right to engage in procreative parenting. See Weinberg, *Risk of a Lifetime*, 33–43; Ingrid Robeyns, "Is Procreation Special?," *Journal of Value Inquiry* 56 (2022): 643–61.

61. Luara Ferracioli, "Citizenship for Children: By Soil, by Blood, or by Paternalism?," *Philosophical Studies* 175 (11) (2018): 2859–77; Luara Ferracioli, *Liberal Self-Determination in a World of Migration* (New York: Oxford University Press, 2022).

62. For instance, Article 30 of the United Nations Convention on the Rights of the Child has it that a child "shall not be denied the right, in community with other members of his or her group, to enjoy his or her own culture, to profess and practice his or her own religion, or to use his or her own language."

63. Isaiah Berlin, *Vico and Herder: Two Studies in the History of Ideas* (London: Hogarth Press, 1976), 195. To be sure, children who are adopted later in their childhood also have an interest in speaking their native language and practicing aspects of the culture they care about, and adoptive parents have a duty to facilitate that process.

Part II, Introduction

1. This is not to suggest that there is robust agreement about which interests of the child are the most central, and there is still work to be done on this question. At the same time, the UN Convention on the Rights of the Child and the UNICEF report on children's well-being provide a list of interests that has already garnered some cross-cultural support. See Paul Bou-Habib and Serena Olsaretti, "Autonomy and Children's Well-being," in Alexander Bagattini and Colin Macleod (eds.), *The Nature of Children's Well-Being: Theory and Practice* (Dordrecht: Springer, 2015), 15–33; Harry Brighouse, "What Rights (If Any) Do Children Have?," in David Archard and Colin Macleod (eds.), *The Moral and Political Status of Children: New Essays* (Oxford: Oxford University Press, 2002), 31–52.
2. See Anca Gheaus, "The 'Intrinsic Goods of Childhood' and the Just Society," in Bagattini and Macleod, *Children's Well-Being*, 5–52 at 36.
3. See Patrick Tomlin, "Saplings or Caterpillars? Trying to Understand Children's Wellbeing," *Journal of Applied Philosophy* 35 (1) (2018): 29–46. Note that my view of childhood qualifies as a so-called special goods view. For a discussion, see Anca Gheaus, "Childhood: Value and Duties," *Philosophy Compass* 16 (12) (2021): e12793.
4. For a discussion of whether skipping childhood would be rational if possible, see Samantha Brennan, "The Goods of Childhood, Children's Rights, and the Role of Parents as Advocates and Interpreters," in Françoise Baylis and Carolyn McLeod (eds.), *Family-Making: Contemporary Ethical Challenges* (Oxford: Oxford University Press, 2014), 29–48.
5. For a discussion of the biological changes that take place in puberty, such that it makes sense to think of childhood and adolescence as distinct life stages, see Sarah-Jayne Blakemore, *Inventing Ourselves: The Secret Life of the Teenage Brain* (London: Penguin Random House, 2019).
6. This is of course compatible with the claim that some level of paternalism toward adolescents can be justified in high-stakes domains on the basis that adolescents have more limited life experience, and haven't had as much opportunity as adults to practice employing their already formed capacity for autonomy. This picture would hold that we are not justified in exercising as much paternalism in the lives of adolescents as we are in the lives of children, but we are justified in exercising more paternalism in the lives of adolescents than we are in the lives of adults. Age (as a proxy for life experience) would then become relevant when justifying some level of

paternalism toward agents who do already have a capacity for autonomy. For a plausible view that takes age into account when deciding whether paternalism is justified (but that accepts more paternalism in the lives of adolescents than I would accept), see Andrew Franklin-Hall, "Becoming an Adult: Autonomy and the Moral Relevance of Life's Stages," *Philosophical Quarterly* 63 (251) (2013): 223–47.

Chapter 4

1. This chapter was previously published as Luara Ferracioli, "Carefreeness and Children's Well-Being," *Journal of Applied Philosophy* 37 (1) (2020): 103–17. Note that some minor changes have been made to the text.
2. In this book I assume that the nature and value of play remains constant through all life stages, although I grant, of course, that children typically need to play more often than adults in order to lead good lives. I therefore follow Michael Ridge in his account of the value and nature of play. According to Ridge, an agent "is playing just in case the agent is engaged in unscripted activity for the fun of it." He also holds that the unscripted dimension of play and the enjoyment that necessarily attaches to it are both intrinsically valuable. He therefore adds that "play is a unified homeostatic cluster such that the intrinsic value of the whole is plausibly greater than the sum of the intrinsic value of its parts. Moreover, it is plausibly a deep feature of human nature, and so on any of the predominant 'nature fulfilment' theories of welfare it will plausibly be an important ingredient in human welfare": Michael Ridge, "Why So Serious? The Nature and Value of Play," *Philosophy and Phenomenological Research* 105 (2): 406–34. For further discussion on play and the goods of childhood, see Samantha Brennan, "The Goods of Childhood, Children's Rights, and the Role of Parents as Advocates and Interpreters," in Françoise Baylis and Carolyn McLeod (eds.), *Family-Making: Contemporary Ethical Challenges* (Oxford: Oxford University Press, 2014), 29–48; Harry Brighouse and Adam Swift, *Family Values: The Ethics of Parent-Child Relationships* (Princeton: Princeton University Press, 2014); Anca Gheaus, "The 'Intrinsic Goods of Childhood' and the Just Society," in Alexander Bagattini and Colin Macleod (eds.), *The Nature of Children's Well-Being: Theory and Practice* (Dordrecht: Springer, 2015).
3. Gheaus, "Intrinsic Goods of Childhood," 51.

4. Ibid. For another philosophical treatment of play that also supports taking play much more seriously in adulthood, see Ridge, "Why So Serious?"
5. See, for instance, Thomas Hurka, *Perfectionism* (Oxford: Clarendon Press, 1993).
6. See, for instance, Jeremy Bentham, *An Introduction to the Principles of Morals and Legislation*, ed. J. Burns and H. L. A. Hart (Oxford: Clarendon Press, [1789] 1996).
7. A brief first defence of hybrid accounts of well-being can be found in the work of T. M. Scanlon. When discussing the role of subjective preferences in adjudicating between equally compelling moral claims, Scanlon makes the point that the more subjective importance one attaches to a moral claim, the stronger the claim becomes, even if its objective value remains the same. See Thomas Scanlon, "Preference and Urgency," *Journal of Philosophy* 72 (19) (1975): 655–69 at 666.
8. These are joint-necessity views: see Christopher Woodard, "Hybrid Theories," in Guy Fletcher (ed.), *The Routledge Handbook of Philosophy of Well-Being* (Abingdon: Routledge, 2016), 161–74.
9. Joseph Raz, *The Morality of Freedom* (Oxford: Clarendon Press, 1986), 292.
10. Shelly Kagan, "Well-Being as Enjoying the Good," *Philosophical Perspectives* 23 (1) (2009): 253–72 at 257.
11. Susan Wolf, "Happiness and Meaning: Two Aspects of the Good Life," *Social Philosophy and Policy* 14 (1) (1997): 207–25.
12. See Martha C. Nussbaum, *Creating Capabilities: The Human Development Approach* (Cambridge, MA: Harvard University Press, 2011); Amartya Sen, *Inequality Re-examined* (Oxford: Clarendon Press, 1992).
13. Serena Olsaretti, "Endorsement and Freedom in Amartya Sen's Capability Approach," *Economics and Philosophy* 21 (1) (2005): 89–108 at 94.
14. Ibid., 98.
15. John Simpson and Edmund Weiner (eds.), *The Oxford English Dictionary*, 2nd ed. (Oxford: Oxford University Press, 1989).
16. For a defence of this choice of term, see Olsaretti, "Endorsement and Freedom," 98.
17. According to psychologists, both affective/emotional well-being and evaluative/cognitive well-being are part of "subjective well-being." See Ed Diener, "Subjective Well-Being," *Psychological Bulletin* 95 (3) (1984): 542–75. For a philosophical account that requires affect, see Jennifer Hawkins, "The Subjective Intuition," *Philosophical Studies* 148 (1) (2010): 62–68. Kagan, "Well-Being as Enjoying," also talks about enjoyment as "taking pleasure in the good," which suggests a similar commitment.

18. There is also an important question about how stable endorsement can be over time when beliefs and emotions pull us in different directions. Here I assume it can be sufficiently stable, but acknowledge that this requires further research. I thank Duncan Ivison for pushing me on this important point.
19. Daniel Kahneman, "Objective Happiness," in Daniel Kahneman, Ed Diener, and Norbert Schwarz (eds.), *Well-Being: The Foundations of Hedonic Psychology* (New York: Russell Sage Foundation, 1999), 3–25.
20. Anca Gheaus, "Children's Vulnerability and Legitimate Authority over Children," *Journal of Applied Philosophy* 35 (1) (2018): 60–75 at 66.
21. Gheaus, "Intrinsic Goods of Childhood," 38.
22. Note that for Gheaus, the endorsement condition might not be necessary, but merely additive. Alternatively, she might believe that adults should not be forced to be carefree, due to the value of state neutrality.
23. Brighouse and Swift, *Family Values*, 69.
24. I am not suggesting that Brighouse and Swift defend this further claim in their work; I am noting only that carefreeness needs to be both necessary and special in order for us to adequately refute it.
25. Peter C. Scales, "Developmental Assets and the Promotion of Well-Being in Middle Childhood," in Asher Ben-Arieh, Ferran Casas, Ivar Frønes, and Jill E. Korbin (eds.), *Handbook of Child Well-Being: Theories, Methods and Policies in Global Perspective* (Dordrecht: Springer, 2014), 1649–78 at 1671. See also Sarah Hannan, "Why Childhood Is Bad for Children," *Journal of Applied Philosophy* 35 (1) (2018): 11–28.
26. Tamar Schapiro, "What Is a Child?," *Ethics* 109 (4) (1999): 715–38 at 729.
27. Ibid.
28. We might only be able to justify the same level of paternalism toward children that can be justified toward adults—that is, only under very special circumstances.
29. Note that both of these children are significantly better off than a child who dropped out of school because she did not enjoy it, and who now enjoys the other aspects of her life. After all, education not only constitutes a good childhood in cases where endorsement obtains, but also plays a vital role in the protection and promotion of many of the current and future interests of children. The lesson here is that, under some circumstances, paternalism in favor of a project will be appropriate even absent positive affect on the part of a child. And this is because children are owed certain goods as a matter of justice irrespective of whether these goods also constitute a good childhood.

30. Diener, "Subjective Well-Being," 548. See also Ed Diener et al., "Intensity and Frequency: Dimensions Underlying Positive and Negative Affect," *Journal of Personality and Social Psychology* 48 (5) (1985): 1253–65.
31. Patrick D. Quinn and Angela L. Duckworth, "Happiness and Academic Achievement: Evidence for Reciprocal Causality," poster presented at the Annual Meeting of the American Psychological Society (2007).
32. Arne Holte et al., "Psychology of Child Well-Being," in Ben-Arieh et al., *Handbook of Child Well-Being*, 513–54 at 596.
33. Here I do not conceive of a lack of carefreeness as a mental illness. This is for two reasons. First, some children are not carefree purely due to their circumstances. Second, recent empirical evidence "indicates that the determinants of wellbeing are in many instances different from the determinants of mental illness": Praveetha Patalay and Emla Fitzsimons, "Correlates of Mental Illness and Wellbeing in Children: Are They the Same? Results from the UK Millennium Cohort Study," *Journal of the American Academy of Child and Adolescent Psychiatry* 55 (9) (2016): 771–83 at 781.
34. This is not to deny that play or education is *instrumentally* valuable for this child, but rather to affirm that, without sufficient positive affective responses on her part, they will not count as intrinsic goods of *her* childhood. Being carefree is required for endorsement of the valuable goods of childhood, and so required for them to *constitute* a good childhood.

Chapter 5

1. Gwen Bradford, "Achievement, Wellbeing, and Value," *Philosophy Compass* 11 (2016): 795–803 at 796–97.
2. Ibid., 796.
3. The ice pop was accidentally created in 1905 by Frank Epperson, an 11-year-old.
4. Bradford, "Achievement, Wellbeing, and Value," 797. See also Gwen Bradford, *Achievement* (Oxford: Oxford University Press, 2015), 26–63.
5. Bradford, "Achievement, Wellbeing, and Value," 797.
6. Ibid.
7. I thank Holly Lawford-Smith for suggesting this possibility to me.
8. Hasko von Kriegstein flags this position: "Effort and Achievement," *Utilitas* 29 (1) (2017): 27–51 at 31.

9. See Thomas Hurka, *Perfectionism* (Oxford: Clarendon Press, 1993); Bradford, *Achievement*.
10. Gwen Bradford, "Achievement," in Hugh LaFollette (ed.), *International Encyclopaedia of Ethics* (Hoboken, NJ: John Wiley & Sons, 2018), 1–7.
11. See Christopher Woodard, "Hybrid Theories," in Guy Fletcher (ed.), *The Routledge Handbook of Philosophy of Well-Being* (Abingdon: Routledge, 2016). See also Susan Wolf, "Happiness and Meaning: Two Aspects of the Good Life," *Social Philosophy and Policy* 14 (1) (1997): 207–25.
12. Of course, the question of what is in fact worthwhile is a complex one. In this book I assume that there is such a thing as objective value, and that philosophical thinking can help us settle the question of which projects and relationships are in fact worthy of our attraction to them.
13. Bradford, "Achievement, Wellbeing, and Value," 801–2.
14. Ibid.
15. Tamar Schapiro, "What Is a Child?," *Ethics* 109 (4) (1999): 715–38 at 729. See Chapter 4 for a more detailed discussion of this point.
16. Bradford, "Achievement, Wellbeing, and Value," 800–801.
17. Matthew Stewart, "Review of *Ernest Hemingway: A New Life*, by James M. Hutchisson," *American Studies* 56 (1) (2017): 229–30.
18. Cody Delistraty, "How Picasso Bled the Women in His Life for Art," *Paris Review*, November 2017. This is not to deny that we might criticize Picasso's behavior on moral grounds. The point is simply to show that Picasso's work will still count as an achievement, even if we think that he violated a stringent duty to treat women with respect and concern.
19. Anca Gheaus, "Childhood: Value and Duties," *Philosophy Compass* 16 (12) (2021): e12793.
20. Ibid.
21. It is certainly common for kids to think they hate an activity when they first try it, then discover that they love it if they persist with it a little longer. This is why it is morally permissible for a parent to introduce an activity to a child, even if the child does not initially seem particularly interested or curious. But once the parent has introduced the activity in question, and the child has a sufficiently good grasp of what is involved, it is up to the child whether or not to pursue it further. I thank Daniel Wodak for suggesting this sort of scenario to me.
22. Of course, children will not love all the aspects of an activity that they enjoy overall. A child might love tennis, but dislike the ten-minute warmup session that precedes her class. The existence of negative affect does not

preclude endorsement, so long as positive affect dominates the child's experience with a particular project.
23. Ed Diener, "Subjective Well-Being," *Psychological Bulletin* 95 (3): 542–75 at 548. See also Ed Diener et al., "Intensity and Frequency: Dimensions Underlying Positive and Negative Affect," *Journal of Personality and Social Psychology* 48 (5) (1985): 1253–65.
24. Thanks to Daniel Wodak for raising this type of case.
25. Nate Jones, "9 Outrageous Dennis Rodman Stories," *Vulture*, April 2020.
26. "Behind the Books: A Conversation with Edwidge Danticat," Random House, 1998, archived from the original on November 4, 2008.
27. Bethonie Butler, "Bill Withers Was in His 30s with a Job Making Toilets: Then 'Ain't No Sunshine' Changed His Life," *Washington Post*, April 4, 2020.
28. Schools have to encourage students to "achieve academically" to at least a reasonable level. They also have to instill important skills and attitudes, such as perseverance, discipline, and commitment. That is the point of schools, after all. But in this case there are strong paternalistic reasons in favor of such interventions. After all, without a good education and the development of pro-work attitudes, children stand no chance of meeting their basic needs and becoming independent in adulthood. However, schools should not pressure children into achieving in extracurricular activities which are not in fact necessary for children to adequately function in adulthood. Opportunities in sports, drama, and music should certainly be made available to pupils, but no child should be made to feel miserable so that schools can brag about the achievements of their existing and past students.
29. Some parents will be excused to some extent due to their own formative experiences causing them to believe that achievements in childhood are in fact required for adults to function in a liberal society. Indeed, some immigrant parents who come from countries with limited socioeconomic opportunities might struggle to see that children can in fact lead good adulthoods without being pressured into achieving in childhood. In such cases, parents are less blameworthy than they would be if they pressured their children to achieve due to greed, narcissism, or a lack of reflection about what a good childhood requires. At the same time, they are not completely off the hook, since there is plenty of evidence in a liberal society that a carefree childhood is compatible with success later on in life. I thank Holly Lawford-Smith for encouraging me to address this point.
30. Bradford, "Achievement, Wellbeing, and Value.

Chapter 6

1. Judy Dunn, *Children's Friendships* (Oxford: Blackwell Publishing, 2004), 3. She goes on to say that there "are three striking features of these early relationships. . . . The first is the stability of the relationships between these very young children, the second is the reciprocal quality of their relationships, and the third is the developing sophistication of their social understanding" (17).
2. Harry Brighouse and Adam Swift, *Family Values: The Ethics of Parent-Child Relationships* (Princeton: Princeton University Press, 2014); Anca Gheaus, "Childhood: Value and Duties," *Philosophy Compass* 16 (12) (2021): e12793. For a discussion of childhood friendship and the usefulness of different adult-focused theories, see Mary Healy, "Should We Take the Friendships of Children Seriously?," *Journal of Moral Education* 40 (4) (2017): 441–56.
3. Dean Cocking and Jeanette Kennett, "Friendship and the Self," *Ethics* 108 (3) (1998): 502–27.
4. Laurence Thomas, "Friendship," *Synthese* 72 (2) (1987): 217–36 at 230.
5. Nancy Sherman, "Aristotle on Friendship and the Shared Life," *Philosophy and Phenomenological Research* 47 (4) (1987): 589–613 at 600.
6. There is also empirical support for the claim that children care deeply about friendships. A study in Australia showed that friendships were Australian children's favorite aspect of their first year at school. See Elizabeth Murray and Linda J. Harrison, "Children's Perspectives on Their First Year of School: Introducing a New Pictorial Measure of School Stress," *European Early Childhood Education Research Journal* 13 (1) (2005): 111–27.
7. I follow Cocking and Kennett here in labeling these two families of views as the mirror view and the secrets view: see "Friendship and the Self."
8. Ibid., 518.
9. *Nichomachean Ethics* 1165b14–35, cited by Cocking and Kennett, "Friendship and the Self," 506. Another aspect of Aristotle's view that makes it hard to accommodate young children is the assumption that moral virtue is necessary for the highest form of friendship: see Diane Hoyos-Valdés, "The Notion of Character Friendship and the Cultivation of Virtue," *Journal of the Theory of Social Behaviour* 48 (1) (2017): 66–82.
10. For instance, it may be crystal clear to the adults around a child that the main reason she has become a vegetarian is to be more like her best friend, even though she may sincerely insist that vegetarianism follows directly from her love of animals.

11. Cocking and Kennett, "Friendship and the Self," 509.
12. According to Nancy Sherman, for Aristotle "agents must choose each other, in part, on the basis of a firm and stable character. Through the particular friendship, the commitments of character will deepen and express themselves in ways peculiar to and conditioned by that friendship. But even so, a well-cultivated sense of virtue must be in place from the start": Sherman, "Aristotle on Friendship," 599.
13. Thomas, "Friendship," 224.
14. Moreover, empirical studies suggest that, for instance, "on the whole, most children do not usually confide in their peers in detail about family troubles": see Dunn, *Children's Friendships*, 73. It is true that sometimes children keep secrets from their parents, but it is plausible that this has less to do with wanting to signal close friendship to a friend and more to do with the creation of important boundaries between them and their parents.
15. Ibid.
16. Cocking and Kennett, "Friendship and the Self," 518.
17. Dunn, *Children's Friendships*, 29.
18. Vivian Gussin Paley, *Bad Guys Don't Have Birthdays: Fantasy Play at Four* (Chicago: University of Chicago Press, 1988).
19. Cocking and Kennett, "Friendship and the Self," 503.
20. Ibid., 509.
21. Ibid., 510.
22. Ibid., 504.
23. Dunn, *Children's Friendships*, 5.
24. Ibid., 44.
25. Judy Dunn presents empirical evidence that children as young as two behave differently with parents, siblings, and friends. She also presents evidence that children employ more other-oriented reasoning when they are acting in the realm of friendship: ibid., 38.
26. See Neil Delaney, "Romantic Love and Loving Commitment: Articulating a Modern Ideal," *American Philosophical Quarterly* 33 (4) (1996): 339–56; Simon Keller, "How Do I Love Thee? Let Me Count the Properties," *American Philosophical Quarterly* 37 (2) (2000): 163–73. See also Thomas, "Friendship."
27. Many philosophers hold that we care about our friends partly due to the good qualities of their character that we are exposed to during our friendship: see Julia Annas, "Plato and Aristotle on Friendship and Altruism," *Mind* 86 (344) (1977): 532–54; Sherman, "Aristotle on Friendship." However, many philosophers also hold that we are often attracted by the

nonmoral features of our friends, such as their humor, charisma, and accomplishments: see Susan Wolf, "Moral Saints," *Journal of Philosophy* 79 (8) (1982): 419–39.

28. Thomas, "Friendship," 218; Jessica Isserow, "On Having Bad Persons as Friends," *Philosophical Studies* 175 (2018): 3099–116 at 3111. Note that Isserow is particularly concerned with the start of friendships, although her account allows us to also fault people morally for persisting with an already existing friendship should the friend reveal herself to have a bad character.
29. Isserow, "Bad Persons as Friends," 3111.
30. Ibid., 3112.
31. Ibid.
32. Thomas, "Friendship," 221.
33. As Cocking and Kennett explain, "The drawing that takes place in friendship need have nothing to do with character improvement, as parents despairing over their adolescent children's friendships will readily attest": "Friendship and the Self," 514. Although Cocking and Kennett do not discuss childhood friendship in their work, they are clearly attuned to how their account does a good job of making sense of friendship between adolescents.
34. See Barbara Herman, "Rules, Motives, and Helping Actions," *Philosophical Studies* 45 (1984): 369–77; Sherman, "Aristotle on Friendship." See also Stephanie Collins, "Duties to Make Friends," *Ethical Theory and Moral Practice* 16 (2013): 907–21.
35. See Healy, "Friendships of Children." See also Jean Piaget, *The Moral Judgment of the Child*, trans. M. Gabain (New York: Free Press [1932] 1965).
36. Cocking and Kennett, "Friendship and the Self," 514.
37. I grant that ultimately this is an important empirical question that we cannot settle from the armchair. For my purposes, it need only be plausible to claim that "bad" exemplars by themselves are unlikely to undermine the development of a child's moral capacities when all the other conditions for healthy moral development are already in place. Thanks to Stephanie Collins and Jessica Isserow for encouraging me to address this point.
38. Serious forms of bullying would also cause a high level of stress and anxiety and so make a carefree childhood impossible. This is why parents are entitled to interfere in such cases.
39. See Chapter 4 for a more detailed discussion.
40. Healy, "Friendships of Children," 453.

41. Gadi Lissak, "Adverse Physiological and Psychological Effects of Screen Time on Children and Adolescents: Literature Review and Case Study," *Environmental Research* 164 (2018): 149–57.
42. Luara Ferracioli, "Why the Family?," *Law, Ethics and Philosophy* 3 (2015): 205–19.
43. This is also why I believe that parents are not morally entitled to deprive their child of a compulsory, secular, and public liberal education: Luara Ferracioli and Rosa Terlazzo, "Educating for Autonomy: Liberalism and Autonomy in the Capabilities Approach," *Ethical Theory and Moral Practice* 17 (4) (2014): 443–55.
44. Although I disagree with Amy Mullin, who thinks that even young children can exercise a great deal of local autonomy, I think she is right in pushing for us to recognize that parents must give children some latitude to make some decisions about their lives, so long as those decisions are in line with children's current and future interests, as well as their ability to lead a good childhood. As she puts it, "Good relationships with young children require a combination of respect for children's already existing autonomy, support for their development of skills and capacities which enhance autonomy, and varieties of caregiver behavior that constrain those activities which appear to threaten (what the caregivers assess as) the children's long-term interests": Amy Mullin, "Children, Autonomy, and Care," *Journal of Social Philosophy* 38 (4) (2007): 536–53 at 549.
45. But, of course, the degree of freedom that parents should afford their children in a particular domain should depend on how serious the consequences would be if children were to make bad decisions in that domain. For a discussion, see David Archard and Suzanne Uniacke, "The Child's Right to a Voice," *Res Publica* 27 (2021): 521–36. There is also empirical support for the claim that having some control over some relationships is important for children's well-being: see Toby Fattore, Jan Mason, and Elizabeth Watson, "Children's Conceptualization(s) of Their Well-Being," *Social Indicators Research* 80 (1) (2007): 5–29; Toby Fattore, Jan Mason, and Elizabeth Watson, "When Children Are Asked about Their Well-Being: Towards a Framework for Guiding Policy," *Child Indicators Research* 2 (1) (2009): 57–77. Thanks to Jessica Isserow for encouraging me to expand on the value of some level of control over one's childhood.
46. The latter response is quite common among parents. One study in Nottingham showed that 35 percent of parents of seven-year-olds had already taken steps to discourage specific friendships. It also showed that 72 percent of mothers indicated that they "would take action to restrict

their child's friendship if they were not happy with it": Dunn, *Children's Friendships*, 140.
47. Do parents have to take on costs even when their children have plenty of siblings to play with? The answer here is yes. Although sibling relationships are valuable in their own right, they are quite distinct from close friendships. And, in fact, one major difference is the dependence of the sibling relationship *on the parent*. Siblings cannot be interpreted and directed in the same way as friends in childhood because parents play a very active role in the sibling relationship, which, in turn, affects the degree of interpretation and direction that is available to each of the siblings.
48. For a discussion on parental attitudes toward childhood friendships which unfortunately indicates that parents don't seem to value childhood friendship as much as children do, see Sigrid Brogaard-Clausen and Sue Robson, "Friendships for Wellbeing? Parents' and Practitioners' Positioning of Young Children's Friendships in the Evaluation of Wellbeing Factors," *International Journal of Early Years Education* 27 (4) (2019): 345–59.
49. Does that mean that if the parent does not support her child's friendships, she ceases to be a moral parent? As I alluded to in the introduction, I am not arguing that parents must ensure that children enjoy the good of friendship (or achievement and carefreeness) to a significant extent at pain of failing to count as a moral parent. However, given that moral parenthood partly depends on the creation of the conditions for children to lead good lives, parents must discharge the obligations I have discussed in Part II of this book at least to a sufficient extent. This means that a parent who is particularly lousy at supporting their child's friendships must do at least a good job when it comes to achievement and carefreeness.

Bibliography

Adopt Change. 2015. "Modern Families: Attitudes and Perceptions of Adoption in Australia." AdoptChange.org.au. Retrieved June 1, 2022.

Ambrose, Margaret. 2021. "'I Started Working Two Jobs': The Real Cost of IVF." *Sydney Morning Herald*, September 24.

Annas, Julia. 1977. "Plato and Aristotle on Friendship and Altruism." *Mind* 86 (344): 532–54.

Archard, David. 1995. "What's Blood Got to Do with It?" *Res Publica* 1 (1): 91–106.

Archard, David. 2010. "The Obligations and Responsibilities of Parenthood." In David Archard and David Benatar, eds., *Procreation and Parenthood: The Ethics of Bearing and Rearing Children*. Oxford: Oxford University Press, 103–14.

Archard, David and Uniacke, Suzanne. 2021. "The Child's Right to a Voice." *Res Publica* 27: 521–36.

Australian Institute of Health and Welfare. 2021. "Child Protection Australia 2019–20." Child Welfare Series no. 74, cat. no. CWS 78. Canberra: AIHW.

Baron, Teresa. 2019. "Nobody Puts Baby in the Container: The Foetal Container Model at Work in Medicine and Commercial Surrogacy." *Journal of Applied Philosophy* 36 (3): 491–505.

Baron, Teresa. 2020. "A Lost Cause? Fundamental Problems for Causal Theories of Parenthood." *Bioethics* 34 (7): 664–70.

Bayne, Tim and Kolers, Avery. 2003. "Toward a Pluralist Account of Parenthood." *Bioethics* 17 (3): 221–42.

Benatar, David. 2006. *Better Never to Have Been: The Harm of Coming into Existence*. New York: Oxford University Press.

Bentham, Jeremy. [1789] 1996. *An Introduction to the Principles of Morals and Legislation*. Ed. J. Burns and H. L. A. Hart. Oxford: Clarendon Press.

Berlin, Isaiah. 1976. *Vico and Herder: Two Studies in the History of Ideas*. London: Hogarth Press.

Blakemore, Sarah-Jayne. 2019. *Inventing Ourselves: The Secret Life of the Teenage Brain*. London: Penguin Random House.

Blustein, Jeffrey. 1997. "Procreation and Parental Responsibility." *Journal of Social Philosophy* 28 (2): 79–86.

Bou-Habib, Paul and Olsaretti, Serena. 2019. "Autonomy and Children's Well-Being." In Alexander Bagattini and Colin Macleod, eds., *The Nature of Children's Well-Being: Theory and Practice*. Dordrecht: Springer, 15–33.

Bradford, Gwen. 2015. *Achievement*. Oxford: Oxford University Press.

Bradford, Gwen. 2016. "Achievement, Wellbeing, and Value." *Philosophy Compass* 11 (12): 795–803.

Bradford, Gwen. 2018. "Achievement." In Hugh LaFollette, ed., *International Encyclopaedia of Ethics*. Hoboken, NJ: John Wiley & Sons, 1–17.

Brake, Elizabeth. 2010. "Willing Parents: A Voluntarist Account of Parental Role Obligations." In David Archard and David Benatar, eds., *Procreation and Parenthood: The Ethics of Bearing and Rearing Children*. Oxford: Oxford University Press, 151–77.

Brandt, Reuven. 2017. "The Transfer and Delegation of Responsibilities for Genetic Offspring in Gamete Provision." *Journal of Applied Philosophy* 34 (5): 665–78.

Brennan, Samantha. 2014. "The Goods of Childhood, Children's Rights, and the Role of Parents as Advocates and Interpreters." In Françoise Baylis and Carolyn McLeod, eds., *Family-Making: Contemporary Ethical Challenges*. Oxford: Oxford University Press, 29–48.

Brennan, Samantha and Noggle, Robert. 1997. "The Moral Status of Children: Children's Rights, Parents, Rights, and Family Justice." *Social Theory and Practice* 23 (1): 1–26.

Brighouse, Harry. 2002. "What Rights (If Any) Do Children Have?" In David Archard and Colin Macleod, eds., *The Moral and Political Status of Children: New Essays*. Oxford: Oxford University Press, 31–52.

Brighouse, Harry and Swift, Adam. 2006. "Parents' Rights and the Value of the Family." *Ethics* 117 (1): 80–108.

Brighouse, Harry and Swift, Adam. 2014. *Family Values: The Ethics of Parent-Child Relationships*. Princeton: Princeton University Press.

Brogaard-Clausen, Sigrid and Robson, Sue. 2019. "Friendships for Wellbeing? Parents' and Practitioners' Positioning of Young Children's Friendships in the Evaluation of Wellbeing Factors." *International Journal of Early Years Education* 27 (4): 345–59.

Butler, Bethonie. 2020. "Bill Withers Was in His 30s with a Job Making Toilets: Then 'Ain't No Sunshine' Changed His Life." *Washington Post*, April 4.

Clayton, Matthew. 2006. *Justice and Legitimacy in Upbringing*. Oxford: Oxford University Press.

Cocking, Dean and Kennett, Jeanette. 1998. "Friendship and the Self." *Ethics* 108 (3): 502–27.

Collins, Stephanie. 2014. "Duties to Make Friends." *Ethical Theory and Moral Practice* 16 (5): 907–21.

Cowden, Mhairi. 2012. "A Need Is Not a Right." *Critical Review of International Social and Political Philosophy* 15 (3): 369–62.

Cowden, Mhairi. 2012. "What's Love Got to Do with It? Why a Child Does Not Have a Right to Be Loved." *Critical Review of International Social and Political Philosophy* 15 (3): 325–45.

Dandicat, Edwidge. 2008. "Behind the Books: A Conversation with Edwidge Danticat [1998]." November. https://web.archive.org/web/20081104091003/http://www.randomhouse.com/vintage/danticat.html.

Delaney, Neil. 1996. "Romantic Love and Loving Commitment: Articulating a Modern Ideal." *American Philosophical Quarterly* 33 (4): 339–56.

Delistraty, Cody. 2017. "How Picasso Bled the Women in His Life for Art." *Paris Review*, November.

De Melo-Martín, Inmaculada. 2014. "The Ethics of Anonymous Gamete Donation: Is There a Right to Know One's Genetic Origins?" *Hastings Center Report* 44 (2): 28–35.

De Melo-Martín, Inmaculada. 2014. "Reproductive Embryo Editing." *Hastings Center Report* 52 (4): 26–33.

De Wispelaere, Jurgen and Weinstock, Daniel. 2012. "Licensing Parents to Protect Our Children." *Ethics and Social Welfare* 6 (2): 195–205.

De Wispelaere, Jurgen and Weinstock, Daniel. 2014. "State Regulation and Assisted Reproduction: Balancing the Interests of Parents and Children." In Françoise Baylis and Carolyn McLeod, eds., *Family-Making: Contemporary Ethical Challenges*. Oxford: Oxford University Press, 131–50.

Diener, Ed. 1984. "Subjective Well-Being." *Psychological Bulletin* 95 (3): 542–75.

Diener, Ed, et al. 1985. "Intensity and Frequency: Dimensions Underlying Positive and Negative Affect." *Journal of Personality and Social Psychology* 48 (5): 1253–65.

Dunn, Judy. 2004. *Children's Friendships*. Oxford: Blackwell Publishing.

Fattore, Toby, Mason, Jan, and Watson, Elizabeth. 2007. "Children's Conceptualization(s) of Their Well-Being." *Social Indicators Research* 80 (1): 5–29.

Fattore, Toby, Mason, Jan, and Watson, Elizabeth. 2009. "When Children Are Asked about Their Well-Being: Towards a Framework for Guiding Policy." *Child Indicators Research* 2 (1): 57–77.

Ferracioli, Luara. 2014. "On the Value of Intimacy in Procreation." *Journal of Value Inquiry* 48 (1): 349–69.

Ferracioli, Luara. 2014. "The State's Duty to Ensure Children Are Loved." *Journal of Ethics and Social Philosophy* 8 (2): 1–19.

Ferracioli, Luara. 2015. "Why the Family?" *Law, Ethics and Philosophy* 3: 205–19.

Ferracioli, Luara. 2018. "Citizenship for Children: By Soil, by Blood, or by Paternalism?" *Philosophical Studies* 175 (11): 2859–77.

Ferracioli, Luara. 2018. "Procreative-Parenting, Love's Reasons and the Demands of Morality." *Philosophical Quarterly* 68 (270): 77–97.
Ferracioli, Luara. 2020. "Carefreeness and Children's Well-Being." *Journal of Applied Philosophy* 37 (1): 103–17.
Ferracioli, Luara. 2022. *Liberal Self-Determination in a World of Migration*. New York: Oxford University Press.
Ferracioli, Luara. Forthcoming. "On the Human Right to Found a Family." In Jesse Tomalty and Kerri Woods, eds., *The Routledge Handbook of the Philosophy of Human Rights*.
Ferracioli, Luara and Terlazzo, Rosa. 2014. "Educating for Autonomy: Liberalism and Autonomy in the Capabilities Approach." *Ethical Theory and Moral Practice* 17 (4): 443–55.
Frankfurt, Harry. 2006. *The Reasons of Love*. Princeton: Princeton University Press.
Franklin-Hall, Andrew. 2013. "Becoming an Adult: Autonomy and the Moral Relevance of Life's Stages." *Philosophical Quarterly* 63 (251): 223–47.
Friedrich, Daniel. 2013. "A Duty to Adopt?" *Journal of Applied Philosophy* 30 (1): 25–39.
Fuscaldo, Giuliana. 2006. "Genetic Ties: Are They Morally Binding?" *Bioethics* 20 (2): 64–76.
Gheaus, Anca. 2011. "Arguments for Nonparental Care for Children." *Social Theory and Practice* 37 (3): 483–509.
Gheaus, Anca. 2012. "The Right to Parent One's Biological Baby." *Journal of Political Philosophy* 20 (4): 432–55.
Gheaus, Anca. 2015. "The 'Intrinsic Goods of Childhood' and the Just Society." In Alexander Bagattini and Colin Macleod, eds., *The Nature of Children's Well-Being: Theory and Practice*. Dordrech: Springer, 35–52.
Gheaus, Anca. 2018. "Biological Parenthood: Gestational, Not Genetic." *Australasian Journal of Philosophy* 96 (2): 225–40.
Gheaus, Anca. 2018. "Children's Vulnerability and Legitimate Authority over Children." *Journal of Applied Philosophy* 35 (1): 60–75.
Gheaus, Anca. 2021. "Childhood: Value and Duties." *Philosophy Compass* 16 (12): e127–93.
Grill, Kalle. 2020. "How Many Parents Should There Be in a Family?" *Journal of Applied Philosophy* 37 (3): 465–84.
Grotevant, Harold D., Perry, Yvette V., and McRoy, Ruth G. 2005. "Openness in Adoption: Outcomes for Adolescents within Their Adoptive Kinship Networks." In David Brodzinsky and Jesús Palacios, eds., *Psychological Issues in Adoption: Research and Practice*. Westport, CT: Praeger Publishers / Greenwood Publishing Group, 167–86.
Hall, Barbara. 1999. "The Origin of Parental Rights." *Public Affairs Quarterly* 13 (1): 73–82.
Hanna, Jason. 2019. "Causal Parenthood and the Ethics of Gamete Donation." *Bioethics* 33 (2): 267–73.

Hannan, Sarah. 2018. "Why Childhood Is Bad for Children." *Journal of Applied Philosophy* 35 (1): 11–28.

Hannan, Sarah and Leland, R. J. 2018. "Childhood Bads, Parenting Goods, and the Right to Procreate." *Critical Review of International Social and Political Philosophy* 21 (3): 366–84.

Hawkins, Jennifer. 2010. "The Subjective Intuition." *Philosophical Studies* 148 (1): 628.

Healy, Mary. 2017. "Should We Take the Friendships of Children Seriously?" *Journal of Moral Education* 40 (4): 441–56.

Helm, Bennett. 2009. "Love." In Edward N. Zalta, ed., *The Stanford Encyclopedia of Philosophy*. Fall ed.

Herman, Barbara. 1984. "Rules, Motives, and Helping Actions." *Philosophical Studies* 45 (3): 369–77.

Hill, J. L. 1991. "What Does It Mean to Be a 'Parent'? The Claims of Biology as a Basis for Parental Rights." *New York University Law Review* 66 (3): 353–420.

Holte, Arne et al. 2014. "Psychology of Child Well-Being." In Asher Ben-Arieh et al., eds., *Handbook of Child Well-Being: Theories, Methods and Policies in Global Perspective*. Dordrecht: Springer, 513–54.

Hoyos-Valdés, Diane. 2017. "The Notion of Character Friendship and the Cultivation of Virtue." *Journal of the Theory of Social Behaviour* 48 (1): 66–82.

Hurka, Thomas. 1993. *Perfectionism*. Oxford: Clarendon Press.

Isserow, Jessica. 2018. "On Having Bad Persons as Friends." *Philosophical Studies* 175 (12): 3099–9116.

Jones, Nate. 2020. "9 Outrageous Dennis Rodman Stories." *Vulture*, April.

Kagan, Shelly. 2009. "Well-Being as Enjoying the Good." *Philosophical Perspectives* 23 (1): 253–72.

Kahneman, Daniel. 1999. "Objective Happiness." In Daniel Kahneman, Ed Diener, and Norbert Schwarz, eds., *Well-Being: The Foundations of Hedonic Psychology*. New York: Russell Sage Foundation, 3–25.

Keller, Simon. 2000. "How Do I Love Thee? Let Me Count the Properties." *American Philosophical Quarterly* 27 (2): 163–73.

Kolodny, Niko. 2003. "Love as Valuing a Relationship." *Philosophical Review* 112 (2): 135–89.

LaFollette, Hugh. 2010. "Licensing Parents Revisited." *Journal of Applied Philosophy* 27 (4): 327–42.

Leighton, Kimberly. 2014. "Analogies to Adoption in Arguments against Anonymous Gamete Donation." In Françoise Baylis and Carolyn McLeod, eds., *Family-Making: Contemporary Ethical Challenges*. Oxford: Oxford University Press, 239–64.

Liao, S. Matthew. 2006. "The Idea of a Duty to Love." *Journal of Value Inquiry* 40 (1): 1–22.

Liao, S. Matthew. 2006. "The Right of Children to Be Loved." *Journal of Political Philosophy* 14 (4): 420–40.

Liao, S. Matthew. 2012. "Why Children Need to Be Loved." *Critical Review of International Social and Political Philosophy* 15 (3): 347–58.

Liao, S. Matthew. 2015. *The Right to Be Loved*. New York: Oxford University Press.

Lissak, Gadi. 2018. "Adverse Physiological and Psychological Effects of Screen Time on Children and Adolescents: Literature Review and Case Study." *Environmental Research* 164: 149–57.

Little, Margaret Olivia. 1999. "Abortion, Intimacy and the Duty to Gestate." *Ethical Theory and Moral Practice* 2 (3): 295–312.

Lotz, Mianna. 2014. "Adoptee Vulnerability and Post-adoptive Parental Obligations." In Françoise Baylis and Carolyn McLeod, eds., *Family-Making: Contemporary Ethical Challenges*. Oxford: Oxford University Press, 198–221.

Macleod, Colin. 1997. "Conceptions of Parental Autonomy." *Politics and Society* 25 (1): 117–40.

Macleod, Colin. 2002. "Liberal Equality and the Affective Family." In David Archard and Colin Macleod, eds., *The Moral and Political Status of Children*. Oxford: Oxford University Press, 212–30.

McLeod, Carolyn. 2017. "The Medical Nonnecessity of In Vitro Fertilization." *International Journal of Feminist Approaches to Bioethics* 10 (1): 78–102.

Millum, Joseph. 2018. *The Moral Foundations of Parenthood*. New York: Oxford University Press.

Mullin, Amy. 2005. *Reconceiving Pregnancy and Childcare: Ethics, Experience, and Reproductive Labor*. Cambridge: Cambridge University Press.

Mullin, Amy. 2007. "Children, Autonomy, and Care." *Journal of Social Philosophy* 38 (4): 536–53.

Murray, Elizabeth and Harrison, Linda J. 2005. "Children's Perspectives on Their First Year of School: Introducing a New Pictorial Measure of School Stress." *European Early Childhood Education Research Journal* 13 (1): 111–27.

Narveson, Jan. 2002. *Respecting Persons in Theory and Practice*. Lanham, MD: Rowman and Littlefield.

Nelson, James Lindemann. 1991. "Parental Obligations and the Ethics of Surrogacy: A Causal Perspective." *Public Affairs Quarterly* 5 (1): 49–61.

Nelson, James Lindemann. 2014. "Special Responsibilities of Parents Using Technologically Assisted Reproduction." In Françoise Baylis and Carolyn McLeod, eds., *Family-Making: Contemporary Ethical Challenges*. Oxford: Oxford University Press, 185–97.

Nussbaum, Martha C. 2011. *Creating Capabilities: The Human Development Approach*. Cambridge, MA: Harvard University Press.

Olsaretti, Serena. 2005. "Endorsement and Freedom in Amartya Sen's Capability Approach." *Economics and Philosophy* 21 (1): 89–108.

O'Neill, Onora. 1979. "Begetting, Bearing, and Rearing." In Onora O'Neill and William Ruddick, eds., *Having Children: Philosophical and Legal Reflections on Parenthood*. New York: Oxford University Press, 25–38.

Overall, Christine. 2012. *Why Have Children? The Ethical Debate*. Cambridge, MA: MIT Press.

Palacios, Jesús and Brodzinsky, David. 2010. "Review: Adoption Research: Trends, Topics, Outcomes." *International Journal of Behavioural Development* 34 (3): 270–84.

Paley, Vivian Gussin. 1988. *Bad Guys Don't Have Birthdays: Fantasy Play at Four*. Chicago: University of Chicago Press.

Patalay, Praveetha and Fitzsimons, Emla. 2016. "Correlates of Mental Illness and Wellbeing in Children: Are They the Same? Results from the UK Millennium Cohort Study." *Journal of the American Academy of Child and Adolescent Psychiatry* 55 (9): 771–83.

Pettit, Philip. 2015. *The Robust Demands of the Good: Ethics with Attachment, Virtue, and Respect*. Oxford: Oxford University Press.

Piaget, Jean. [1932] 1965. *The Moral Judgment of the Child*. Trans. M. Gabain. New York: Free Press.

Porter, Lindsey. 2014. "Why and How to Prefer a Causal Account of Parenthood." *Journal of Social Philosophy* 45 (2): 182–202.

Protasi, Sara. 2016. "Loving People for Who They Are (Even When They Don't Love You Back)." *European Journal of Philosophy* 24 (1): 214–34.

Purdy, Laura. 1989. "Surrogate Mothering: Exploitation or Empowerment?" *Bioethics* 3 (1): 18–34.

Quinn, Patrick D. and Duckworth, Angela L. 2007. "Happiness and Academic Achievement: Evidence for Reciprocal Causality." Poster presented at the Annual Meeting of the American Psychological Society.

Rachels, Stuart. 2014. "The Immorality of Having Children." *Ethical Theory and Moral Practice* 17 (3): 567–82.

Raz, Joseph. 1986. *The Morality of Freedom*. Oxford: Clarendon Press.

Ridge, Michael. 2022. "Why So Serious? The Nature and Value of Play." *Philosophy and Phenomenological Research* 105 (2): 406–34.

Rieder, Travis N. 2015. "Procreation, Adoption and the Contours of Obligation." *Journal of Applied Philosophy* 32 (3): 293–309.

Robeyns, Ingrid. 2022. "Is Procreation Special?" *Journal of Value Inquiry* 56: 643–61.

Rulli, Tina. 2014. "The Unique Value of Adoption." In Françoise Baylis and Carolyn McLeod, eds., *Family Making: Contemporary Ethical Challenges*. Oxford: Oxford University Press, 110–28.

Rulli, Tina. 2016. "Preferring a Genetically-Related Child." *Journal of Moral Philosophy* 13 (6): 669–98.

Rulli, Tina. 2016. "What Is the Value of Three-Parent IVF?" *Hastings Center Report* 46: 38–47.

Sawhill, Isabel V. 2014. *Drifting into Sex and Parenthood without Marriage*. Washington, DC: Brookings Institution Press.

Scales, Peter C. 2014. "Developmental Assets and the Promotion of Well-Being in Middle Childhood." In Asher Ben-Arieh et al., eds., *Handbook of Child Well-Being: Theories, Methods and Policies in Global Perspective*. Dordrecht: Springer, 1649–78.

Scanlon, Thomas. 1975. "Preference and Urgency." *Journal of Philosophy* 72 (19): 655–69.

Schapiro, Tamar. 1999. "What Is a Child?" *Ethics* 109 (4): 715–38.

Scheffler, Samuel. 1982. *The Rejection of Consequentialism*. Oxford: Clarendon Press.

Sen, Amartya. 1992. *Inequality Re-examined*. Oxford: Clarendon Press.

Sherman, Nancy. 1987. "Aristotle on Friendship and the Shared Life." *Philosophy and Phenomenological Research* 47 (4): 589–613.

Shields, Liam. 2016. "How Bad Can a Good Enough Parent Be?" *Canadian Journal of Philosophy* 46 (2): 163–82.

Shields, Liam. 2019. "Parental Rights and the Importance of Being Parents." *Critical Review of International Social and Political Philosophy* 22 (2): 119–33.

Shpall, Sam. 2014. "Moral and Rational Commitment." *Philosophy and Phenomenological Research* 88 (1): 146–72.

Shpall, Sam. 2023. "Parental Love and Procreation." *Philosophical Quarterly* 73 (1): 206–26.

Simpson, John and Weiner, Edmund, eds. 1989. *The Oxford English Dictionary*. 2nd ed. Oxford: Oxford University Press.

Sparrow, Robert. 2006. "Cloning, Parenthood, and Genetic Relatedness." *Bioethics* 20 (6): 308–18.

Stewart, Matthew. 2017. "Review of Ernest Hemingway: A New Life, by James M. Hutchisson." *American Studies* 56 (1): 229–30.

Straehle, Christine. 2016. "Is There a Right to Surrogacy?" *Journal of Applied Philosophy* 33 (2): 146–59.

Thomas, Laurence. 1987. "Friendship." *Synthese* 72 (2): 217–36.

Tomlin, Patrick. 2018. "Saplings or Caterpillars? Trying to Understand Children's Wellbeing." *Journal of Applied Philosophy* 35 (1): 29–46.

Uniacke, Suzanne. 1987. "*In Vitro* Fertilization and the Right to Reproduce." *Bioethics* 1 (3): 241–54.

Vallentyne, Peter. 2003. "The Rights and Duties of Childrearing." *William and Mary Bill of Rights Journal* 11 (3): 991–1009.

Velleman, David. 2008. "Persons in Prospect." *Philosophy and Public Affairs* 36 (3): 245–66.

Vlastos, Gregory. 1972. "The Individual as an Object of Love in Plato." In his *Platonic Studies*. Princeton: Princeton University Press, 3–34.

Von Kriegstein, Hasko. 2017. "Effort and Achievement." *Utilitas* 29 (1): 27–51.

Walsh, Joseph. 2017. "Commitment and Partialism in the Ethics of Care." *Hypatia* 32 (4): 817–32.

Weinberg, Rivka. 2008. "The Moral Complexity of Sperm Donation." *Bioethics* 22 (3): 166–78.

Weinberg, Rivka. 2015. *The Risk of a Lifetime: How, When, and Why Procreation May Be Permissible*. New York: Oxford University Press.

Wilkinson, Stephen. 2018. "Exploitation in International Paid Surrogacy Arrangements." *Journal of Applied Philosophy* 33 (2): 125–45.

Wolf, Susan. 1982. "Moral Saints." *Journal of Philosophy* 79 (8): 419–39.

Wolf, Susan. 1997. "Happiness and Meaning: Two Aspects of the Good Life." *Social Philosophy and Policy* 14 (1): 207–25.

Wolf, Susan. 2010. *Meaning in Life and Why It Matters*. Princeton: Princeton University Press.

Woodard, Christopher. 2016. "Hybrid Theories." In Guy Fletcher, ed., *The Routledge Handbook of Philosophy of Well-Being*. Abingdon: Routledge, 161–74.

Wright, Amy Conley, Luu, Betty, and Cashmore, Judith. 2021. "Adoption in Australia: Past, Present and Considerations for the Future." *Australasian Law Journal* 95: 67–90.

Young, Thomas. 2001. "Overconsumption and Procreation: Are They Morally Equivalent?" *Journal of Applied Philosophy* 18 (2): 183–92.

Index

For the benefit of digital users, indexed terms that span two pages (e.g., 52–53) may, on occasion, appear on only one of those pages.

abortion, 55, 56
abuse and neglect. *See* child abuse and neglect
achievement, 3, 83–84, 85, 106, 108–26, 127
   in adulthood, 113–16
   in childhood, 116–24
   implications for action, 124–26
   instrumental, 109, 117–21, 126
   intrinsic, 109, 121–22, 126
   motives for, 113–16
   parents' formative experiences and, 177n.29
   perfectionist account of, 112, 116–17
   well-being and, 109–13
adolescents, 85–86, 171–72n.6
adoption, 3, 4–5, 7–8, 53–54, 78–79, 83
   counseling and mental health support in, 71–72
   cross-cultural, 75–79, 170n.62, 170n.63
   implications for action, 69–73
   inclusion desideratum and, 36–37
   interracial, 77
   legal parenthood status in, 72–73
   legal support for, 71
   the liberal state and, 26–27, 53–54, 55, 63, 65–78
   in mixed families, 21
   moral commitment and, 30, 44, 45–46, 48–49
   moral parenthood and, 32–34, 36–37, 53–54, 73
   objections to some practices in, 73–78
   open, 71, 72–73, 75–76, 78–79, 169n.54
   parental leave and, 55, 70–71
   parental love and, 18–20, 21, 26–27, 65–67, 68–69
   procreative parenting compared with, 6, 8, 20, 21, 26–27
   rates of, 53
   screening procedures for, 65, 167–68n.31
adulthood, 84, 85
   achievement in, 113–16
   carefreeness and, 85, 88, 92–98
   childhood achievement and, 122–24
   friendship in, 128, 136–38
   play and, 87–88, 96
anonymous egg donation, 58
anonymous gamete donation, 62–63, 166nn.24, 25
anonymous sperm donation, 58
antinatalist challenge, 11
antiparenting challenge, 11
Aristotle, 130, 178n.9, 179n.12
authoritative decisions
   achievement and, 113–14, 117–19, 124–25, 126
   via positive affect, 100–3

bad parenting, 47–48. *See also* child abuse and neglect
biological parents. *See* procreative parenting
bodily autonomy, 56, 78
bodily integrity, 56, 62, 83–84
Bradford, Gwen, 109, 110, 112–13, 116–17, 126
Brake, Elizabeth, 155n.3, 155n.5, 156n.14
Brighouse, Harry, 98–99, 127

INDEX

capabilities approach, 90–91
carefreeness, 3, 83–84, 85, 87–107, 108, 127
  achievement and decrease in, 108, 126
  adulthood and, 85, 88, 92–98
  defined, 92
  a good childhood and, 98–105
  implications for action, 105–6
  requirements for, 92–93
  two ways of understanding, 92
  well-being and, 89–91
care uncertainty, 58–62
causal theories, 30, 31–33, 43–44, 51–52, 156n.15
  dual-interest desideratum and, 35, 36
  inclusion desideratum and, 36–37
  parental proliferation and, 50
  parental scarcity and, 47, 49
  relationship desideratum and, 38
child abuse and neglect, 47–48, 49, 53
Cocking, Dean, 127, 128, 129–30, 131, 132, 134, 135, 141
cognitive abilities
  achievement and, 118
  carefreeness and, 100–3
commercial surrogacy, 58, 61, 62–63, 71, 166n.25
commitment theory, 39. *See also* moral commitment
competency. *See* parental competency
consent, 31–32. *See also* voluntarist theories
  dual-interest desideratum and, 35–36
  moral commitment and, 30, 43–44
  parental proliferation and, 50
  pluralist theories on, 32
  relationship desideratum and, 38–39
contraception, 55, 169n.48
Convention on the Rights of the Child, 87
co-procreators, 57–64, 164nn.11, 12
  care uncertainty and, 58–62
  conditions for and against collaboration by, 58–60
  defined, 57, 164n.11
  the liberal state and, 62–64
core interests, 3–4, 22–23, 83–84. *See also* interests of the child
cost-taking
  for achievement in children, 125–26

  for friendship in children, 137, 146–47
  moral commitment and, 49
  parental love and, 12, 14–15, 66–67
Cowden, Mhairi, 69
credit condition, 109–10, 121, 126
cross-cultural adoption, 75–79, 170n.62, 170n.63

Danticat, Edwidge, 122–23
difficulty condition, 109, 110–11, 121, 126
drawing view of friendship, 128, 129–30, 133–36, 139–40, 147
dual comparative view of child redistribution, 10
dual-interest desideratum, 33–34
  explained, 34–36
  parental scarcity and, 48–49
dual-interest theory of the family, 14–15, 22, 44, 153n.32
Dunn, Judy, 127, 133
duties. *See* moral duties

education, 4, 90, 174n.29, 177n.28
  achievement in, 119, 124
  carefreeness and, 103, 104
egg donation, 8, 57, 58. *See also* gamete donation
endorsement. *See* subjective endorsement
environmental impact of procreation, 5, 6, 7, 8, 9, 11, 150n.7

fantasy (imaginative) play, 132–33
fertility clinics, 58–60, 61–62, 63, 78
foster care, 53, 67, 68–69, 78
Frankfurt, Harry, 66
friendship, 3, 83–84, 85, 106, 127–47
  in adulthood, 128, 136–38
  in childhood, 139–43
  co-creation in, 139, 141
  drawing view of, 128, 129–30, 133–36, 139–40, 147
  empirical support for children's feelings toward, 178n.6
  implications for action, 143–47
  mirror view of, 128, 129–31, 133–34, 136
  moral grounds and, 139–42, 144, 146
  obsessive, 138, 142

parental love compared with, 13, 15, 17, 137
prudential grounds and, 139–40
secrets view of, 128, 129–30, 131–34, 136
well-being and, 129–36

gamete donation, 8, 31. *See also* egg donation; sperm donation
anonymous, 62–63, 166nn.24, 25
care uncertainty and, 59, 61
the liberal state and, 55, 56, 57, 62–63
genetic connection, 6, 7–8, 31, 45
children's right to know, 56, 72
inclusion desideratum and, 36–37
moral commitment and, 45
pluralist theories on, 32
redistribution challenge on, 9, 10, 25
gestation, 31, 155n.5, 159–60n.31
co-procreators in (*see* co-procreators)
inclusion desideratum and, 36–37
moral commitment and, 44–45
pluralist theories on, 32
in procreative parenting, 6, 7–8, 9, 10, 25–26, 44–45
redistribution challenge on, 9, 10, 25–26
relationship desideratum and, 38–39
in surrogacy, 38–39
Gheaus, Anca, 7, 24–26, 87–88, 95–97, 116–17, 159–60n.31

healthcare, 56, 78
Healy, Mary, 143
Hemingway, Ernest, 115
historical-relationship properties, 16–17, 63
homosexual couples, 75
hybrid account of well-being, 88, 89, 173n.7, *See also* joint-necessity hybrid account of well-being

inclusion desideratum, 33–34, 36–37
instrumental achievement, 109, 117–21, 126
interests of the child, 34, 35, 50–51, 83–84, 171n.1, *See also* core interests
interests of the parents, 34

interracial adoption, 77
intrinsic achievement, 109, 121–22, 126
intrinsic qualities of children, 16–18, 20, 23, 24, 63
in vitro fertilization (IVF), 54, 55, 167n.28
Isserow, Jessica, 137–38

joint-necessity hybrid account of well-being
achievement and, 109, 112, 114–15
arguments in support of, 89–91
carefreeness and, 89–91, 93, 96–97, 99, 100

Kagan, Shelly, 89–90
Kennett, Jeanette, 127, 128, 129–30, 131, 132, 134, 135, 141

legal parenthood, 32–33, 36
for adoptive parents, 72–73
defined, 31
parental scarcity and, 48–49
Liao, S. Matthew, 153n.34, 168n.32, 169n.46
liberal state, 3, 30, 48–49
achievement fostered by, 117, 124
adoption and, 26–27, 53–54, 55, 63, 65–78
carefreeness fostered by, 105–6
objections to facilitation of parenting by, 73–78
procreation and, 4–5, 53–64
reproductive technologies and practices, 54, 55–64, 78, 166nn.24, 25, 166–67n.27
support for core interests, 3–4
Light between Oceans, A (film and novel), 29, 37–38, 51–52, 162n.45
love
children's right to, 65–66, 168n.33, 168n.41
friendship, 13, 137
parental (*see* parental love)
romantic, 13, 15, 17, 138, 152n.24
unconditional, 12, 17–18, 23, 24

matchmakers. *See* romantic matchmakers

meaningful life
  adoption and, 66–68
  friendship and, 138
  procreative parenting and, 6, 9, 11
  worthwhile projects and relationships and, 89–90
Médecins Sans Frontières (MSF), 39–40, 42
mediocre parents, 48–49, 160n.36
Millum, Joseph, 157n.18
mirror view of friendship, 128, 129–31, 133–34, 136
mitochondria donation, 8, 149n.2
monist theories, 32–33, 157n.19, *See also* causal theories; voluntarist theories
  defined, 32
  desiderata for, 33–39
moral commitment, 30, 33, 39–52
  to a child, 42–46
  immoral actions incompatible with, 40, 42, 43, 158n.27
  objections to theory of, 46–51
  prevention of, 162n.44
  promises as, 157–58n.23
  theory of, 39–42
moral complacency, 137–38, 140–41
moral duties, 154n.1
  adoption and, 3
  moral commitment and, 46, 47
  moral parenthood and, 30, 31–32
  Parental love and moral duties, 69
  procreative parenting and, 20
moral parenthood, 3, 4, 29–30, 53–54, 83
  bad parenting and, 47–48
  causal theories on (*see* causal theories)
  co-procreators and, 58, 59
  defined, 30
  desiderata for a theory of, 33–39 (*see also* dual-interest desideratum; inclusion desideratum; relationship desideratum)
  mediocre parenting and, 48–49
  moral commitment and (*see* moral commitment)
  moral parenthood and adoption, 32–34, 36–37, 53–54, 73
  moral parenthood and procreation, 27, 33–34, 36–37, 53–54
  parental work and, 157n.18
  undermining of other moral parents and, 161n.42
  voluntarist theories on (*see* voluntarist theories)
moral permissibility, 4–5, 7, 9, 31–32, 42–43
moral rights, 31–33, 160–61n.37
  moral commitment and, 30, 36, 46, 47
  to procreation, 9
MSF. *See* Médecins Sans Frontières
Mullin, Amy, 181n.44
My Girl? (film), 131

negative affect, 104, 120
Nelson, James Lindemann, 59
normative reasons for parental love, 16, 18, 21, 26–27, 63, 137, 153n.28

objective goods
  achievement and, 112, 113, 118, 121, 126
  carefreeness and, 88, 89–90, 91, 93, 94, 96–97, 100
  joint-necessity hybrid account of well-being on, 89–90, 91, 93, 112
Olsaretti, Serena, 90–91
open adoption, 71, 72–73, 75–76, 78–79, 169n.54
open parenting, 73
opportunity costs
  achievement and, 126
  procreation and, 6, 7
  reproductive technologies and practices and, 63–64
  worthwhile projects and relationships and, 102–3
Overall, Christine, 7, 24

Paley, Vivian, 133
parental competency
  assessment of, 58–60, 164–65nn.17, 18, 166n.26
  dual-interest desideratum and, 34, 36
  procreative parenting and, 22–24
parental leave, 55, 70–71
parental love
  adoption and, 18–20, 21, 26–27, 65–67, 68–69

compared with other types of love, 13–14, 15
depth of, 12, 13–14, 15, 19, 20, 22, 137
procreative parenting and, 7, 12–15, 16–20, 21, 22, 23, 24, 63
property view of, 16–17
reasons for, 16–20
relationship view of, 16–17
robustness of, 12, 13–14, 15, 19, 20, 22, 137, 152n.24
weighty pro tanto reason for, 7, 12, 17–18, 20, 21, 22, 23, 24, 27, 154n.43
parental proliferation, 46, 49–51, 161n.40
parental scarcity, 46–49, 160n.34
parental work, 157n.18
paternalism, 86, 90
achievement and, 121, 124–26
toward adolescents, 171–72n.6
carefreeness and, 100, 101, 103, 106
friendship and, 128, 138, 139–47, 181nn.44, 45, 181–82n.46, 182nn.47, 48, 182n.49
between liberal state and parentless children, 74–75
moral commitment and, 42–44, 51
moral parenthood and, 30, 31–32
perfectionist account of achievement, 112, 116–17
permissibility. *See* moral permissibility
Pettit, Philip, 152n.24
philosophical theories, 4–5
on achievement, 110, 112, 114
on carefreeness, 93
on children's right to love, 65–66
on friendship, 127, 128, 129, 133, 147
on a meaningful life, 67
on moral parenthood, 30, 31–32
on play, 87
on well-being, 89–90
Picasso, 115, 176n.18
play, 87–88, 99, 104, 105–6, 123, 172n.2
in adulthood, 87–88, 96
fantasy (imaginative), 132–33
pluralist theories, 32–33
positive affect
achievement and, 118, 120–22, 126
carefreeness required for, 99, 104–5

friendship and, 142
subjective endorsement and, 99, 100–3, 104
pregnancy. *See* gestation
procreation challenge, 6
alternative responses to, 24
difficulty meeting, 11
explained, 8–9
withstanding, 20–21
procreative parenting, 3, 4–5, 6–28, 31, 83
alternative responses to challenges, 24–26
challenges to, 6–11, 20–24 (*see also* procreation challenge; redistribution challenge)
defined, 7–8, 149n.3
the liberal state and (*see* liberal state, procreation and)
moral commitment and, 30, 44–46, 49
moral parenthood and, 27, 33–34, 36–37, 53–54
not superior to other forms of parenting, 20–21
parental love and (*see under* parental love)
parental scarcity and, 49
value of, 6, 9, 11, 12–15, 18, 20, 21, 23–24, 27
promises as moral commitments, 157–58n.23
property view of parental love, 16–17

Raz, Joseph, 89–90
redistribution challenge, 7
alternative responses to, 24–26
difficulty meeting, 11
explained, 9–11
withstanding, 21–24
relationship desideratum, 33–34, 37–39
relationship view of parental love, 16–17
reproductive technologies and practices, 54, 55–64, 78, 166nn.24, 25, 166–67n.27
resource allocation, 3–4, 63–64
Ridge, Michael, 172n.2
Rodman, Denis, 122–23
romantic love, 13, 15, 17, 138, 152n.24
romantic matchmakers, 57, 60

Rulli, Tina, 8

sacrifice
  for achievement in children, 125–26
  for friendships in children, 13, 137
  parental love and, 12, 14–15, 16, 66–67
  social workers and, 14
Scanlon, T. M., 173n.7
secrets view of friendship, 128, 129–30, 131–34, 136
self-disclosure, 131–32
self-knowledge, 130–31
Shapiro, Tamar, 101–2
Sherman, Nancy, 129
Shields, Liam, 10
Shpall, Sam, 154n.43
skipping childhood, 85, 171n.4
social parenthood, 31, 32–33, 36, 48–49
social workers, 14, 48, 68–69
sperm donation, 6, 8, 57, 165n.21, *See also* gamete donation
  anonymous, 58
  care uncertainty and, 60
state. *See* liberal state
stepparents, 7–8, 20
sterilization procedures, 56
Straehle, Christine, 57, 70–71
subjective endorsement
  achievement and, 112, 113, 114–15, 117–18
  carefreeness and, 88, 89–91, 93–94, 95–98, 99–103, 104
  joint-necessity hybrid account of well-being on, 89–91, 93, 96, 112
  positive affect and, 99, 100–3, 104
  stability of, 174n.18
  of worthwhile projects and relationships, 95–96, 97–98, 99–100, 102–3, 112, 114–15
surrogacy, 8, 31, 57
  care uncertainty and, 59, 61
  commercial, 58, 61, 62–63, 71, 166n.25
  co-procreator role and, 164n.12
  the liberal state and, 54, 55, 56, 57, 62–63
  reasons not to participate in, 58
  relationship desideratum and, 38–39
Swift, Adam, 98–99, 127

Thomas, Laurence, 129, 131, 137–38
trans men, 56, 63–64

unconditional love, 12, 17–18, 23, 24
Uniacke, Suzanne, 56
Universal Declaration of Human Rights, 87

valuable goods. *See* worthwhile projects and relationships
value expression, 40, 41–42, 43–44, 45–46
value recognition, 39–41, 42–44, 158n.24, 158n.26
Velleman, David, 150–51n.9
voluntarist theories, 30, 31–32, 51–52, 160n.34, 161n.40
  dual-interest desideratum and, 35–36
  parental proliferation and, 50
  parental scarcity and, 47, 49
  relationship desideratum and, 38

well-being. *See also* hybrid account of well-being
  achievement and, 109–13
  carefreeness and, 89–91
  friendship and, 129–36
Weinberg, Rivka, vii, 154–55n.2, 160n.36, 165n.19, 169n.50, 170n.60
Withers, Bill, 122–23
Wolf, Susan, 89–90
worthwhile projects and relationships, 86, 97, 105
  achievement and, 112–13, 114–15, 117–18, 126
  carefreeness and, 95–96, 97–98, 99–100, 102–3
  a meaningful life and, 67, 68, 89–90
  moral commitment and, 41–42, 44
  subjective endorsement of, 95–96, 97–98, 99–100, 102–3, 112, 114–15